Mastering Machine Learning with Rust

A Practical Guide to High-Performance Machine Learning for Rust Programmers and AI Developers

Phillips Jeremy

Table of Contents

Preface...6

Chapter 1: Introduction..9

    1.1 The Growing Demand for High-Performance ML...................... 9

    1.2 Rust's Strengths.. 15

    1.3 Why Rust for Machine Learning? Addressing Performance
Bottlenecks...23

Chapter 2: Rust Essentials for Machine Learning....................29

    2.1 Core Concepts..29

    2.2 Structs and Enums... 35

    2.3 Trait...43

    2.4 Generics.. 51

    2.5 Error Handling..56

    2.6 Modules and Crates...66

Chapter 3: Setting Up Your Rust ML Environment.....................76

    3.1 Installing Rust and Cargo.................................... 76

    3.2 Managing Dependencies with Cargo.toml..................... 88

    3.3 Introduction to Key Numerical and Data Crates (e.g., ndarray,
rand).. 96

    3.4 Setting Up a Basic Rust Project for ML..................... 105

    3.5 Tips for Efficient Rust Development.........................123

Chapter 4: Data Handling and Preprocessing with Rust.............. 134

    4.1 Reading Data from Various Sources (CSV, JSON, etc.) in Rust....
134

    4.2 Efficient Data Structures for Numerical and Categorical Data..153

    4.3 Data Cleaning Techniques.......................................162

    4.4 Feature Scaling and Normalization in Rust............................ 176

    4.5 Feature Encoding... 183

    4.6 Working with DataFrames.. 193

Chapter 5: Linear Algebra in Rust: The Bedrock of ML..................200

    5.1 Vectors and Matrices in Rust (ndarray basics)........................ 200

    5.4 Matrix Transpose, Inverse, and Determinant..........................207

    5.3 Dot Products and Vector Norms................................. 218

    5.4 Matrix Transpose, Inverse, and Determinant..........................222

5.5 Eigenvalues and Eigenvectors...................................... 231

5.6 Applications of Linear Algebra in Machine Learning.................236

Chapter 6: Fundamental Machine Learning Algorithms in Rust (Part 1: Supervised Learning)..242

6.1 Linear Regression...242

6.2 Logistic Regression... 257

6.3 Basic Tree-Based Methods (Conceptual Overview and Potential Rust Libraries)... 269

Chapter 7: Fundamental Machine Learning Algorithms in Rust (Part 2: Unsupervised Learning).. 275

7.1 Clustering..275

7.2 Dimensionality Reduction.. 288

Chapter 8: Leveraging Rust for Performance Optimization in ML.305

8.1 Memory Management and Data Layout for Efficiency..............305

8.2 Parallelism with Rayon for ML Tasks..................................... 312

8.3 Utilizing SIMD for Vectorized Computations in Rust................320

8.4 Profiling and Benchmarking Rust ML Code............................327

8.5 Optimizing Data Access Patterns... 334

8.6 Case Studies in Performance Optimization............................ 341

Chapter 9: Neural Networks in Rust.................................... 350

9.1 Fundamentals of Neural Networks... 350

9.2 Implementing Feedforward Neural Networks in Rust.............. 354

9.3 Backpropagation Algorithm...364

9.4 Optimization Algorithms..369

9.5 Training Neural Networks.. 376

9.6 Evaluating Neural Network Performance................................381

9.7 Introduction to Popular Neural Network Architectures.............390

Chapter 10: Working with Deep Learning Frameworks (Rust Bindings)... 397

10.1 Overview of Popular Deep Learning Frameworks (TensorFlow, PyTorch)..397

10.2 Exploring Existing Rust Bindings for Deep Learning Frameworks... 406

10.3 Using Foreign Function Interface (FFI) for Interoperability..... 412

10.4 Leveraging Pre-trained Models in Rust................................ 421

10.5 Building Custom Layers or Operations in Rust and Integrating with Frameworks...427

Chapter 11: Deploying ML Models Built with Rust.........................437

11.1 Model Serialization and Deserialization in Rust......................437

11.2 Building Standalone Executables for Model Inference...........449

11.3 Deploying Rust ML Models to Servers (Web APIs with Rust Frameworks)..456

11.4 Integrating ML Models into Existing Rust Applications...........465

11.5 Considerations for Edge Deployment with Rust.....................470

Chapter 12: Exploring Advanced ML Techniques in Rust.............476

12.1 Introduction to Reinforcement Learning Concepts and Potential Rust Implementations..476

12.2 Natural Language Processing with Rust................................481

12.3 Computer Vision in Rust: Image Processing Crates and Deep Learning Integration..488

12.4 Generative Models..495

12.5 Ethical Considerations in High-Performance ML...................499

Chapter 13: The Rust ML Ecosystem: Libraries and Tools............506

13.1 Numerical Computation Libraries (e.g., ndarray, nalgebra)....506

13.2 Data Manipulation and Analysis Crates................................515

13.3 Machine Learning Model Building Libraries...........................524

13.4 Visualization Tools and Integration with Rust........................530

13.5 Community Resources and Projects in Rust ML....................535

Chapter 14: The Future of High-Performance ML with Rust..........540

14.1 Current Research and Development in Rust for ML...............540

14.2 Open Challenges and Opportunities.....................................543

14.3 The Role of Rust in Edge AI and Embedded Systems...........546

14.4 Predictions for the Rust ML Ecosystem................................550

14.5 Getting Involved in the Rust ML Community.........................553

Conclusion...557

Preface

How exciting that you're picking up this book! We're about to embark on a fascinating exploration of machine learning, powered by the incredible Rust programming language. This combination might seem a bit unexpected at first. For many, machine learning brings Python to mind. But get ready to have your perspective broadened!

Introduction

Machine learning is changing how we interact with technology and the world around us. It's fueling everything from recommendation systems that predict what movies you'll love to sophisticated tools that help doctors diagnose diseases. As these applications become more complex and data-intensive, the need for speed and efficiency becomes critical. That's where Rust comes into the picture.

Background and Motivation

Rust is a modern systems programming language known for its speed, reliability, and memory safety. It lets developers write code that performs exceptionally well, without sacrificing safety. In areas like operating systems and game development, Rust has been making waves, and now it's poised to make a significant impact in the field of machine learning.

You might be wondering, "Why Rust for machine learning?" Well, traditional languages often struggle to deliver the performance needed for the most demanding ML tasks. Rust provides that performance boost, enabling the development of faster, more efficient ML systems. This is especially important for applications where every millisecond counts.

Purpose and Scope

This book is designed to equip you with the knowledge and skills to harness Rust's power for machine learning. We'll start with the fundamentals, ensuring you have a solid grasp of both Rust's core concepts and the essential principles of machine learning. From there, we'll progress to more advanced topics, showing you how to build and optimize high-performance ML systems using Rust.

Our goal is to be practical and hands-on. We want you to not only understand the theory but also gain the ability to implement real-world ML solutions with Rust.

Target Audience

This book is crafted for two primary audiences:

- **Rust programmers** who are eager to apply their skills to the exciting field of machine learning.
- **AI developers** who want to leverage Rust's performance to create more efficient and robust machine learning applications.

Whether you're a seasoned developer or relatively new to either Rust or machine learning, you'll find valuable insights and practical guidance here. A basic understanding of programming concepts will be helpful, but we'll explain both Rust and machine learning concepts clearly as we go.

Invitation to Read

We're genuinely thrilled to have you join us on this exciting exploration. We believe that Rust has the potential to revolutionize the way we build machine learning systems, and we're excited to share that with you. So, get ready to roll up your sleeves, write some Rust code, and unlock the power of high-performance machine learning! Let's get started!

Chapter 1: Introduction

Hey there, and welcome to the first chapter! We're kicking off our exploration into the exciting intersection of Rust and machine learning. In this chapter, we'll lay the foundation for why this combination is so powerful and why it's becoming increasingly important in the world of AI.

1.1 The Growing Demand for High-Performance ML

Okay, let's talk about why everyone's so obsessed with making machine learning faster and more powerful. It's not just about bragging rights or some abstract concept; it's about very real needs and challenges that are popping up all over the place.

The Explosion of Data

Think about how much data we create every single day. It's mind-boggling! We're talking about everything from social media posts and streaming videos to data from sensors in factories and hospitals. This massive increase in data is often called "big data," and it's one of the key drivers behind the demand for high-performance ML.

To make that mountain of data useful, we need machine learning. ML algorithms can find patterns, make predictions, and extract valuable insights. But here's the catch: the more data we have, the more computationally intensive these algorithms become. It's like trying to find a specific grain of sand on an entire beach—it takes a lot of effort!

Real-World Example: Recommendation Systems

Let's consider recommendation systems, something many of us interact with daily. Companies like Amazon, Netflix, and Spotify use ML to suggest products, movies, or songs we might like. These systems analyze our past behavior, preferences, and even the behavior of other users with similar tastes.

Now, think about the sheer scale of these platforms. Amazon has hundreds of millions of products, Netflix has thousands of movies and shows, and Spotify has tens of millions of songs. To provide accurate and timely recommendations to each user, these systems need to process enormous amounts of data and perform complex calculations in real-time.

If the ML algorithms behind these recommendation systems are slow, you, as a user, would experience frustrating delays. Imagine clicking on a product page on Amazon and having to wait several seconds for recommendations to load. You'd probably get impatient and leave the site! That's where high-performance ML comes in. Companies invest heavily in optimizing their ML systems to deliver fast and accurate recommendations, enhancing user experience and driving sales.

The Need for Speed: Real-Time Applications

Beyond handling large datasets, many modern applications require ML to operate in real-time. This means that the ML algorithms need to process information and produce results almost instantaneously.

Here are a few examples:

- Autonomous Driving: Self-driving cars rely on ML to perceive their surroundings, detect objects, and make driving decisions. These systems need to process data from cameras, lidar, and radar sensors in milliseconds to ensure the safety of the passengers and other drivers. A delay of even a fraction of a second could have catastrophic consequences.

- Fraud Detection: Banks and financial institutions use ML to detect fraudulent transactions. These systems analyze transaction patterns and user behavior to identify suspicious activity. To prevent fraud effectively, they need to do this in real-time, before the transaction is completed.
- Voice Assistants: When you talk to Siri, Alexa, or Google Assistant, your voice is processed by an ML model that understands your request and generates a response. This interaction needs to feel natural and seamless, which requires very low latency.

In all these cases, high-performance ML is not just about making things faster; it's about enabling the application to function at all.

Exercise: Real-Time Requirements

Think of three other real-world applications that demand real-time ML.

For each application, describe:

- The ML task involved.
- Why low latency is crucial.
- What the potential consequences of slow ML processing would be.

The Complexity of Modern ML Models

As we try to solve more complex problems with machine learning, the models themselves are becoming increasingly sophisticated. Deep learning, for instance, involves training neural networks with many layers, requiring a huge number of calculations.

Consider these examples:

- Image Recognition: State-of-the-art image recognition models, used in applications like facial recognition and medical image analysis, can have hundreds of layers. Training these models on large datasets can take days or even weeks without high-performance computing.
- Natural Language Processing (NLP): Large language models, like those used in chatbots and machine translation, have billions or even trillions of parameters. The computational resources needed to train and run these models are enormous.

To make progress in these areas, researchers and engineers need access to high-performance ML tools and techniques.

Code Example: Simple Performance Comparison

To illustrate the difference that efficient code can make, let's look at a very basic example. We'll compare two ways of performing a simple matrix multiplication in Python. Python isn't known for its speed, but this will give you a general idea.

```python
import numpy as np

import time


# Create two large matrices

size = 1000

matrix1 = np.random.rand(size, size)

matrix2 = np.random.rand(size, size)
```

```python
# Method 1: Using a loop (slow)

start_time = time.time()

result_loop = np.zeros((size, size))

for i in range(size):

    for j in range(size):

        for k in range(size):

            result_loop[i, j] += matrix1[i, k] * matrix2[k, j]

end_time = time.time()

loop_time = end_time - start_time


# Method 2: Using NumPy's built-in function (fast)

start_time = time.time()

result_numpy = np.dot(matrix1, matrix2)

end_time = time.time()

numpy_time = end_time - start_time


print(f"Time using loop: {loop_time:.2f} seconds")

print(f"Time using NumPy: {numpy_time:.2f} seconds")


# Verify that the results are the same (within a small
tolerance)
```

```
if np.allclose(result_loop, result_numpy, atol=1e-6):

    print("Results are the same")

else:

    print("Results are different")
```

When you run this code, you'll see that the NumPy version is significantly faster than the loop version. This is because NumPy is highly optimized for numerical computations. Even in Python, which is generally slower than Rust, optimized libraries make a huge difference. Now, you can begin to see how a language like Rust, which is designed for performance, can provide even greater gains.

The Cost of Inefficiency

Finally, it's important to remember that inefficiency in ML has a cost. It can mean:

- Longer training times, which delays development and experimentation.
- Increased energy consumption, which is bad for the environment and increases operating costs.
- The need for more expensive hardware, such as powerful GPUs, to achieve acceptable performance.

High-performance ML helps to reduce these costs, making machine learning more sustainable and accessible.

1.2 Rust's Strengths

Let's explore what makes Rust stand out. It's a language that has garnered a lot of attention, and for good reason. Rust brings a unique combination of features to the table, making it a compelling choice for a wide range of applications, including machine learning. At its core, Rust provides three key strengths: safety, speed, and concurrency.

Safety: Preventing the Dreaded Bugs

When programmers talk about "safety" in programming languages, they're often referring to memory safety. Memory safety is all about how a program manages the computer's memory. If a program isn't memory-safe, it can lead to a whole host of problems, with some of the most common and dangerous being:

- Null pointer dereferences: This happens when a program tries to access a memory location that doesn't actually exist, often because a pointer is "null" (meaning it doesn't point to anything). This can cause the program to crash.
- Buffer overflows: This occurs when a program writes more data to a buffer (a region of memory) than it can hold, potentially overwriting other important data or even executable code. This can lead to crashes, security vulnerabilities, and unpredictable behavior.
- Data races: These happen in concurrent programs when multiple threads try to access the same memory location at the same time, and at least one of them is writing to it. This can lead to corrupted data and unpredictable results.

These kinds of bugs can be incredibly difficult to track down, and they can have serious consequences. In critical systems, like operating systems or medical devices, memory errors can lead to system failures or even endanger lives.

Rust takes a very different approach to memory management than languages like C or C++. Instead of relying on the programmer to manually manage memory (which is error-prone) or using a garbage collector (which can introduce performance overhead), Rust employs a system of ownership, borrowing, and lifetimes.

Ownership, Borrowing, and Lifetimes: Rust's Safety Mechanisms

These concepts might sound a bit intimidating at first, but they're the key to Rust's safety.

Let's break them down:

- Ownership: In Rust, every value has a variable that's its "owner." When the owner goes out of scope, the value is automatically dropped (freed from memory). This ensures that memory is always cleaned up properly, preventing memory leaks.
- Borrowing: Instead of transferring ownership, you can "borrow" a value. Borrowing allows you to access a value without taking ownership of it. Rust has strict rules about borrowing to prevent data races. For example, you can have multiple immutable borrows of a value, or one mutable borrow, but not both at the same time.
- Lifetimes: Lifetimes are annotations that specify how long a reference (a pointer) is valid. The compiler uses lifetimes to ensure that references don't outlive the data they point to, preventing dangling pointers.

These rules are checked by the Rust compiler at compile time. If you try to write code that violates these rules, the compiler will give you an error, and your program won't even compile. This might seem strict, but it catches potential bugs early in the development process, making your code much more reliable.

Code Example: Ownership and Borrowing

Here's a simple Rust example that demonstrates ownership and borrowing:

```
Rust
```

```
fn main() {
```

```rust
// `s` owns the String data.

let s = String::from("hello");


// `s` is moved to `take_ownership`, and `s`
is no longer valid here.

take_ownership(s);


// This would cause a compile error:

// println!("{}", s);


let x = 5; // `x` is a copyable type (i32).


// `x` is copied to `makes_copy`. `x` is
still valid here.

makes_copy(x);

println!("{}", x); // This is OK.


let mut t = String::from("world");

change_string(&mut t);   //borrow t as mutable

println!("{}", t);

}
```

```rust
fn take_ownership(some_string: String) {

    println!("{}", some_string);

    // `some_string` is dropped here.

}



fn makes_copy(some_integer: i32) {

    println!("{}", some_integer);

    // `some_integer` is dropped here.

}



fn change_string(some_string: &mut String) {

    some_string.push_str(", world");

}
```

In this example:

- When s is passed to take_ownership, ownership of the String data is transferred. After the function call, s is no longer valid in main.
- When x is passed to makes_copy, the i32 value is copied. x is still valid in main.
- The change_string function borrows t as a mutable reference, allowing the function to modify the original String.

Exercise: Ownership and Functions

Write a Rust function that takes a String as an argument and returns a new String that is the reverse of the input string. Pay close attention to ownership and borrowing.

Speed: Performance Without Compromise

Rust's commitment to safety doesn't come at the cost of performance. Rust is a compiled language, which means that Rust code is translated directly into machine code that your computer's processor can understand. This results in very fast execution speeds, often comparable to languages like C and C++.

Here are some of the reasons why Rust is so fast:

- No garbage collection: Unlike languages with garbage collectors (like Java or Python), Rust doesn't have a runtime process that periodically cleans up unused memory. This eliminates a source of performance overhead, allowing Rust programs to run more predictably and efficiently.
- Zero-cost abstractions: Rust is designed to allow you to write high-level code that compiles down to efficient machine code. This means you can use abstractions (like iterators and generics) without sacrificing performance.
- Low-level control: Rust provides fine-grained control over memory management, allowing you to optimize your code for specific hardware and use cases.

Rust's speed makes it an excellent choice for applications where performance is critical, such as:

- High-performance computing: Scientific simulations, financial modeling, and other computationally intensive tasks.
- Game development: Building games with demanding graphics and physics simulations.

- Embedded systems: Programming devices with limited resources, where efficiency is paramount.
- Web servers: Handling large numbers of concurrent requests with low latency.

Concurrency: Fearless Parallelism

Modern computers have multiple cores, and to take full advantage of this processing power, programs need to be able to execute tasks concurrently (at the same time). Concurrency can significantly improve performance, but it also introduces the risk of data races, which, as we discussed, can lead to nasty bugs.

Rust's safety guarantees extend to its concurrency model. The ownership and borrowing system ensures that it's impossible to have data races in safe Rust code. This allows you to write concurrent programs with confidence, without having to worry about the usual pitfalls.

Rust provides several tools for writing concurrent code, including:

- Threads: Rust provides a standard library for creating and managing threads.
- Channels: Channels allow threads to communicate with each other by sending and receiving messages.
- Atomic types: Atomic types provide a way to safely share data between threads.

Code Example: Concurrency with Threads

Here's a simple example of using threads in Rust:

```
Rust

use std::thread;
```

```rust
use std::time::Duration;


fn main() {

    let handle = thread::spawn(|| {

        for i in 1..10 {

            println!("Hello from spawned thread!
{}", i);


thread::sleep(Duration::from_millis(1));

        }

    });


    for i in 1..5 {

        println!("Hello from the main thread!
{}", i);

        thread::sleep(Duration::from_millis(1));

    }


    handle.join().unwrap(); // Wait for the
spawned thread to finish.

}
```

In this example, a new thread is created that prints numbers from 1 to 9, while the main thread prints numbers from 1 to 4. The handle.join().unwrap() call ensures that the main thread waits for the spawned thread to finish before exiting.

Exercise: Concurrent Sum

Write a Rust program that calculates the sum of a large array of numbers using multiple threads. Divide the array into chunks, and have each thread sum its chunk. Then, combine the results from each thread to get the final sum.

Real-World Example: Web Servers

High-performance web servers, like those built with Rust's Tokio framework, need to handle many client requests concurrently. Rust's safety and concurrency features make it an excellent choice for this kind of application. A web server written in Rust can efficiently manage thousands of connections without crashing or experiencing data races, ensuring a smooth and responsive experience for users.

Rust's safety, speed, and concurrency make it a powerful language for a wide range of applications, including those that demand high performance and reliability. By preventing common bugs, providing low-level control, and enabling fearless parallelism, Rust empowers developers to build efficient, robust, and scalable systems.

1.3 Why Rust for Machine Learning? Addressing Performance Bottlenecks

You might be wondering, with languages like Python being so popular in the machine learning space, why should we consider Rust? That's a great question! While Python has a rich ecosystem of libraries and tools for ML, it often falls short when it comes to performance, especially as models and datasets grow larger and more complex. Rust, on the other hand, offers a unique combination of features that make it well-suited to tackle these performance bottlenecks.[1]

The Performance Bottleneck in Machine Learning

Before we discuss how Rust helps, let's understand the performance challenges in machine learning.

There are several key areas where performance bottlenecks can arise:

- Data Processing: Machine learning models learn from data, and often, this data needs significant preprocessing.[2] This can involve cleaning, transforming, and organizing the data, which can be computationally intensive, especially with large datasets.[3]
- Model Training: Training a machine learning model involves feeding it data and adjusting its parameters until it learns to make accurate predictions.[4] This process can require a lot of computation, particularly for complex models like deep neural networks.[5]
- Inference: Once a model is trained, it can be used to make predictions on new data.[6] In some applications, like real-time systems, these predictions need to be generated very quickly.[7] This is called inference, and it can also be a performance bottleneck.
- Resource Constraints: In some cases, ML models need to run on devices with limited resources, such as mobile phones or embedded systems.[8] In these situations, efficiency is crucial.

How Rust Addresses These Bottlenecks

Rust's design provides several advantages that directly address these performance challenges:

- Speed: Rust is a compiled language that produces highly optimized machine code. This results in very fast execution, often comparable to C or C++. This speed advantage is crucial for all stages of the ML pipeline, from data processing to model training and inference.

- Memory Efficiency: Rust's ownership system ensures that memory is managed efficiently without the need for a garbage collector.[9] This eliminates the overhead associated with garbage collection, making Rust a great choice for memory-intensive ML tasks.[10]
- Parallelism: Modern ML often relies on parallel processing to speed up computations.[11] Rust's concurrency features make it easier to write parallel code that can take full advantage of multi-core processors, without the risk of data races.[12]
- Low-Level Control: Rust provides a level of control over hardware that is often necessary for optimizing performance.[13] This allows developers to fine-tune their code for specific hardware and use specialized instructions.

Code Example: Parallel Data Processing with Rust

Let's look at an example of how Rust can be used to speed up data processing using parallelism. Imagine you have a large vector of numbers that you need to square and then sum. A simple approach would be to iterate over the vector and perform the calculations sequentially. However, with Rust's Rayon library, you can parallelize this process.

```rust
Rust


use rayon::prelude::*;


fn main() {

    // Create a large vector of numbers.
```

```
    let data: Vec<i32> =
(0..10_000_000).collect();


    // Calculate the sum of the squares in
parallel using Rayon.

    let sum_of_squares = data

        .par_iter() // Convert the vector into a
parallel iterator.

        .map(|&x| x * x) // Square each number.

        .sum::<i64>(); // Sum the squares.


    println!("Sum of squares: {}",
sum_of_squares);

}
```

In this example, par_iter() converts the vector into a parallel iterator, which automatically divides the data into chunks and processes them on multiple threads. This can significantly reduce the time it takes to perform the calculation, especially for large datasets.

Real-World Example: High-Performance Inference

Companies that provide machine learning as a service, such as cloud providers, need to perform inference at massive scale.[14] They might receive millions of requests per second, each requiring a prediction from a trained model. To handle this load, they need inference systems that are incredibly fast and efficient.

Rust's performance characteristics make it an excellent choice for building these high-performance inference systems.[15] By using Rust, companies can minimize latency (the time it takes to generate a prediction) and maximize throughput (the number of predictions that can be served per second).[16] This translates to a better user experience and lower infrastructure costs.

Exercise: Parallel Matrix Multiplication in Rust

As we saw in the previous chapter, matrix multiplication is a fundamental operation in many machine learning algorithms.[17] Write a Rust function that performs matrix multiplication in parallel using Rayon. Compare its performance to a sequential implementation.

Rust's Growing Ecosystem for ML

While Rust's ML ecosystem is still evolving, there are a growing number of libraries and tools that leverage its performance advantages.

These include:

- ndarray: A Rust library for efficient numerical computation with n-dimensional arrays.[18]
- Linfa: A Rust machine learning framework that provides implementations of various ML algorithms.[19]
- Burn: A flexible and comprehensive deep learning framework built in Rust.[20]

As the Rust ML ecosystem continues to develop, we can expect to see even more innovative and high-performance solutions emerge.

Rust's speed, memory efficiency, parallelism, and low-level control make it an excellent language for addressing the performance bottlenecks in machine learning. Whether it's processing large datasets, training complex models, or performing real-time inference, Rust can help developers build more efficient, reliable, and scalable ML systems.[21] As the demand for high-performance ML grows, Rust is poised to play an increasingly important role in the future of this field.

Chapter 2: Rust Essentials for Machine Learning

Alright, let's get into the heart of Rust and see what makes it so special, especially when we're thinking about using it for machine learning. This chapter is all about the Rust fundamentals that will become your best friends as you start building ML systems.

2.1 Core Concepts

Okay, let's talk about something super important in Rust: how it handles memory. If you've programmed in other languages, you might be used to either manually managing memory (like in C or C++) or relying on a garbage collector to do it for you (like in Java or Python). Rust does things a bit differently, with a system that's all about ownership, borrowing, and lifetimes.

Why Does This Matter for Machine Learning?

You might be wondering why we're spending so much time on memory management in a machine learning book. Well, in ML, we often deal with huge datasets and complex models. Efficiently managing how memory is used can make a big difference in how fast our code runs and how much memory it consumes. Rust's approach can give us a serious edge.

Ownership: Who's in Charge?

At its core, Rust's memory management is based on this idea of ownership. Every piece of data in a Rust program has a single, clear owner. You can think of it like this: imagine you have a pet. You're responsible for taking care of it, feeding it, and making sure it's okay. When you're done with the pet, you're also responsible for making sure it's properly taken care of (e.g., finding it a new home or, well, you get the idea).

In Rust, when the owner of a piece of data goes out of scope (like when a function finishes running), that data is automatically dropped, meaning its memory is freed. This happens without you having to write any extra code. It's automatic and efficient.

Here's a simple example:

Rust

```
fn main() {

    let my_string = String::from("Hello, Rust!");
// `my_string` is the owner.

    println!("{}", my_string);

} // `my_string` goes out of scope here, and the
memory is freed.
```

In this case, my_string owns the string data "Hello, Rust!". When main finishes, my_string goes out of scope, and Rust automatically frees the memory used by the string.

Move vs. Copy

Now, what happens when you assign one variable to another? In Rust, there are two possibilities: the data is either moved or copied.

- Move: When data is moved, the ownership is transferred from one variable to another. The original variable is no longer valid.
- Copy: When data is copied, a new, independent copy of the data is created. Both the original and the new variable are valid.

Copying happens with simple types like integers and floating-point numbers. These types are stored directly on the stack, and copying them is cheap.

Moving happens with more complex types like Strings, Vectors, and custom data structures. These types store their data on the heap, and moving them involves transferring ownership of the pointer to that data.

Here's an illustration:

Rust

```rust
fn main() {

    let x = 5; // i32 is a copyable type.

    let y = x; // `x` is copied.

    println!("x = {}, y = {}", x, y); // Both `x`
and `y` are valid.


    let s1 = String::from("Hello"); // `s1` owns
the String data.

    let s2 = s1; // `s1` is moved to `s2`.

    // println!("{}", s1); // This would cause an
error: `s1` is no longer valid.

    println!("{}", s2); // `s2` is valid.

}
```

Borrowing: Sharing Data Without Taking Ownership

Sometimes, you want to access data without taking ownership of it. This is where borrowing comes in. Borrowing lets you create a *reference* to a value, which allows you to read or modify the value without taking ownership.

There are two kinds of borrowing:

- Immutable borrowing: You can create multiple immutable references to a value. This allows you to read the value but not modify it.
- Mutable borrowing: You can create a single mutable reference to a value. This allows you to modify the value.

Rust has a key rule: you can't have both a mutable borrow and any other borrows (mutable or immutable) of the same value at the same time. This rule prevents data races, which, as we discussed, can lead to nasty bugs.

Here's an example:

Rust

```
fn main() {

    let mut greeting = String::from("Hello");


    let greeting_ref = &greeting; // Immutable
borrow.

    println!("{}", greeting_ref); // You can read
the value through the reference.
```

```rust
    let mutable_greeting_ref = &mut greeting; //
Mutable borrow.

    mutable_greeting_ref.push_str(", world!"); //
You can modify the value through the reference.

    println!("{}", mutable_greeting_ref);

    println!("{}", greeting);

}
```

Lifetimes: Avoiding Dangling Pointers

Lifetimes are a more advanced concept, but they're crucial for understanding how Rust prevents a specific kind of error called a dangling pointer. A dangling pointer is a reference that points to a memory location that has already been freed.

Rust uses lifetime annotations to specify the relationships between the lifetimes of different references. The compiler then checks these annotations to ensure that no reference outlives the data it points to.

Here's a simplified example:

Rust

```rust
fn main() {

    let string1 = String::from("long string");

    let result;

    {

        let string2 = String::from("short");
```

```
        result = longest(string1.as_str(),
string2.as_str());

        println!("The longest string is '{}'",
result);

    } //string2 goes out of scope

    //println!("The longest string is '{}'",
result); //result is a dangling pointer

}



fn longest<'a>(x: &'a str, y: &'a str) -> &'a str
{

    if x.len() > y.len() {

        x

    } else {

        y

    }

}
```

The <'a> syntax declares a lifetime parameter. The function longest takes two string slices with lifetime 'a and returns a string slice with the same lifetime 'a. This means the returned string slice will live as long as the shortest of the input string slices.

Why This Matters for Machine Learning

In machine learning, we often work with large datasets and complex data structures. Rust's ownership, borrowing, and lifetime rules help us write code that is both efficient and safe. We can avoid unnecessary copying, minimize memory usage, and prevent data races when working with multiple threads. This is especially important when dealing with the performance-critical aspects of machine learning, such as training large models or performing real-time inference.

2.2 *Structs and Enums*

When you're building machine learning models, you need ways to organize your data. Rust provides two powerful tools for this: structs and enums.

Structs: Building Custom Data Types

A struct (short for "structure") is a way to create a custom data type that groups together related values. You can think of it like a blueprint for creating objects with specific properties.

Here's an example of a struct that could represent a data point in a machine learning dataset:

Rust

```
struct DataPoint {

    features: Vec<f64>,

    label: i32,

}



fn main() {

    let point = DataPoint {

        features: vec![1.0, 2.0, 3.0],
```

```
        label: 0,

    };



    println!("Features: {:?}", point.features);

    println!("Label: {}", point.label);

}
```

In this example, the DataPoint struct has two fields: features, which is a vector of floating-point numbers, and label, which is an integer. You can then create instances of this struct, like the point variable in main.

More on Structs

Let's expand a bit on structs. You can make structs with various types, and nest them.

Rust

```
struct TrainingConfig {

    learning_rate: f64,

    epochs: u32,

    batch_size: u32,

}



struct NeuralNetworkModel {

    config: TrainingConfig,
```

```rust
    weights: Vec<Vec<f64>>, // A vector of
matrices

    biases: Vec<f64>,

}


fn main() {

    let my_config = TrainingConfig {

        learning_rate: 0.01,

        epochs: 100,

        batch_size: 64,

    };


    let mut my_model = NeuralNetworkModel {

        config: my_config,

        weights: vec![vec![0.1, 0.2], vec![0.3,
0.4]],

        biases: vec![0.0, 0.0],

    };


    println!("Learning Rate: {}",
my_model.config.learning_rate);

    println!("Weights: {:?}", my_model.weights);
```

```rust
    // You can also change values.

    my_model.config.learning_rate = 0.005;

    println!("New Learning Rate: {}",
my_model.config.learning_rate);

}
```

In this example, we define a TrainingConfig struct and nest it inside the NeuralNetworkModel struct. This is a common pattern in machine learning, where you might have various hyperparameters and model parameters that you want to group together.

Methods

You can also define methods on structs. Methods are functions that are associated with a particular struct. They allow you to define behavior for objects of that struct.

Rust

```rust
impl DataPoint {

    fn distance_to(&self, other: &DataPoint) ->
f64 {

        let mut sum = 0.0;

        for i in 0..self.features.len() {

            let diff = self.features[i] -
other.features[i];

            sum += diff * diff;
```

```
        }

        sum.sqrt()

    }

}


fn main() {

    let point1 = DataPoint {

        features: vec![1.0, 2.0, 3.0],

        label: 0,

    };

    let point2 = DataPoint {

        features: vec![4.0, 5.0, 6.0],

        label: 1,

    };


    let distance = point1.distance_to(&point2);

    println!("Distance between points: {}",
distance);

}
```

In this example, we define a method called distance_to on the
DataPoint struct. This method calculates the Euclidean distance
between two data points. The &self parameter is a reference to the

instance of the DataPoint struct. It allows the method to access the data within the struct.

Enums: Representing Different States

An enum (short for "enumeration") is a way to define a type that can take on a fixed set of values. Enums are useful for representing data that can be in one of several different states.

Here's an example of an enum that could represent the different types of a machine learning model:

Rust

```rust
enum ModelType {

    LinearRegression,

    DecisionTree,

    NeuralNetwork,

}


fn main() {

    let model_type = ModelType::NeuralNetwork;


    match model_type {

        ModelType::LinearRegression =>
println!("Model type: Linear Regression"),

        ModelType::DecisionTree =>
println!("Model type: Decision Tree"),
```

```
        ModelType::NeuralNetwork =>
println!("Model type: Neural Network"),

    }

}
```

In this example, the ModelType enum can take on one of three values: LinearRegression, DecisionTree, or NeuralNetwork. You can then use a match statement to handle each of these cases. The match statement is crucial for working with enums. It allows you to write code that handles each possible value of the enum.

Enums with Data

Enums are even more powerful because they can hold data. This allows you to represent more complex states.

Rust

```
enum Message {

    Quit,                       // No data
associated.

    Move { x: i32, y: i32 },    // An anonymous
struct

    Write(String),              // A single
String.

    ChangeColor(i32, i32, i32), // Three i32
values.

}


fn main() {
```

```rust
    let message1 = Message::Quit;

    let message2 = Message::Move{x: 10, y: 20};

    let message3 =
Message::Write(String::from("Hello, world"));


    process_message(message1);

    process_message(message2);

    process_message(message3);
}



fn process_message(msg: Message) {

    match msg {

        Message::Quit => println!("Quit"),

        Message::Move { x, y } => println!("Move
to x={}, y={}", x, y),

        Message::Write(text) => println!("Write:
{}", text),

        Message::ChangeColor(r, g, b) =>

            println!("Change color to r={}, g={},
b={}", r, g, b),

    }

}
```

Enums are a powerful tool for modeling data that can exist in various states, each potentially carrying different information.

Why This Matters for Machine Learning

Structs and enums allow you to create clear, organized, and efficient data structures for your machine learning models and data. Whether you're representing individual data points, different model types, or the various stages of a training process, these tools help you write code that is both readable and performant.

2.3 Trait

In Rust, a *trait* is a way to define a set of methods that a type must implement. You can think of it like an interface in other languages. Traits allow you to define shared behavior that different types can have.

Here's a simple example:

Rust

```
trait Model {

    fn train(&mut self, features: &Vec<Vec<f64>>,
labels: &Vec<i32>);

    fn predict(&self, features: &Vec<Vec<f64>>)
-> Vec<i32>;

}
```

In this example, we define a trait called Model that has two methods: train and predict. Any type that implements the Model trait must provide implementations for these two methods. Traits do not provide default implementations. They only declare the method signatures.

Here's how you might implement this trait for a simple linear regression model:

Rust

```rust
struct LinearRegressionModel {

    weights: Vec<f64>,

    bias: f64,

}



impl LinearRegressionModel{

    fn new() -> Self{

        LinearRegressionModel{

            weights: Vec::new(),

            bias: 0.0,

        }

    }

}



impl Model for LinearRegressionModel {

    fn train(&mut self, features: &Vec<Vec<f64>>,
labels: &Vec<i32>) {

        // Implementation of the training
algorithm (e.g., gradient descent).
```

```rust
        println!("Linear Regression Model
Trained");

        self.weights = vec![0.5, 0.2]; //dummy

        self.bias = 0.1;

    }



    fn predict(&self, features: &Vec<Vec<f64>>)
-> Vec<i32> {

        // Implementation of the prediction
logic.

        println!("Linear Regression Model
Prediction");

        let mut predictions = Vec::new();

        for feature in features{

            let prediction = 0;

            predictions.push(prediction);

        }

        predictions

    }

}
```

This tells Rust that our LinearRegressionModel struct adheres to the behavior defined by the Model trait. The impl Model for LinearRegressionModel block provides the actual implementation of the train and predict methods for the LinearRegressionModel struct. A struct can implement multiple traits.

More on Traits

Let's look at a more detailed example. Suppose you have different kinds of data sources for your machine learning models, like CSV files and databases.

You can define a trait for reading data:

Rust

```
trait DataSource {

    fn read_data(&self, path: &str) ->
Result<Vec<Vec<f64>>, String>;

}



struct CSVFileSource {

    delimiter: char,

}



impl DataSource for CSVFileSource {

    fn read_data(&self, path: &str) ->
Result<Vec<Vec<f64>>, String> {

        // Implementation for reading data from a
CSV file.
```

```rust
        println!("Reading data from CSV file:
{}", path);

        Ok(vec![vec![1.0, 2.0], vec![3.0, 4.0]])
// Dummy data

    }

}


struct DatabaseSource {

    connection_string: String,

    query: String,

}


impl DataSource for DatabaseSource {

    fn read_data(&self, path: &str) ->
Result<Vec<Vec<f64>>, String> {

        // Implementation for reading data from a
database.

        println!("Reading data from database with
connection string: {}", self.connection_string);

        Ok(vec![vec![5.0, 6.0], vec![7.0,
8.0]])// Dummy data

    }

}
```

```rust
fn main() {

    let csv_source = CSVFileSource { delimiter:
',' };

    let db_source = DatabaseSource {

        connection_string:
"your_db_connection_string".to_string(),

        query: "SELECT * FROM
your_table".to_string(),

    };



    let csv_data =
csv_source.read_data("data.csv").unwrap();

    let db_data =
db_source.read_data("").unwrap(); //path not
needed



    println!("CSV Data: {:?}", csv_data);

    println!("Database Data: {:?}", db_data);

}
```

In this example, the DataSource trait defines a read_data method that takes a path and returns a Result containing the data as a Vec<Vec<f64>> or an error as a String. The CSVFileSource and DatabaseSource structs then implement this trait, providing their own specific implementations of how to read data from their respective sources.

Default Implementations

Traits can also provide default implementations for some or all of their methods. This allows a type that implements the trait to use the default implementation or provide its own custom implementation.

```rust
Rust

trait Logger {

    fn log(&self, message: &str);


    fn log_error(&self, message: &str) {

        self.log(&format!("ERROR: {}", message));

    }

}



struct ConsoleLogger;


impl Logger for ConsoleLogger {

    fn log(&self, message: &str) {

        println!("{}", message);

    }
```

```rust
}


fn main() {

    let logger = ConsoleLogger;

    logger.log("Hello, world!");

    logger.log_error("Something went wrong!");

}
```

In this example, the Logger trait defines a log method and a log_error method. The log_error method has a default implementation that simply calls the log method with an "ERROR: " prefix. The ConsoleLogger struct implements the Logger trait and provides a custom implementation for the log method. It uses the default implementation of log_error.

Why This Matters for Machine Learning

Traits are incredibly useful for machine learning because they allow you to define common interfaces for different models and algorithms. This makes your code more modular and reusable. For example, you could define a trait for different optimization algorithms (like gradient descent, Adam, etc.) and then use any of those algorithms to train different models.

2.4 Generics

Generics are a way to write code that can work with different types. They allow you to define functions, structs, and enums that are parameterized by one or more types.

Here's a simple example:

Rust

```rust
fn print_vector<T: std::fmt::Debug>(vector:
&Vec<T>) {

    for element in vector {

        println!("{:?}", element);

    }

}


fn main() {

    let int_vector = vec![1, 2, 3];

    let float_vector = vec![1.0, 2.0, 3.0];

    let string_vector = vec!["hello", "world"];


    print_vector(&int_vector);

    print_vector(&float_vector);

    print_vector(&string_vector);

}
```

In this example, the print_vector function uses a generic type parameter T. This allows the function to work with vectors of any type that implements the Debug trait. The T: std::fmt::Debug part specifies that the type T must implement the Debug trait. This is necessary because the println!("{:?}", element) statement uses the Debug trait to format the elements for printing.

More on Generics

Let's expand on how generics can be used in different contexts:

Generic Structs

You can define structs that are generic over one or more types:

Rust

```
struct Point<T> {

    x: T,

    y: T,

}


impl<T> Point<T> {

    fn new(x: T, y: T) -> Self {

        Point { x, y }

    }

}


fn main() {

    let int_point = Point { x: 10, y: 20 };

    let float_point = Point { x: 10.5, y: 20.5 };
```

```rust
    println!("Integer Point: x = {}, y = {}",
int_point.x, int_point.y);

    println!("Float Point: x = {}, y = {}",
float_point.x, float_point.y);


    let my_point = Point::new(100, 200);

    println!("My Point: x = {}, y = {}",
my_point.x, my_point.y);

}
```

In this example, the Point struct is generic over the type T. This allows you to create Point structs with different types for the x and y coordinates. The impl<T> block allows you to define methods on the generic struct Point<T>.

Generic Enums

Enums can also be generic:

Rust

```rust
enum Option<T> {

    Some(T),

    None,

}



fn main() {

    let some_int: Option<i32> = Option::Some(10);
```

```rust
    let some_float: Option<f64> =
Option::Some(10.5);

    let none_string: Option<String> =
Option::None;


    match some_int {

        Option::Some(value) => println!("Some
int: {}", value),

        Option::None => println!("No int value"),

    }


    match some_float {

        Option::Some(value) => println!("Some
float: {}", value),

        Option::None => println!("No float
value"),

    }


    match none_string {

        Option::Some(value) => println!("Some
string: {}", value),

        Option::None => println!("No string
value"),
```

```
    }

}
```

The Option<T> enum is a standard Rust enum that represents a value that may or may not be present. It's generic over the type T, which allows it to hold any type of value.

Generic Traits

Traits themselves can also be generic. For example, the Iterator trait is generic:

```Rust

trait MyIterator<T> {

    fn next(&mut self) -> Option<T>;

}
```

Why This Matters for Machine Learning

Generics enable you to write highly reusable and flexible code. Imagine you're building a machine learning library. With generics, you can define a generic function to train a model, and that function can work with various model types and data types. This avoids code duplication and makes your library more versatile.

Here are some more specific examples of how generics can be beneficial in machine learning:

- Generic Model Training: You could define a generic train function that takes a model and a dataset as input, where the model and dataset can be of different types.
- Generic Data Processing: You could write generic functions to perform data cleaning, normalization, and feature extraction, which can work with different data types and structures.

- Generic Loss Functions: You could define generic loss functions that can be used to train different types of models.

By using generics effectively, you can create a set of reusable components that can be combined in various ways to build different machine learning models and applications. This can significantly reduce development time and improve the maintainability of your code.

2.5 Error Handling

Error handling is a critical aspect of any software development, and machine learning is no exception. In Rust, error handling is a first-class citizen, and the language provides powerful tools to help you write robust and reliable code.

Rust uses a type called Result<T, E> to represent the outcome of an operation that might fail.

Result has two variants:

- Ok(T): Indicates that the operation was successful and returns a value of type T.
- Err(E): Indicates that the operation failed and returns an error value of type E.

Here's a basic example:

Rust

```
use std::fs::File;

use std::io::{self, Read};



fn read_username_from_file() -> Result<String,
io::Error> {
```

```rust
    let mut file = File::open("username.txt")?;
// ? propagates the error

    let mut s = String::new();

    file.read_to_string(&mut s)?;

    Ok(s)

}


fn main() {

    let username_result =
read_username_from_file();


    match username_result {

        Ok(username) => println!("Username: {}",
username),

        Err(error) => println!("Error reading
username: {}", error),

    }

}
```

In this example, the read_username_from_file function returns a Result that either contains the username as a String (if the file is read successfully) or an io::Error (if an error occurs).

The ? operator is a handy shortcut for propagating errors. If File::open or file.read_to_string returns an Err, the ? operator will return that error from the read_username_from_file function.

More on Rust Error Handling

Let's look more deeply into error handling.

The Result Type

The Result type is generic, which makes it very flexible. The T in Result<T, E> represents the type of the value that is returned when the operation is successful, and the E represents the type of the error that is returned when the operation fails.

For example, Result<i32, String> represents an operation that might return an integer (i32) on success or a string (String) on failure.

Handling Errors with match

The match statement is a powerful way to handle Result values. It allows you to explicitly handle both the Ok and Err cases.

Rust

```
fn parse_number(s: &str) -> Result<i32,
std::num::ParseIntError> {

    s.parse::<i32>()

}



fn main() {

    let number_result = parse_number("10");

    match number_result {

        Ok(number) => println!("Parsed number:
{}", number),
```

```
        Err(error) => println!("Error parsing
number: {}", error),

    }



    let invalid_result = parse_number("abc");

    match invalid_result {

        Ok(number) => println!("Parsed number:
{}", number),

        Err(error) => println!("Error parsing
number: {}", error),

    }

}
```

In this example, the parse_number function attempts to parse a string into an integer using s.parse::<i32>(). This operation can fail if the string doesn't represent a valid integer, in which case it returns a ParseIntError. The match statement in main handles both the success and failure cases.

Error Propagation with the ? Operator

The ? operator provides a concise way to propagate errors up the call stack. If a function returns a Result, you can use ? to return the error from the current function if the Result is an Err.

```
Rust

use std::fs::File;

use std::io::{self, Read};
```

```rust
fn read_file_contents(filename: &str) ->
Result<String, io::Error> {

    let mut file = File::open(filename)?;

    let mut contents = String::new();

    file.read_to_string(&mut contents)?;

    Ok(contents)

}



fn main() {

    let contents_result =
read_file_contents("my_file.txt");

    match contents_result {

        Ok(contents) => println!("File
contents:\n{}", contents),

        Err(error) => println!("Error reading
file: {}", error),

    }

}
```

In this example, the read_file_contents function attempts to open a file and read its contents into a string. Both File::open and file.read_to_string can return an io::Error. The ? operator is used to propagate any errors from these operations. If either operation fails, the read_file_contents function will return the corresponding io::Error.

Custom Error Types

For more complex applications, you might want to define your own custom error types. This allows you to provide more specific and informative error messages.

Rust

```rust
use std::fmt;



#[derive(Debug)]

enum MyError {

    FileNotFound(String),

    InvalidData(String),

    Other(String),

}



impl fmt::Display for MyError {

    fn fmt(&self, f: &mut fmt::Formatter) ->
fmt::Result {

        match self {

            MyError::FileNotFound(filename) =>

                write!(f, "File not found: {}",
filename),
```

```rust
            MyError::InvalidData(message) =>
                write!(f, "Invalid data: {}",
message),
            MyError::Other(message) =>
                write!(f, "Other error: {}",
message),
        }
    }
}


fn process_data(data: &str) -> Result<i32,
MyError> {
    if data.is_empty() {
        Err(MyError::InvalidData("Data is
empty".to_string()))
    } else {
        // Assume processing logic here...
        if data == "error" { //Simulated error
            Err(MyError::Other("Something went
wrong!".to_string()))
        }
        else{
            Ok(data.len() as i32)
```

```rust
        }


    }

}


fn read_and_process_file(filename: &str) ->
Result<i32, MyError> {

    let contents =
std::fs::read_to_string(filename)

        .map_err(|e|
MyError::FileNotFound(format!("{}: {}", filename,
e)))?;

    let result = process_data(&contents)?;

    Ok(result)

}


fn main() {

    let result =
read_and_process_file("my_file.txt");

    match result {

        Ok(processed_value) =>
println!("Processed value: {}", processed_value),
```

```
        Err(error) => println!("Error: {}",
error),

    }

}
```

In this example, we define a custom error type MyError using an enum. This enum has three variants, each representing a different type of error that can occur in our application. We then implement the fmt::Display trait for MyError, which allows us to print user-friendly error messages. The macro derives the Debug trait for MyError, enabling easy printing of error details with println!

The process_data function can now return a MyError::InvalidData if the input data is invalid. The read_and_process_file function uses map_err to convert an io::Error from std::fs::read_to_string into a MyError::FileNotFound, providing more context.

Error Handling in ML Pipelines

In machine learning, errors can occur in various stages of the pipeline:

- Data loading: The data file might not exist, or the data might be in an unexpected format.
- Data preprocessing: The data might contain missing values or inconsistencies.
- Model training: The training process might fail to converge, or the model might encounter numerical instability.
- Inference: The input data for prediction might be invalid or malformed.

Rust's error handling mechanisms can help you write robust ML pipelines that can gracefully handle these errors. For example, you could define custom error types to represent specific errors that can occur in your ML pipeline, and then use Result and match to handle these errors appropriately. This might involve logging the error, retrying the operation, or returning a default value.

Why This Matters for Machine Learning

Robust error handling is essential to ensure that your ML systems are reliable and can function correctly in the face of unexpected input or conditions. By using Rust's powerful error handling tools, you can build ML pipelines that are less likely to crash or produce incorrect results, leading to more trustworthy and dependable applications.

2.6 Modules and Crates

As your machine learning projects grow in size and complexity, you'll need ways to organize your code into manageable pieces. Rust provides two key tools for this: modules and crates.

- Modules: Modules allow you to organize code within a single crate (a Rust project). You can use modules to group related functions, structs, and enums into logical units.
- Crates: A crate is a collection of Rust source code. A crate can be a binary executable or a library. Crates are the basic unit of code distribution in Rust.

Here's a basic example of a module:

```
Rust

// Create a module named `my_module`.

mod my_module {

    // This function is only visible within
`my_module`.

    fn internal_function() {
```

```rust
        println!("This is an internal
function.");

    }


    // This function is visible outside
`my_module`.

    pub fn public_function() {

        println!("This is a public function.");

        internal_function(); // You can call
internal functions from public ones.

    }

}


fn main() {

    // You can't call `internal_function` from
here.

    my_module::public_function(); // But you can
call `public_function`.

}
```

In this code, the mod keyword is used to define a module named my_module. Inside the module, internal_function is private, meaning it can only be called from within my_module. public_function is declared as public with the pub keyword, so it can be called from outside the module.

More on Modules

Let's look at how modules can be structured in more complex ways and how they interact with files.

Module Nesting

Modules can be nested to create a hierarchical organization of your code. This allows you to create a clear and intuitive structure for your project.

Rust

```rust
mod parent_module {

    pub fn parent_function() {

        println!("This is a function in the
parent module.");

    }


    pub mod child_module {

        pub fn child_function() {

            println!("This is a function in the
child module.");

            super::parent_function(); // Access
function in parent

        }

    }

}
```

```
fn main() {

    parent_module::parent_function();


parent_module::child_module::child_function();

}
```

In this example, child_module is nested inside parent_module. The child_function can access the parent_function using the super keyword.

Modules and Files

In larger projects, it's common to define modules in separate files. Rust provides a convention for this:

- If you have a module named my_module, you can create a file named my_module.rs or a directory named my_module/ containing a file named mod.rs.

For example, let's say you have the following file structure:

my_project/

  src/

    main.rs

    my_module.rs

    my_module/

      child_module.rs

Here's how the code might look:

`src/main.rs`:

Rust

```rust
mod my_module; // Declare the module

use my_module::public_function;


fn main() {

    public_function();

}
```
```src/my_module.rs`:


```rust
pub fn public_function() {

    println!("This is a public function from
my_module.");

    internal_function();

}


fn internal_function() {

    println!("This is an internal function from
my_module.");
```
```

```
}
```

```
pub mod child_module; // Declare child module
```

```
```src/my_module/child_module.rs`:
```

```
```rust

pub fn child_function() {

    println!("This is a public function from
child_module.");

}
```

In this setup, main.rs declares and uses the my_module from my_module.rs. The my_module.rs file declares a nested module child_module, whose code resides in child_module.rs.

Crates: Building and Distributing Rust Code

A crate is the basic unit of compilation and distribution in Rust. Every Rust project is a crate, whether it's a binary executable or a library.

- Binary crates are programs that you can run. They have a main function and are typically used for applications.
- Library crates are collections of code that can be used by other Rust programs. They don't have a main function and are typically used for reusable components.

Cargo: Rust's Build System and Package Manager

Cargo is the standard tool for managing Rust projects.

It handles tasks such as:

- Building your code
- Managing dependencies (external libraries)
- Running tests
- Generating documentation

A Cargo.toml file is used to configure a Rust project. It contains information about the project, such as its name, version, and dependencies.

Here's a basic Cargo.toml file:

```ini
Ini, TOML

[package]

name = "my_project"

version = "0.1.0"

authors = ["Your Name <your.email@example.com>"]

edition = "2021"


[dependencies]

# Add dependencies here, e.g.:

# rayon = "1.5.1"
```

To build a Rust project with Cargo, you can use the cargo build command. This will compile your code and create an executable in the target/debug directory. For optimized builds, use cargo build --release.

To add a dependency to your project, you can add it to the [dependencies] section of your Cargo.toml file. Cargo will automatically download and link the dependency when you build your project.

Real-World Example: Organizing a Machine Learning Library

Let's consider how you might organize a Rust machine learning library using modules and crates.

Imagine you're building a library that provides various machine learning algorithms.

You could structure your project as follows:

my_ml_library/

  Cargo.toml

  src/

    lib.rs

    models/

      linear_regression.rs

      decision_tree.rs

      neural_network.rs

    algorithms/

      gradient_descent.rs

      adam.rs

    utils/

data_loading.rs

preprocessing.rs

In this structure:

- The Cargo.toml file defines the library crate.
- The src/lib.rs file is the entry point for the library and declares the modules.
- The models/ directory contains modules for different machine learning models.
- The algorithms/ directory contains modules for different optimization algorithms.
- The utils/ directory contains modules for utility functions, such as data loading and preprocessing.

This modular structure makes the library easier to navigate, understand, and maintain. Users of the library can import and use specific modules as needed.

Why This Matters for Machine Learning

As you build more complex ML projects, you'll likely have many different components, such as data loading modules, model definitions, training algorithms, and evaluation metrics. Modules and crates help you organize this code into logical units, making it easier to navigate, understand, and maintain. They also promote code reuse and prevent naming conflicts.

Chapter 3: Setting Up Your Rust ML Environment

Alright, let's get our hands dirty and set up our Rust environment so we can start building some cool machine learning stuff! This chapter will walk you through the process step by step.

3.1 Installing Rust and Cargo

To begin our exploration of using Rust, especially for machine learning, the very first thing we need to do is set up our development environment. Think of this as preparing your workshop before starting a big project. In the Rust "workshop," we need two essential tools: Rust itself, which is the programming language, and Cargo, which is Rust's build system and package manager.

Why Rustup?

You might be wondering why the installation process involves something called "Rustup." It's a fair question! You see, Rust is a language that evolves quite rapidly. New versions are released frequently, bringing improvements, new features, and bug fixes. To manage these different versions of Rust effectively, we use Rustup.

Rustup is a command-line tool that acts as a Rust manager. It simplifies the process of installing Rust, keeping it updated, and even switching between different versions of Rust if you need to work on different projects. It also installs Cargo along with Rust, so you get both tools in one go.

Think of Rustup as your personal Rust conductor, orchestrating the different versions and components to ensure everything works harmoniously. It's the recommended and most convenient way to get Rust on your system.

Installation on macOS and Linux

If you're working on a macOS or Linux system, the installation process is quite straightforward and primarily involves using your terminal.

1. Open your terminal:
   - macOS: You can find the Terminal application in /Applications/Utilities/.
   - Linux: The location might vary slightly depending on your distribution, but you can usually find it by searching for "Terminal" in your applications menu or by using a keyboard shortcut like Ctrl+Alt+T.
2. Download and run the Rustup installation script:
   - In your terminal, carefully type or, even better, copy and paste the following command:

Bash

```
curl --proto '=https' --tlsv1.2 -sSf https://sh.rustup.rs | sh
```

Now, let's break down this command to understand what it does:

- curl: This is a versatile command-line tool used for transferring data from or to a server. In this case, we're using it to download the Rustup installation script from a specific address on the internet (the Rust website).
- --proto '=https': This part of the command ensures that curl uses the HTTPS protocol for the download. HTTPS provides a secure connection, encrypting the

data being transferred and protecting it from eavesdropping.

- o --tlsv1.2: This specifies that curl should use TLS version 1.2, which is a cryptographic protocol that provides secure communication over a network.
- o -s: This option makes curl silent, meaning it won't display a progress bar or other unnecessary output.
- o -S: This option tells curl to show error messages if the download fails.
- o -f: This option instructs curl to fail silently (without displaying an error message) if the server returns an HTTP error code (like 404 Not Found). However, combined with -S, it will still show the error if there's a problem with the connection itself.
- o |: This is the pipe operator. It takes the output from the command on the left (in this case, the downloaded script) and sends it as input to the command on the right.
- o sh: This is the command that invokes the shell, which is a program that interprets and executes commands. In this case, it executes the downloaded Rustup installation script.

In essence, this command securely downloads the Rustup installation script and then runs it in your terminal.

3. Follow the on-screen instructions:
   - o Once you execute the command, the installation script will start running. It will display some information about the installation process and then prompt you to make a choice.
   - o You'll typically be presented with a few options, such as:

- 1) Proceed with installation (default)
- 2) Customize installation
- 3) Cancel installation
  - For most users, the default option (1) is perfectly fine. It will install the stable version of Rust, which is the recommended version for general use. If you have specific needs or want to install a different version, you can choose option 2 to customize the installation.
  - After you make your choice, the installer will download the necessary files and install Rust, Cargo, and other components on your system. This process might take a few minutes, depending on your internet speed.
4. Set up your environment (if necessary):
  - After the installation is complete, Rustup will usually try to configure your system so that you can easily use Rust and Cargo from your terminal. This involves adding the directories where Rust and Cargo are installed to your system's PATH environment variable.
  - The PATH is a list of directories where your operating system looks for executable files. When you type a command like rustc or cargo in your terminal, your system searches the directories listed in the PATH to find the corresponding program.
  - Rustup generally handles this PATH configuration automatically. However, in some cases, you might need to take an extra step to ensure the changes take effect. The installer will often display a message like this:

To start using Rust, you need to open a new terminal, or run:

source $HOME/.cargo/env

- This means you need to update your current terminal session with the new PATH settings. You can do this by "sourcing" your shell's configuration file.
- Here's how to do it:
  - Bash: If you're using the Bash shell (which is common on many Linux distributions and was the default on older macOS versions), run this command:

Bash

source ~/.bashrc

  - Zsh: If you're using the Zsh shell (which is the default on newer macOS versions), run this command:

Bash

source ~/.zshrc

- Other shells: If you're using a different shell, the configuration file might be different (e.g., .profile, .bash_profile). The installer message should tell you the correct file to source.
- Alternatively, you can simply close your current terminal and open a new one. This will usually have the same effect, as a new terminal session will read the updated configuration file.
  - To find out which shell you are using, echo the SHELL environment variable

Bash

echo $SHELL

Installation on Windows

If you're on a Windows system, the installation process involves downloading and running an installer executable.

1. Open your web browser:
   - Open your preferred web browser (e.g., Chrome, Firefox, Edge) and go to the official Rust website: www.rust-lang.org.
2. Click the "Get Started" button:
   - On the Rust website's homepage, you'll find a prominent button that says "Get Started" or something similar. Click on it. This will take you to the installation page.
3. Download the Rustup installer:
   - On the installation page, look for the section related to Windows. You'll see a link to download the rustup

installer. The filename will typically end with .exe, which indicates an executable file.

- o You might be presented with two options: a 32-bit installer and a 64-bit installer. It's crucial to download the correct one for your system architecture.
- o Here's how to determine whether you need the 32-bit or 64-bit version:
  - Press the Windows key on your keyboard.
  - Type "System Information" and press Enter.
  - In the System Information window, find the "System Type" entry.
  - If it says "x64-based PC," you have a 64-bit system, and you should download the 64-bit installer.
  - If it says "x86-based PC," you have a 32-bit system, and you should download the 32-bit installer.
  - If you're unsure, downloading the 64 bit installer and running it will usually give a clear error if your system is 32 bit.

4. Run the installer:
   - o Once the download is complete, locate the downloaded .exe file (it's likely in your "Downloads" folder) and double-click it to run the installer.
   - o The installer will guide you through the installation process[1] with a series of prompts and dialog boxes.

5. Follow the on-screen instructions:
   - o The installer will display a welcome message and ask you to click "Next" to continue. You'll typically be presented with options to customize the installation, but the default settings are usually fine for most users.
   - o The installer will then download the necessary files and install Rust, Cargo, and other components on

your system. This might take a few minutes, depending on your internet speed.

6. Restart your terminal or command prompt:
   - After the installation is finished, it's a good practice to restart your terminal or command prompt (either Command Prompt or PowerShell) to ensure that the changes to your system's PATH environment variable take effect.
   - This step is similar to sourcing your shell's configuration file on macOS and Linux. Restarting the terminal ensures that your system recognizes the newly installed Rust and Cargo commands.

Verifying the Installation

After you've completed the installation process for your operating system, it's essential to confirm that Rust and Cargo have been installed correctly and are accessible from your command line.

1. Open a terminal or command prompt:
   - macOS and Linux: Open the Terminal application.
   - Windows: Open either Command Prompt or PowerShell. You can usually find these by searching for them in the Start menu.
2. Check the Rust version:
   - In your terminal or command prompt, type the following command and press Enter:

Bash

```
rustc --version
```

- This command instructs the Rust compiler (rustc) to display its version number. If Rust is installed correctly and your system can find the rustc executable, you should see output similar to this:

rustc 1.75.0 (18c0b9e52 2023-12-18)

- The exact version number might be different depending on the latest stable release of Rust. The important thing is that you see a version number and no error messages.
3. Check the Cargo version:
   - In your terminal or command prompt, type the following command and press Enter:

Bash

cargo --version

- This command asks Cargo to display its version number. If Cargo is installed correctly and your system can find the cargo executable, you should see output similar to this:

cargo 1.75.0 (18c0b9e52 2023-12-18)

- Again, the version number might vary, but you should see a version and no errors.

If you see the version numbers for both rustc and cargo without any errors, it means that Rust and Cargo have been successfully installed and configured on your system. You're now ready to start writing Rust code!

What Just Happened?

To summarize, here's what happened during the installation:

- You used a tool called Rustup (either by running a script or an executable) to automate the installation process.
- Rustup downloaded and installed the Rust compiler (rustc), the Cargo build system and package manager, and other essential tools and libraries.
- Rustup configured your system's PATH environment variable (or you did it manually by restarting your terminal) to make the Rust and Cargo commands accessible from your command line.

Troubleshooting Common Issues

While the installation process is generally smooth, you might encounter some issues along the way.

Here are some common problems and how to address them:

- Internet connection problems: The installer needs to download files from the Rust website, so a stable internet connection is essential. If you experience download errors, check your connection and try again.
- Permission issues: On some systems, especially when installing software system-wide, you might encounter permission errors.
  - macOS and Linux: If you see errors related to permissions, try running the installation command with sudo (e.g., sudo curl ... | sudo sh). This will give the command administrator privileges. However, be

very cautious when using sudo, and only do so if you understand the command you're running.

- o Windows: On Windows, the installer usually prompts you for administrator privileges if needed. Make sure you're logged in to an administrator account.
- Antivirus or firewall interference: In rare cases, your antivirus software or firewall might interfere with the installation process by blocking the download or execution of the installer. You can try temporarily disabling them to see if that resolves the issue, but remember to re-enable them afterward.
- PATH not updated: If you can't run rustc or cargo after the installation, it's likely that your system's PATH variable wasn't updated correctly.
  - o Restart your terminal or command prompt: This is the simplest solution and often works.
  - o Manually add Rust and Cargo to your PATH: The installation output usually shows the location where Rust and Cargo were installed. You can add this location to your PATH manually. The exact steps for doing this vary slightly depending on your operating system, and you can find detailed instructions online by searching for "how to set PATH on [your operating system]".
- Installer crashes or hangs: If the installer crashes or hangs, try downloading it again from the Rust website. If the problem persists, try restarting your computer and running the installer again.
- Specific error messages: If you encounter a specific error message during the installation, the best approach is to search for that exact message online. Other users have likely encountered the same problem, and you can often find solutions or workarounds in online forums or documentation.

Where to Find More Help

If you're still having trouble installing Rust, don't worry! The Rust community is known for being very friendly and helpful.

Here are some excellent resources where you can find assistance:

- The official Rust documentation: The official Rust website (www.rust-lang.org) has comprehensive documentation, including detailed installation instructions and troubleshooting tips for various platforms.
- The Rust forum: The Rust forum (users.rust-lang.org) is a great place to ask questions and get help from other Rust users. You can search for existing threads or start a new one describing your problem.
- Online communities: You can also find help on websites like Stack Overflow, Reddit (r/rust), and various Discord servers or chat groups dedicated to Rust.

Remember to provide as much information as possible about your problem, including your operating system, the exact error messages you're seeing, and the steps you've already taken to try to resolve it. This will help others assist you more effectively.

Okay, let's discuss how to manage project dependencies using Cargo and the Cargo.toml file.

3.2 Managing Dependencies with Cargo.toml

When you start building more complex Rust applications, especially in machine learning, you'll rarely rely solely on the code you write yourself. You'll often need to use external libraries, also known as "dependencies" or "crates" in the Rust ecosystem, to provide functionality like numerical computation, data manipulation, or specific machine learning algorithms.

Cargo, Rust's build system and package manager, makes managing these dependencies incredibly easy. It uses a file called Cargo.toml to keep track of which libraries your project needs and which versions to use.

Understanding the Cargo.toml File

The Cargo.toml file is a central configuration file for your Rust project. It's written in TOML (Tom's Obvious, Minimal Language), which is designed to be easy to read and write. This file tells Cargo everything it needs to know about your project, including its name, version, and, most importantly, its dependencies.

Let's break down a typical Cargo.toml file:

Ini, TOML

```
[package]

name = "my_ml_project" # The name of your
project.  This is how other crates will refer to
your project, if it were a library.

version = "0.1.0"     # The initial version of
your project.  Follows Semantic Versioning.

authors = ["Your Name <your.email@example.com>"]
# Your name and email address.

edition = "2021"     # The Rust edition used for
this project.  Important for language features.

# See more keys and their definitions at
https://doc.rust-lang.org/cargo/reference/manifes
t.html
```

```
[dependencies] # This section lists your
project's dependencies.

# Add dependencies here, e.g.:

ndarray = "0.15.1"

rand = "0.8.5"

# specific version

serde = { version = "1.0", features = ["derive"]
} # Example with features.
```

- [package] Section: This section contains metadata about your project itself.
  - name: The name of your project. Cargo uses this name for various purposes, such as when building your crate or publishing it to crates.io (the Rust package registry).
  - version: The current version of your project. Rust projects, and crates in general, follow Semantic Versioning (SemVer), which we'll discuss in more detail later.
  - authors: A list of the authors of the project.
  - edition: The Rust edition used for the project. Rust has editions, which are like yearly snapshots of the language. This setting ensures that your code is compiled with the features and behavior of the specified edition.
- [dependencies] Section: This is where you declare the external libraries (crates) that your project relies on.
  - Each line in this section specifies a dependency and its version.
  - ndarray = "0.15.1": This line tells Cargo that your project depends on the ndarray crate, version 0.15.1.

Cargo will download this crate and make it available to your code.

○ rand = "0.8.5": Similarly, this adds a dependency on the rand crate.

○ Dependencies can also be specified with more complex syntax, as shown with serde.

Adding Dependencies

Adding a dependency to your project is as simple as adding a line to the [dependencies] section of your Cargo.toml file and then building your project.

For example, let's say you want to use the ndarray crate for numerical computations and the rand crate for random number generation in your machine learning project. You would add these lines to your Cargo.toml:

Ini, TOML

```
[dependencies]

ndarray = "0.15.1"

rand = "0.8.5"
```

Once you've added these lines, you need to tell Cargo to fetch these dependencies. You do this by running the following command in your project's root directory (the directory containing the Cargo.toml file):

Bash

cargo build

Cargo will then:

1. Read the Cargo.toml file.
2. Download the specified versions of the ndarray and rand crates from crates.io (the central repository for Rust crates).
3. Compile the downloaded crates.
4. Link the compiled crates with your project, making them available for you to use in your Rust code.

Now, you can import and use the ndarray and rand crates in your Rust code:

```rust
Rust

use ndarray::Array2;

use rand::Rng;



fn main() {

    // Create a 2x3 matrix using ndarray.

    let mut matrix = Array2::<f64>::zeros((2,
3));

    println!("Matrix:\n{}", matrix);



    // Generate a random number using rand.

    let mut rng = rand::thread_rng();

    let random_number = rng.gen_range(0.0..1.0);

    println!("Random number: {}", random_number);
```

```
// Assign a value to the matrix

matrix[[0, 0]] = random_number;

println!("Matrix:\n{}", matrix);
```

}

Semantic Versioning (SemVer)

When you specify a version for a dependency in your Cargo.toml file, you're not just giving Cargo a random string. You're using a system called Semantic Versioning (SemVer), which is a standard way of versioning software.

SemVer defines a version number as having three parts:

- Major: The first number (e.g., 1.0.0, the "1" is the major version).
- Minor: The second number (e.g., 1.2.0, the "2" is the minor version).
- Patch: The third number (e.g., 1.2.3, the "3" is the patch version).

The numbers have the following meaning:

- Patch: Patch releases are for bug fixes that don't change the API (the way you use the library). For example, if a crate has a bug and the authors release a new version that fixes it, only the patch number will increase (e.g., from 1.2.0 to 1.2.1).
- Minor: Minor releases are for new features that are backward compatible with the previous version. This means that if you update from 1.2.0 to 1.3.0, your code that used version 1.2.0 should still compile and work correctly.

- Major: Major releases are for changes that are not backward compatible. This means that if you update from 1.0.0 to 2.0.0, your code might break and require changes to work with the new version.

Specifying Version Requirements

In your Cargo.toml file, you don't always have to specify an exact version. Cargo allows you to use various operators to specify a range of acceptable versions. This gives you some flexibility while still ensuring that your project works with compatible versions of the dependencies.

Here are some common ways to specify version requirements:

- "=" or no operator: Exact version. For example, ndarray = "0.15.1" means you want exactly version 0.15.1.
- ">=": Minimum version. For example, ndarray = ">=0.15.0" means you want version 0.15.0 or any later version.
- "<=": Maximum version. For example, ndarray = "<=0.16.0" means you want version 0.16.0 or any earlier version.
- ">" and <: Exclusive minimum and maximum versions (not inclusive).
- ~: Compatible release. For example, ndarray = "~0.15.0" is equivalent to >=0.15.0, <0.16.0. This is often a good choice because it allows Cargo to update to the latest patch release within the same minor version.
- *: Any version. This is generally not recommended, as it can lead to compatibility issues.

Example: Version Requirements

Let's say the latest version of ndarray is 0.16.2. If you specify your dependency in Cargo.toml as:

- ndarray = "0.15.1": You'll only use version 0.15.1.
- ndarray = ">=0.15.0": Cargo might use version 0.16.2, as it's greater than 0.15.0.
- ndarray = "~0.15.0": Cargo will use the latest 0.15.x version, likely 0.15.1, but not 0.16.0.
- ndarray = "*": Cargo could use any version, including 0.16.2, which might introduce breaking changes.

Features

Some crates provide optional features that you can enable or disable. Features allow you to customize which parts of a crate are included in your project, which can be useful for reducing the size of your compiled code or enabling specific functionality.

You can specify features in your Cargo.toml file using the following syntax:

Ini, TOML

```
[dependencies]

serde = { version = "1.0", features = ["derive"]
}
```

In this example, we're using the serde crate, and we're enabling the "derive" feature. This feature allows us to automatically generate code for serializing and deserializing data using the #[derive(Serialize, Deserialize)] attribute.

If you don't specify any features, Cargo will use the default features of the crate.

Workspaces

For larger projects with multiple related crates, Cargo workspaces provide a way to manage them together. A workspace allows you to define a single Cargo.toml file that manages multiple crates, which can be useful for:

- Sharing dependencies between crates.
- Building multiple crates with a single command.
- Organizing a project with a modular architecture.

Cargo and the Cargo.toml file provide a powerful and convenient way to manage dependencies in your Rust projects. By understanding how to specify dependencies and version requirements, you can ensure that your projects use the correct versions of external libraries and that they build consistently across different environments.

3.3 Introduction to Key Numerical and Data Crates (e.g., ndarray, rand)

When you're working on machine learning projects in Rust, you'll often need to perform numerical computations, handle arrays of data, and generate random numbers. Fortunately, the Rust ecosystem provides several excellent crates (libraries) that make these tasks easier and more efficient. Let's take a closer look at two of the most important ones: ndarray and rand.

ndarray: N-Dimensional Arrays

At the heart of many machine learning tasks is the manipulation of numerical data, often organized in the form of arrays. Whether you're dealing with vectors, matrices, or higher-dimensional tensors, you need a data structure that can efficiently store and process this information. That's where the ndarray crate comes in.

ndarray provides an n-dimensional array type for Rust. If you're familiar with NumPy in Python, you can think of ndarray as its Rust counterpart. It allows you to create and work with arrays of any number of dimensions, making it a fundamental tool for numerical computation in Rust.

Key Features of ndarray

Let's explore some of the most important features of ndarray:

Array Creation:

- ndarray offers various ways to create arrays, depending on your needs. You can create arrays from:
    - Vectors: You can easily convert a Rust Vec (a growable vector) into an ndarray::Array1 (a 1-dimensional array, or vector).
    - Slices: You can create an ndarray::ArrayView from a Rust slice, which allows you to work with a portion of an existing array without copying the data.
    - Specific values: You can create arrays filled with zeros, ones, or a specific value using convenient functions.
    - Raw data: For more advanced use cases, you can create arrays from raw memory buffers.
    - From a shape and a vector: Convert a vector with the data and a tuple with the shape into an array.

Array Operations:

- ndarray provides a rich set of methods for performing operations on arrays, including:
    - Element-wise arithmetic: You can perform addition, subtraction, multiplication, division, and other arithmetic operations on arrays of the same shape.
    - Matrix multiplication: ndarray includes efficient implementations of matrix multiplication, which is a fundamental operation in many machine learning algorithms.

- Slicing: You can extract sub-arrays from an array using slicing, allowing you to work with specific portions of the data.
- Reshaping: You can change the shape of an array without changing its underlying data, which is useful for transforming data into the desired format for different operations.
- Reduction operations: Compute sums, means, maxes, mins, etc.

Broadcasting:

- ndarray supports a powerful feature called broadcasting, which allows you to perform operations on arrays with different shapes under certain conditions.
- Broadcasting essentially expands the dimensions of the smaller array to match the larger array, enabling element-wise operations. This can significantly simplify your code and improve performance.

Code Example: Working with ndarray

Let's look at a code example that demonstrates some of the key features of ndarray:

Rust

```rust
use ndarray::Array2; // Import the Array2 type
for 2-dimensional arrays.

use ndarray::arr2;    // Import the arr2! macro
for convenient array creation.
```

```rust
fn main() {
    // Create a 2x3 matrix with specified
    elements using the arr2! macro.
    let matrix: Array2<f64> = arr2(&[
        [1.0, 2.0, 3.0],
        [4.0, 5.0, 6.0],
    ]);
    println!("Matrix:\n{}", matrix);


    // Create a 3x1 vector (1-dimensional array
    with 3 elements).
    let vector = ndarray::array![1.0, 2.0, 3.0];
    println!("Vector:\n{}", vector);


    // Matrix multiplication using the dot
    method.
    let result = matrix.dot(&vector);
    println!("Result of matrix
    multiplication:\n{}", result);


    // Create a new matrix with zeros.
    let mut zeros_matrix =
    Array2::<f64>::zeros((2, 2)); //shape tuple
    println!("Zeros Matrix:\n{}", zeros_matrix);

    // Modify elements using indexing.
    zeros_matrix[[0, 0]] = 5.0;
```

```rust
    zeros_matrix[[1, 1]] = 10.0;

    println!("Modified Zeros Matrix:\n{}",
zeros_matrix);


    // Array slicing

    let row = matrix.row(0);

    println!("First row of matrix:\n{}", row);


    // Element-wise addition

    let matrix_ones = Array2::<f64>::ones((2,
3));

    let added_matrix = matrix + matrix_ones;

    println!("Matrix after element wise
addition:\n{}", added_matrix);

}
```

In this example, we:

- Create a 2x3 matrix using the arr2! macro, which provides a convenient way to define arrays with initial values.
- Create a 3x1 vector using the array! macro.
- Perform matrix multiplication using the dot method.
- Create a matrix filled with zeros using Array2::zeros.
- Modify elements of the matrix using indexing.
- Demonstrate array slicing to extract a row.
- Perform element-wise addition of two matrices.

This example showcases how ndarray simplifies working with multi-dimensional arrays in Rust, providing a foundation for implementing various numerical computations and machine learning algorithms.

rand: Random Number Generation

Random numbers are essential for many tasks in machine learning.

You need them for:

- Initializing the parameters of your models.
- Shuffling your data to prevent bias during training.
- Splitting your data into training and testing sets.
- Sampling from probability distributions.
- Implementing algorithms that involve randomness, such as random forests or genetic algorithms.

The rand crate provides a comprehensive set of tools for generating random numbers in Rust. It offers a variety of random number generators and distributions, allowing you to generate the specific type of random numbers you need for your application.

Key Features of rand

Here are some of the key features of the rand crate:

Random Number Generators (RNGs):

- rand provides different types of random number generators, each with its own characteristics.
- ThreadRng: This is a thread-local random number generator that is usually the most convenient and efficient choice for general-purpose random number generation.
- OsRng: This generator uses the operating system's random number source, which is typically cryptographically secure but might be slower.

Distributions:

- rand allows you to generate random numbers from various probability distributions, including:
    - Uniform distribution: Generates numbers with equal probability within a given range.
    - Normal (Gaussian) distribution: Generates numbers from the bell-shaped curve, which is commonly used in statistics and machine learning.
    - Other distributions: rand also supports other distributions like the Bernoulli, Binomial, Exponential, and more.

Sampling:

- The core functionality of rand revolves around the concept of sampling. You use a random number generator, combined with a distribution, to sample random values.

Code Example: Generating Random Numbers with rand

Let's look at a code example that demonstrates how to use the rand crate to generate different types of random numbers:

Rust

```rust
use rand::Rng;              // Import the Rng trait
for random number generation.

use rand::distributions::Uniform; // Import the
Uniform distribution.
```

```rust
fn main() {
    // Get a thread-local random number
generator.
    let mut rng = rand::thread_rng();


    // Generate a random integer.  The gen method
can generate a variety of primitive types.
    let random_integer: i32 = rng.gen();
    println!("Random integer: {}",
random_integer);


    // Generate a random floating-point number
between 0 and 1 (exclusive).
    let random_float: f64 =
rng.gen_range(0.0..1.0); //range syntax
    println!("Random float (0..1): {}",
random_float);


    // Generate a random number from a uniform
distribution within a specified range.
    let uniform_distribution = Uniform::new(10.0,
20.0); //range 10-20
    let random_in_range: f64 =
rng.sample(uniform_distribution);
    println!("Random float (10..20): {}",
random_in_range);


    // Generate a random boolean value.
    let random_bool: bool = rng.gen();
```

```
    println!("Random bool: {}", random_bool);
}
```

In this example, we:

- Obtain a thread-local random number generator using rand::thread_rng().
- Generate a random integer using the gen method.
- Generate a random floating-point number within the range 0..1 using gen_range.
- Generate a random floating-point number from a uniform distribution within a specified range using Uniform and sample.
- Generate a random boolean value using gen.

This example illustrates how rand provides a flexible and convenient way to generate various types of random numbers in Rust, which is essential for implementing machine learning algorithms and other applications that involve randomness.

Beyond ndarray **and** rand

While ndarray and rand are fundamental for numerical computation and random number generation, you might also encounter other Rust crates that are useful for machine learning, depending on your specific needs:

- serde: This crate is used for serializing and deserializing data, which is the process of converting data between different formats (e.g., from a Rust struct to a JSON string, or vice versa). serde is very useful for loading and saving datasets, model parameters, and other data.
- csv: This crate provides functionality for reading and writing CSV files, which are a common format for storing tabular data. If your machine learning project involves working with data in CSV format, this crate can be very helpful.

- plotters: This crate allows you to create plots and visualizations in Rust. Visualizing your data and model results is an important part of the machine learning workflow, and plotters provides a way to do this directly in Rust.

3.4 Setting Up a Basic Rust Project for ML

When you embark on a machine learning project in Rust, you'll need a well-organized structure to manage your code, dependencies, and build process. Cargo, Rust's powerful build system and package manager, provides a standard way to set up your projects, ensuring consistency and ease of use.

Creating a New Cargo Project

The foundation of any Rust project is a Cargo project. Cargo handles everything from creating the project structure to building your code and managing external libraries.

1. Open your terminal or command prompt:
   - Ensure that you have Rust and Cargo installed on your system, as we discussed in the previous section.
   - Navigate to the directory where you want to create your project. This could be a dedicated folder for your Rust projects or any other location where you prefer to keep your code. For instance, to create the project in a folder named "ml_projects" in your home directory, you would use the following command:

Bash

```
cd ~/ml_projects
```

2. Use cargo new to generate the project:
   - ○ In your terminal, execute the following command:

Bash

cargo new rust_ml_project

   - ○ This command instructs Cargo to create a new project named "rust_ml_project". Cargo will generate a directory with this name and populate it with the essential files and folders for a basic Rust project.
   - ○ Feel free to replace "rust_ml_project" with a more descriptive name that reflects the purpose of your project. For example, if you're working on a project for image classification, you might name it "image_classifier_rs".

3. Navigate into the project directory:
   - ○ After Cargo has created the project, change your current directory to the newly created project directory:

Bash

cd rust_ml_project

   - ○ This step is crucial because it places you in the root directory of your project, where you'll find the Cargo.toml file and the src directory, which are the core components of a Rust project.

Understanding the Project Structure

Cargo follows a standard project structure that promotes organization and maintainability. When you create a new project with cargo new, it sets up the following directory structure:

rust_ml_project/

    Cargo.toml

    src/

      main.rs

    target/

    .git/

Let's break down the purpose of each of these files and directories:

- Cargo.toml: This is the manifest file, the heart of your Rust project. It's written in TOML (Tom's Obvious, Minimal Language), a simple and human-readable configuration format. The Cargo.toml file contains metadata about your project, such as:
    - The project's name (name)
    - The project's version (version)
    - The authors of the project (authors)
    - The Rust edition used for the project (edition)
    - And, most importantly, a list of your project's dependencies (external libraries)
- src/: This directory houses the source code for your project.
    - main.rs: For a binary crate (an executable program), main.rs is the entry point of your application. It contains the main function, which is the first function that is executed when your program starts.

If you're building a command-line application or a standalone program, your code will reside in main.rs.

- lib.rs: If you're building a library crate (a reusable collection of code), lib.rs is the entry point of your library. It declares the modules and functions that make up your library's public API, which other Rust programs can use.

- target/: This directory is where Cargo stores the output of the build process. When you compile your Rust code, Cargo places the resulting executable (for a binary crate) or library files in the target/ directory. You generally don't need to interact with this directory directly; Cargo manages it for you.

- .git/: This directory is created if you initialize your project as a Git repository, which is a common practice for version control. It contains all the necessary files and metadata for Git to track the changes in your project's code.

Adding Dependencies to Cargo.toml

In most machine learning projects, you'll rely on external libraries to provide functionality that you don't want to implement yourself.

For example, you might use a library for:

- Efficient numerical computations (like matrix operations)
- Handling and processing data in various formats
- Implementing specific machine learning algorithms
- Visualizing your data or model results

Cargo makes it easy to manage these external libraries, which are called "dependencies" or "crates" in the Rust ecosystem. You declare the dependencies that your project needs in the Cargo.toml file.

Open Cargo.toml **in a text editor:**

- Use your preferred text editor to open the Cargo.toml file located in the root directory of your project. Popular choices include:
  - Visual Studio Code (VS Code)
  - Sublime Text
  - Atom
  - Notepad (on Windows)
  - Nano or Vim (in the terminal on macOS and Linux)

Specify your dependencies:

- In the Cargo.toml file, locate the [dependencies] section. This section is where you list the crates that your project depends on.
- Add the names and versions of the crates you want to use. For example, to add the ndarray crate (for numerical computations) and the rand crate (for random number generation), you would add the following lines:

```
Ini, TOML
```

```
[dependencies]

ndarray = "0.15.1"

rand = "0.8.5"
```

- Each line specifies the name of the crate and the version you want to use. Cargo uses Semantic Versioning (SemVer) to manage crate versions, which ensures compatibility and helps you avoid breaking changes.

Save the Cargo.toml **file:**

- After adding your dependencies, save the Cargo.toml file.

Writing Your Machine Learning Code

With your project set up and your dependencies declared, you can now start writing the Rust code for your machine learning application or library.

Open src/main.rs **or** src/lib.rs**:**

- Use your text editor to open the appropriate file, depending on whether you're building a binary crate (application) or a library crate:
    - src/main.rs: For an executable program
    - src/lib.rs: For a reusable library

Import the necessary crates:

- At the beginning of your Rust file, use the use keyword to import the crates and modules that you want to use in your code. For example, to use ndarray and rand, you would add the following lines:

```
Rust
```

```rust
use ndarray::Array2; // Import the Array2 struct
from ndarray

use rand::Rng;      // Import the Rng trait from
rand
```

Write your machine learning code:

- Now you can write the Rust code that implements your machine learning logic. This might involve:
  - Loading and preprocessing data
  - Defining and training machine learning models
  - Performing predictions or inference
  - Evaluating model performance
  - Visualizing your results
- Here's a simple example of a src/main.rs file that uses ndarray and rand to generate a random matrix:

```
Rust
```

```rust
use ndarray::Array2;

use rand::Rng;


fn main() {

    // Define the dimensions of the matrix
```

```rust
    let rows = 3;

    let cols = 4;



    // Create a matrix with random values between
0 and 1

    let mut rng = rand::thread_rng(); // Get a
thread-local random number generator

    let matrix =
Array2::<f64>::from_shape_fn((rows, cols), |_|
rng.gen_range(0.0..1.0));



    // Print the matrix to the console

    println!("Random Matrix ({}x{}):\n{}", rows,
cols, matrix);

}
```

Building and Running Your Project

Cargo provides commands to build your code and run your application or library.

Open your terminal or command prompt:

- Navigate to the root directory of your project (the directory containing the Cargo.toml file).

Build the project:

- To compile your Rust code and create an executable (for a binary crate) or a library, use the following command:

Bash

cargo build

- Cargo will read your Cargo.toml file, download any dependencies you've specified, and compile your code. The compiled output will be placed in the target/debug directory by default.

Run the project (for binary crates):

- If you're building an application (i.e., your project has a src/main.rs file), you can run it with the following command:

Bash

cargo run

- Cargo will first build your project (if necessary) and then execute the resulting executable. In the example above, it will print a 3x4 matrix of random numbers to the console.

Example: Setting Up a Library Project for ML Utilities

Let's illustrate how to set up a library project that provides reusable utility functions for machine learning.

Create a new Cargo project (library):

Bash

```
cargo new --lib ml_utils_rs

cd ml_utils_rs
```

- The --lib flag tells Cargo to create a library crate, which is designed to be used by other Rust programs.

Add dependencies to Cargo.toml **(if needed):**

- If your library depends on other crates (like ndarray for numerical operations), add them to your Cargo.toml file:

Ini, TOML

```
[package]

name = "ml_utils_rs"

version = "0.1.0"

authors = ["Your Name <your.email@example.com>"]

edition = "2021"
```

```
[dependencies]

ndarray = "0.15.1"
```

Write your library code in src/lib.rs**:**

- Open the src/lib.rs file and implement the utility functions that your library will provide. For example, you might create a function to normalize data:

Rust

```
use ndarray::Array1;


/// Normalizes a 1-dimensional array (vector)
using min-max scaling.

///

/// # Arguments

///

/// * `data` - A 1-dimensional array of f64
values to normalize.

/// * `min`  - The minimum value in the original
data.

/// * `max`  - The maximum value in the original
data.
```

```rust
///

/// # Returns

///

/// A new 1-dimensional array with the normalized
values, or an error string on failure.

pub fn normalize_array(data: &Array1<f64>, min:
f64, max: f64) -> Result<Array1<f64>, String> {

    if min >= max {

        return Err("min must be less than
max".to_string());

    }


    if data.is_empty() {

        return Ok(Array1::zeros(0));

    }


    let normalized_data: Array1<f64> =
data.map(|&x| (x - min) / (max - min));

    Ok(normalized_data)

}


#[cfg(test)]
```

```rust
mod tests {

    use super::*;

    use ndarray::array;


    #[test]

    fn test_normalize_array() {

        let data = array![1.0, 2.0, 3.0, 4.0,
5.0];

        let min = 1.0;

        let max = 5.0;

        let expected = array![0.0, 0.25, 0.5,
0.75, 1.0];

        let result = normalize_array(&data, min,
max).unwrap();

        assert_eq!(result, expected);

    }


    #[test]

    fn test_normalize_array_invalid_input() {

        let data = array![1.0, 2.0, 3.0, 4.0,
5.0];

        let min = 5.0;
```

```rust
        let max = 1.0;

        let result = normalize_array(&data, min,
max);

        assert!(result.is_err());

        assert_eq!(result.unwrap_err(), "min must
be less than max".to_string());

    }

     #[test]

    fn test_normalize_array_empty_input() {

        let data = array![];

        let min = 5.0;

        let max = 1.0;

        let result = normalize_array(&data, min,
max).unwrap();

        assert_eq!(result, Array1::zeros(0));

    }

}
```

Build your library:

Bash

cargo build

- This will compile your library code, making it ready to be used by other Rust programs.

Using Your Library in Another Project

To use your library in another Rust project (e.g., a machine learning application), you need to add it as a dependency in the application's Cargo.toml file.

Create a new Cargo project (application):

Bash

cargo new my_ml_app

cd my_ml_app

Add your library as a path dependency:

- In the Cargo.toml file of your application project, add your library as a dependency using a path dependency, which tells Cargo where to find the library on your file system:

```
Ini, TOML


[package]

name = "my_ml_app"

version = "0.1.0"

authors = ["Your Name <your.email@example.com>"]
```

```
edition = "2021"
```

```
[dependencies]
```

```
ml_utils_rs = { path = "../ml_utils_rs" } #
Adjust the path if necessary
```

- The path attribute specifies the relative path to the directory containing your library's Cargo.toml file. Make sure to adjust the path if your library is located in a different directory.

Use your library in your application code:

- In your src/main.rs file, import and use the functions from your library:

```
Rust
```

```
use ndarray::array;
```

```
use ml_utils_rs::normalize_array; // Import the
normalize_array function
```

```
fn main() {

    let data = array![1.0, 2.0, 3.0, 4.0, 5.0];

    let min_val = 1.0;
```

```rust
    let max_val = 5.0;


    let normalized_data = normalize_array(&data,
min_val, max_val);

    match normalized_data {

        Ok(normalized) => println!("Normalized
data: {}", normalized),

        Err(err) => println!("Error: {}", err),

    }

}
```

Build and run your application:

Bash

cargo build

cargo run

- This will build your application, which uses the
  normalize_array function from your custom library.

By following these steps, you can set up well-structured Rust
projects for your machine learning endeavors, whether you're
building standalone applications or reusable libraries. Cargo's
project management capabilities ensure that your code is
organized, your dependencies are handled correctly, and your
build process is streamlined.

3.5 Tips for Efficient Rust Development

As you progress in your Rust journey, especially when building machine learning applications, you'll want to adopt practices and utilize tools that enhance your efficiency. Let's discuss some key tips to help you write Rust code more effectively.

Choosing the Right Editor or IDE

The tool you use to write your code can significantly impact your productivity. A good editor or IDE can provide features that streamline the development process, making it faster, more enjoyable, and less prone to errors.

A powerful editor or IDE typically offers the following features:

- Syntax Highlighting: This feature colors different parts of your code (keywords, variables, etc.), making it easier to read and understand the structure. Imagine reading a document where all the important words are bolded and in a different color; that's what syntax highlighting does for code.
- Code Completion (or Autocompletion): As you type, the editor suggests possible completions for keywords, function names, variable names, and more. This saves you a lot of typing and helps you avoid typos. It's like having a helpful assistant that anticipates what you want to write.
- Code Formatting: Consistent code formatting is crucial for readability. A good editor can automatically format your code according to predefined rules, ensuring that indentation, spacing, and line breaks are consistent. This makes your code easier to read and maintain.
- Error Detection and Hints: Modern editors can detect syntax errors and even some logical errors as you type, providing immediate feedback and helping you catch

mistakes early on. They can also offer hints and suggestions for how to fix the errors or improve your code.

- Debugging Support: A debugger allows you to step through your code line by line, inspect the values of variables, and understand the program's execution flow. This is invaluable for finding and fixing bugs, especially in complex code.
- Integration with Build Tools: For Rust, this means seamless integration with Cargo. You should be able to easily build, run, and test your code from within the editor, without having to switch to the command line.

Here are some of the most popular and effective editors and IDEs for Rust development:

- Visual Studio Code (VS Code) with the Rust (rust-analyzer) extension: VS Code is a free, open-source, and highly customizable editor that has gained immense popularity in the Rust community. It's lightweight yet powerful, and with the Rust (rust-analyzer) extension, it provides excellent Rust support.
  - The rust-analyzer provides features like code completion, go-to-definition (jump to the source code of a function or variable), find-all-references (find all places where a variable or function is used), and more.
  - VS Code also has a rich ecosystem of extensions for other tools, like Git, which is very useful for version control.
- IntelliJ IDEA with the Rust plugin: IntelliJ IDEA is a commercial, full-fledged IDE that offers comprehensive support for Rust through a dedicated plugin. It provides advanced features such as:
  - Smart code completion and refactoring (restructuring your code)
  - Deep code analysis to detect potential issues
  - Integrated debugger with advanced features

- ○ Version control integration
- ○ If you're already familiar with the IntelliJ IDEA ecosystem or prefer a more feature-rich IDE, this is an excellent choice.
- Vim/Emacs with Rust plugins: Vim and Emacs are highly configurable and extensible text editors that are popular among experienced developers who value efficiency and customization.
  - ○ With the right plugins, you can transform these editors into powerful Rust development environments.
  - ○ These editors are known for their modal editing (in Vim) and extensive keyboard shortcuts, which can significantly speed up your coding workflow once you become proficient.

The best editor or IDE for you depends on your personal preferences and workflow. I encourage you to try out a few different options and see which one feels most comfortable and productive for you.

Becoming Proficient with Cargo

Cargo is the cornerstone of Rust development. It's the tool you'll use every day to manage your projects, build your code, and handle dependencies. Investing time in mastering Cargo will pay off handsomely in the long run.

Here are some of the most common and essential Cargo commands:

- cargo build: This command compiles your Rust code. It takes your source code and translates it into an executable program (for a binary crate) or a library that can be used by other programs.

- cargo run: This command first builds your project (if it hasn't been built already) and then executes the resulting executable. It's a convenient way to quickly test and run your code during development.
- cargo test: Rust has a built-in testing framework, and this command runs all the tests in your project. Writing tests is crucial for ensuring the correctness of your code, and Cargo makes it easy to execute them.
- cargo check: This command performs a quick check of your code to ensure that it compiles without errors, but it doesn't generate any output files. It's faster than cargo build and can be useful for catching errors early in the development process.
- cargo doc: This command generates documentation for your project and its dependencies. The documentation is created in HTML format, which you can then view in your web browser. This is invaluable for understanding how to use your own code and the libraries you depend on.
- cargo new: As we discussed earlier, this command creates a new Cargo project with a standard directory structure, setting up all the necessary files and configurations for you.
- cargo fmt: This command formats your code according to the official Rust style guidelines, ensuring consistency and readability. We'll talk more about code formatting later.
- cargo clippy: This command runs the Clippy linter, which we'll also discuss later.

To truly master Cargo, I recommend exploring the official Cargo documentation, which provides a wealth of information on all its features and options: https://doc.rust-lang.org/cargo/

Using rustfmt to Format Your Code

Clean and consistent code formatting is essential for readability and maintainability. When code is well-formatted, it's easier to understand, debug, and collaborate with others. Rust provides a tool called rustfmt that automatically formats your code according to the official Rust style guidelines.

Using rustfmt is incredibly simple. Once you have Rust installed, you can format your code by running this command in your project's root directory:

Bash

cargo fmt

This command will reformat all your Rust source files to adhere to the standard Rust style, ensuring consistent indentation, spacing, line breaks, and other formatting rules.

Many editors and IDEs also have plugins or integrations that can automatically format your code whenever you save a file. This can be a huge time-saver and ensures that your code is always formatted correctly without you having to think about it.

By adopting rustfmt as a standard practice, you can eliminate any debates about code style and ensure that your codebase is consistently formatted, making it a pleasure to work with.

Leveraging clippy for Lints

While the Rust compiler is excellent at catching syntax errors and enforcing Rust's safety rules, there's another tool that can help you write even better Rust code: Clippy.

Clippy is a linting tool that analyzes your code for potential errors, stylistic issues, and opportunities for improvement. Think of it as a super-compiler that catches things that the regular compiler might miss.

Clippy can help you:

- Catch common mistakes: Clippy can detect subtle bugs, such as unnecessary clones, inefficient use of iterators, and potential logic errors.
- Write more idiomatic Rust: Clippy encourages you to use Rust features in the way they were intended, leading to more expressive and efficient code.
- Improve performance: Clippy can suggest ways to optimize your code for better performance, such as using more efficient data structures or algorithms.
- Enforce best practices: Clippy helps you adhere to the best practices and coding conventions recommended by the Rust community.

To run Clippy on your project, use this command:

Bash

```bash
cargo clippy
```

Clippy will analyze your code and print any warnings or suggestions it finds. It's highly recommended to pay close attention to Clippy's output and address the issues it identifies. By doing so, you'll write code that is not only correct but also more robust, efficient, and maintainable.

Writing Tests

Testing is a fundamental aspect of software development, and Rust provides excellent support for writing tests. Writing tests ensures that your code works as expected, helps you catch bugs early on, and makes it easier to refactor your code in the future.

Rust has a built-in testing framework that allows you to write two main types of tests:

- Unit tests: These tests verify the behavior of individual functions, modules, or small units of code. They are typically written close to the code they test and are focused on testing specific logic.
- Integration tests: These tests verify how different parts of your code work together. They often involve testing the interaction between multiple modules or crates and are placed in a separate directory.

A test function in Rust is annotated with the #[test] attribute.

Here's a simple example of a unit test:

Rust

```rust
fn add(x: i32, y: i32) -> i32 {

    x + y

}



#[cfg(test)]

mod tests {

    use super::*; // Import the code you want to test



    #[test]

    fn test_add_positive_numbers() {
```

```rust
        assert_eq!(add(2, 3), 5);

    }



    #[test]

    fn test_add_negative_and_positive_numbers() {

        assert_eq!(add(-1, 1), 0);

    }



    #[test]

    fn test_add_negative_numbers() {

        assert_eq!(add(-1, -1), -2);

    }

}
```

In this example, the #[test] attribute marks the test_add_positive_numbers, test_add_negative_and_positive_numbers, and test_add_negative_numbers functions as test functions. Inside each test function, we use the assert_eq! macro to check if the result of the add function matches the expected value.

To run the tests in your project, use the following command:

Bash

cargo test

Cargo will compile your test code and execute all the functions marked with the #[test] attribute. It will then report the results, indicating which tests passed and which ones failed.

Writing comprehensive tests is crucial for building reliable and maintainable machine learning applications. It ensures that your models and data processing logic work correctly and helps you catch potential issues before they lead to problems in production.

Reading the Documentation

The official Rust documentation is an invaluable resource for learning the language, its standard library, and the vast ecosystem of crates. It's comprehensive, well-organized, and regularly updated.

Here are some key parts of the documentation that you should familiarize yourself with:

- The Rust Programming Language Book: This book provides a thorough introduction to Rust, covering everything from the basics to advanced concepts like ownership, borrowing, lifetimes, and generics. It's an excellent starting point for anyone learning Rust.
- The Rust Standard Library: This section documents all the types, traits, and functions provided by the Rust standard library, which is the foundation of any Rust program. You'll find information on working with collections, input/output, concurrency, and more.
- Cargo Documentation: This section explains how to use Cargo to manage your projects, build your code, handle dependencies, run tests, and generate documentation. It's essential for understanding how to work effectively with Rust projects.
- Crates.io: This is the central package registry for Rust crates. You can search for crates to use in your projects and view their documentation.

The official Rust documentation is available online at https://doc.rust-lang.org/. Make it a habit to consult the documentation whenever you have questions about the language or a particular crate.

Engaging with the Rust Community

The Rust community is widely known for being welcoming, helpful, and active. Connecting with other Rust developers can significantly accelerate your learning, provide support when you encounter challenges, and keep you updated on the latest developments in the Rust world.

Here are some excellent ways to engage with the Rust community:

- The Rust Forum: The official Rust forum (users.rust-lang.org) is a web-based platform where you can ask questions, share your projects, and participate in discussions about Rust.
- Reddit: The r/rust subreddit is a popular online community where you can find news, articles, tutorials, and discussions related to Rust.
- Discord: There are numerous Discord servers dedicated to Rust, where you can chat with other Rust developers in real-time, ask questions, and get help.
- Meetups and conferences: Attending Rust meetups and conferences, either online or in person, is a great way to meet other Rust developers, learn from experts, and network with people who share your passion for the language.

Don't hesitate to ask questions, share your code, and contribute to the community in any way you can. The Rust community is a valuable resource that can greatly enhance your Rust development journey

Chapter 4: Data Handling and Preprocessing with Rust

Welcome to the exciting, and often crucial, stage of a machine learning project: handling and preprocessing data! In this chapter, we'll explore how Rust can be used to efficiently and effectively manage your data, getting it ready for the modeling phase.

4.1 Reading Data from Various Sources (CSV, JSON, etc.) in Rust

In the world of programming, and especially in fields like machine learning, data rarely comes in a format that your program can use directly. It often resides in external sources like files, databases, or web APIs. Therefore, the ability to read and parse data from different formats is a fundamental skill. Rust, with its focus on reliability and performance, provides excellent tools for this task.

Let's discuss how to read data from some of the most common formats

CSV: Comma Separated Values

CSV is a simple and widely used format for storing tabular data. Think of it as a simplified spreadsheet where each row is a record, and the values within each record are separated by commas.

For instance, imagine you have a CSV file named "temperatures.csv" containing temperature readings:

Code snippet

date,city,temperature_celsius

2024-07-28,London,20.5

2024-07-28,New York,25.0

2024-07-28,Tokyo,28.0

2024-07-29,London,21.0

2024-07-29,New York,26.5

The first row is the header, specifying the column names: date, city, and temperature_celsius. Each subsequent row represents a temperature reading for a specific date and city.

Reading CSV Data with the csv Crate

Rust provides the csv crate to handle CSV files efficiently. To use it, you'll need to add it as a dependency to your Cargo.toml file:

```Ini, TOML
[package]

# ... other package information ...



[dependencies]

csv = "1.3.0" # Or the latest version from
crates.io
```

Now, let's write a Rust function to read this temperature data from the CSV file:

```Rust
use std::error::Error;

use std::io;

use csv::Reader;
```

```rust
// Represents a single temperature reading.

struct TemperatureReading {

    date: String,

    city: String,

    temperature_celsius: f64,

}



fn read_temperature_data(filename: &str) ->
Result<Vec<TemperatureReading>, Box<dyn Error>> {

    // 1. Create a CSV reader from the file path.

    let mut reader =
Reader::from_path(filename)?;


    // 2. Store the temperature readings.

    let mut readings = Vec::new();


    // 3. Iterate over the records (rows) in the
CSV file.

    for result in reader.records() {

        // 4. Handle potential errors while
reading each record.
```

```rust
    let record = result?;


    // 5. Extract and parse the data from
each record.
    let date = record[0].to_string();

    let city = record[1].to_string();

    let temperature_celsius: f64 =
record[2].parse()?;


    // 6. Create a TemperatureReading struct
and add it to the vector.
    let reading = TemperatureReading {

        date,

        city,

        temperature_celsius,

    };

    readings.push(reading);

    }


    Ok(readings)

}
```

```rust
fn main() {

    // 1. Call the function to read the CSV data.

    match
read_temperature_data("temperatures.csv") {

        Ok(readings) => {

            // 2. Process the vector of
TemperatureReading structs.

            for reading in readings {

                println!(

                    "Date: {}, City: {},
Temperature: {:.1}°C",

                    reading.date, reading.city,
reading.temperature_celsius

                );

            }

        }

        Err(e) => {

            // 3. Handle any errors that occurred
during the process.

            eprintln!("Error reading temperature
data: {}", e);

        }

    }
```

```
}
```

Let's break down this code:

Define a struct:

- We define a struct named TemperatureReading to represent a single temperature reading. This struct has fields for date, city, and temperature_celsius, which correspond to the columns in our CSV data.

read_temperature_data function:

- This function takes the filename of the CSV file as a string and returns a Result<Vec<TemperatureReading>, Box<dyn Error>>.
  - Result is used for error handling.
  - Ok(Vec<TemperatureReading>) indicates that the function was successful and returns a vector of TemperatureReading structs.
  - Err(Box<dyn Error>) indicates that an error occurred, and it returns a boxed trait object representing the error.

Create a CSV reader:

- let mut reader = Reader::from_path(filename)?;
  - We create a csv::Reader using Reader::from_path, passing the filename.
  - The ? operator propagates any errors that occur during file opening.

- The mut keyword makes the reader mutable because we'll be reading data from it.

Initialize a vector:

- let mut readings = Vec::new();
    - We create an empty vector named readings to store the TemperatureReading structs that we'll create from the CSV data.

Iterate over records:

- for result in reader.records() { ... }
    - We iterate over the rows of the CSV file using reader.records(), which returns an iterator. Each item in the iterator is a Result<csv::StringRecord, csv::Error>, representing either a successful row read or an error.

Handle record errors:

- let record = result?;
    - Inside the loop, we use the ? operator to handle potential errors when reading each row. If a row cannot be read, the function returns the error.

Extract and parse data:

- We extract the data from each field of the record (which is a csv::StringRecord) and convert it to the appropriate data type.
    - let date = record[0].to_string();
    - We get the date from the first column (index 0) and convert it to a String.
    - let city = record[1].to_string();
    - We get the city from the second column (index 1) and convert it to a String.
    - let temperature_celsius: f64 = record[2].parse()?;
    - We get the temperature from the third column (index 2), which is initially a string, and use parse() to convert it into a 64-bit floating-point number (f64). The ? operator handles any potential parsing errors (e.g., if the temperature value is not a valid number).

Create a struct and add it to the vector:

- We create a TemperatureReading struct using the extracted data.
- We push the reading struct onto the readings vector.

Return the result:

- Ok(readings): If the loop completes without errors, we return the readings vector, which now contains all the temperature readings from the CSV file.

Handle errors in main:

- In the main function, we call read_temperature_data and use a match statement to handle the Result.
  - If read_temperature_data returns Ok(readings), we iterate over the vector of TemperatureReading structs and print the data.
  - If read_temperature_data returns an Err(e), we print an error message to the standard error stream (eprintln!).

JSON: JavaScript Object Notation

JSON is a text-based format that is widely used for representing structured data, especially in web APIs. It's human-readable and easy for machines to parse. JSON organizes data as key-value pairs, similar to a dictionary in Python or an object in JavaScript.

For example, the temperature data could also be represented in JSON like this:

JSON

```
[

  {

    "date": "2024-07-28",

    "city": "London",

    "temperature_celsius": 20.5

  },

  {
```

```json
    "date": "2024-07-28",

    "city": "New York",

    "temperature_celsius": 25.0
  },
  {

    "date": "2024-07-28",

    "city": "Tokyo",

    "temperature_celsius": 28.0
  },
  {

    "date": "2024-07-29",

    "city": "London",

    "temperature_celsius": 21.0
  },
  {

    "date": "2024-07-29",

    "city": "New York",

    "temperature_celsius": 26.5
  }
]
```

This JSON represents an array of temperature reading objects. Each object has keys like "date", "city", and "temperature_celsius" with their corresponding values.

Reading JSON Data with the serde_json **Crate**

Rust provides the serde_json crate, which leverages the powerful Serde serialization and deserialization framework, to work with JSON data.

To use serde_json, **add these dependencies to your Cargo.toml:**

Ini, TOML

```
[dependencies]

serde = { version = "1.0", features = ["derive"]
} # Required for Serde's derive macros

serde_json = "1.0"
```

Now, let's write a function to read the temperature data from a JSON string:

Rust

```
use serde::Deserialize;

use serde_json::{Result, Value};



// 1. Define a struct to represent the structure
of a single temperature reading object in the
JSON.

#[derive(Debug, Deserialize)]
```

```rust
struct TemperatureReading {

    date: String,

    city: String,

    temperature_celsius: f64,

}



fn read_temperature_data_from_json(json_str:
&str) -> Result<Vec<TemperatureReading>> {

    // 2. Parse the JSON string into a
    serde_json::Value.

    let json_value: Value =
    serde_json::from_str(json_str)?;


    // 3. Ensure the JSON data is a JSON array.

    let temperature_readings_array = json_value

        .as_array()

        .ok_or("Expected a JSON array of
    temperature readings")?;


    // 4. Deserialize each JSON object in the
    array into a TemperatureReading struct.

    let mut temperature_readings = Vec::new();
```

```rust
    for reading_value in
temperature_readings_array {

        let reading: TemperatureReading =
serde_json::from_value(reading_value.clone())?;

        temperature_readings.push(reading);

    }



    Ok(temperature_readings)

}



fn main() {

    // 5. A JSON string representing an array of
temperature readings.

    let json_data = r#"[

      {

        "date": "2024-07-28",

        "city": "London",

        "temperature_celsius": 20.5

      },

      {

        "date": "2024-07-28",

        "city": "New York",
```

```
      "temperature_celsius": 25.0

    },

    {

      "date": "2024-07-28",

      "city": "Tokyo",

      "temperature_celsius": 28.0

    },

    {

      "date": "2024-07-29",

      "city": "London",

      "temperature_celsius": 21.0

    },

    {

      "date": "2024-07-29",

      "city": "New York",

      "temperature_celsius": 26.5

    }

  ]"#;


  // 6. Call the function to read the JSON
data.
```

```
    match
read_temperature_data_from_json(json_data) {

        Ok(readings) => {

            // 7. Process the vector of
TemperatureReading structs.

            for reading in readings {

                println!("Date: {}, City: {},
Temperature: {:.1}°C", reading.date,
reading.city, reading.temperature_celsius);

            }

        }

        Err(e) => {

            // 8. Handle any errors.

            eprintln!("Error reading JSON data:
{}", e);

        }

    }

}
```

Let's break down this code:

Define a struct:

- We define a struct named TemperatureReading with fields that match the keys in the JSON objects.
- The #[derive(Debug, Deserialize)] annotation does the following:

- o Debug: Enables us to easily print the struct using println!("{:?}"), which is helpful for debugging and inspecting the data.
- o Deserialize: This is where Serde's magic happens. It automatically generates the code to convert a JSON value into a TemperatureReading struct. The field names in the struct *must* match the keys in the JSON data for this to work correctly.

read_temperature_data_from_json function:

- This function takes a JSON string as input and returns a Result<Vec<TemperatureReading>, serde_json::Error>.
  - o serde_json::Error is the error type used by serde_json for JSON-specific errors.
  - o We aim to return a Vec<TemperatureReading>, a vector of TemperatureReading structs, because our JSON data represents an array of temperature readings.

Parse the JSON string:

- let json_value: Value = serde_json::from_str(json_str)?;
  - o We use serde_json::from_str to parse the JSON string (json_str) into a serde_json::Value.
  - o serde_json::Value is a type that can hold any valid JSON value (object, array, string, number, boolean, or null). It's a flexible way to represent JSON data.
  - o The ? operator handles any potential parsing errors.
- Extract the array:
  let temperature_readings_array = json_value .as_array()

.ok_or("Expected a JSON array of temperature readings")?; We use json_value.as_array() to try to convert the json_value into a JSON array.

.ok_or("Expected a JSON array") converts the Option returned by as_array() into a Result. If json_value is not a JSON array, as_array() returns None, and we create an Err with a descriptive message.
The operator then propagates this error if the JSON is not an array.

Deserialize the array of temperature readings:

- We create an empty vector temperature_readings to store the parsed TemperatureReading structs.
- We iterate over the elements of the temperature_readings_array (which we expect to be JSON objects representing individual temperature readings).
- let reading: TemperatureReading = serde_json::from_value(reading_value.clone())?;
  - For each element in the array, we use serde_json::from_value to convert that JSON value into a TemperatureReading struct.
  - The ? operator handles any deserialization errors that might occur if the JSON object doesn't match the structure of the TemperatureReading struct.
  - We use clone() because from_value takes ownership of the value, and we need to use the reading_value multiple times in the loop.

Return the result:

- Ok(temperature_readings): If everything goes well, we return the vector of TemperatureReading structs.

Handle errors in main:

- We define a sample JSON string. The r#""# syntax creates a raw string literal, which allows you to include unescaped double quotes and other special characters. This is often convenient for writing JSON strings in Rust code.
- We call read_temperature_data_from_json to parse the JSON string.
- We use a match statement to handle the Result:
- If the parsing is successful (Ok(readings)), we iterate over the vector of TemperatureReading structs and print each reading's details.
  - If an error occurs (Err(e)), we print an informative error message to the standard error stream.

Key Concepts from the JSON Example

- Serde: Serde is a powerful framework that enables you to serialize and deserialize Rust data structures to and from various formats, including JSON. The #[derive(Deserialize)] annotation automatically generates the code to handle the conversion from JSON to your Rust struct.
- serde_json::Value: This type represents a JSON value. It can hold any valid JSON data, such as objects, arrays, strings, numbers, and booleans. It's useful for working with JSON data of unknown or complex structure.

- Error Handling: We use Rust's Result type and the ? operator to handle potential errors during JSON parsing and data extraction, ensuring our program is robust.

Beyond CSV and JSON

While CSV and JSON are very common, you'll encounter other data formats.

Here are a few important ones:

- Parquet: A columnar storage format optimized for large datasets and efficient data processing. It's often used in big data ecosystems like Hadoop and Spark. Rust crates like parquet are available for working with Parquet files.
- Arrow: A language-agnostic columnar memory format designed for efficient data transfer and processing. It's often used in conjunction with Parquet and other data processing tools. The arrow crate in Rust provides support for working with Arrow data.

The choice of data format often depends on factors like:

- Data source: Data from a database might require a different approach than data from a web API.
- Data size and structure: For massive datasets, columnar formats like Parquet and Arrow can offer significant performance advantages.
- Tooling and framework requirements: Some machine learning tools or data processing frameworks might have specific format preferences.

4.2 Efficient Data Structures for Numerical and Categorical Data

When working with machine learning in Rust, choosing the right data structures to store your data is crucial for performance and efficiency. Machine learning deals with two primary types of data: numerical and categorical, each requiring different storage and manipulation strategies.

Numerical Data

Numerical data represents quantities or measurements. Examples include:

- Temperature readings
- Stock prices
- Sensor measurements
- Image pixel intensities

Efficiently storing and processing numerical data is paramount in machine learning, as models often involve complex mathematical operations on large datasets.

ndarray for Numerical Data

In Rust, the ndarray crate is the go-to solution for handling numerical data. It provides an n-dimensional array type, similar to NumPy arrays in Python, offering powerful features and excellent performance.

Key Features of ndarray

- N-dimensional arrays: ndarray can represent arrays of any dimension, from simple vectors to multi-dimensional tensors. This is essential for representing various types of data, such as:
  - 1D arrays: For feature vectors or time series data.
  - 2D arrays: For matrices, commonly used to represent datasets with rows as samples and columns as features.
  - 3D arrays: For image data (height, width, color channels) or time series with multiple variables.

- Higher dimensions: For more complex data, like volumetric data or batched inputs in neural networks.
- Efficient memory layout: ndarray arrays are stored in contiguous memory blocks, which allows for efficient access and vectorized operations. This is crucial for performance, as modern CPUs can process data much faster when it's stored in a contiguous manner.
- Broadcasting: ndarray supports broadcasting, a powerful feature that allows you to perform operations on arrays with different shapes under certain conditions. This can significantly simplify your code and improve performance by avoiding explicit loops.
- Slicing and views: ndarray provides flexible ways to access subsets of an array without copying the underlying data. This is essential for working with large datasets, where copying can be expensive.
- Integration with Rust's ecosystem: ndarray integrates well with other Rust crates, such as rayon for parallel computation, enabling you to leverage Rust's performance and safety features.

Code Example: Using ndarray **for Numerical Data**

Let's look at an example of creating and manipulating numerical data using ndarray:

Rust

```
use ndarray::Array2; // Import the 2D array type.



fn main() {

    // 1. Create a 2x3 matrix with f64 (64-bit
floating-point) elements.
```

```rust
    let data: Array2<f64> =
Array2::from_shape_vec(

        (2, 3), // Shape: 2 rows, 3 columns

        vec![1.0, 2.0, 3.0, 4.0, 5.0, 6.0], //
Data: elements in row-major order

    )

    .unwrap(); // unwrap because the shape and
data are known to be compatible


    println!("Original Matrix:\n{}", data);


    // 2. Perform element-wise operations.

    let squared_data = data.map(|&x| x * x); //
Square each element

    println!("Squared Data:\n{}", squared_data);


    // 3. Calculate the sum of all elements.

    let sum = data.sum();

    println!("Sum of elements: {}", sum);


    // 4. Access a specific element.

    let element_1_2 = data[[0, 1]]; // Access
element at row 0, column 1 (value 2.0)
```

```
    println!("Element at (0, 1): {}",
element_1_2);
```

```
    // 5. Create a slice (view) of the matrix.

    let row_0 = data.row(0); // Get the first row

    println!("First row:\n{}", row_0);

}
```

In this example:

1. We create a 2x3 matrix with f64 (64-bit floating-point) elements using Array2::from_shape_vec. We provide the shape of the matrix as a tuple (2, 3) and the data as a vector, which is arranged in row-major order. The unwrap() call is used because we know the provided shape and data are compatible, and the creation will not fail.
2. We perform an element-wise operation using the map method. The closure |&x| x * x squares each element of the matrix.
3. We calculate the sum of all elements using the sum method.
4. We access a specific element using the [[row, column]] indexing syntax.
5. We create a view of the first row using the row method. This allows us to access the row's data without copying it.

Categorical Data

Categorical data represents values that can only take on a limited number of categories or labels.

Examples include:

- Colors: "red", "green", "blue"
- City names: "London", "New York", "Tokyo"

- Product categories: "Electronics", "Clothing", "Books"
- Movie genres: "Comedy", "Drama", "Action"

Unlike numerical data, categorical data doesn't have a natural ordering or scale. You can't perform arithmetic operations on categories (e.g., "red" + "blue" doesn't make sense).

Rust's enum for Categorical Data

Rust's enum (enumeration) type is a perfect fit for representing categorical data. An enum allows you to define a type that can take on a fixed set of possible values, each representing a category.

Code Example: Using enum for Categorical Data

Here's how you can use an enum to represent product categories:

Rust

```
use std::fmt; // Import the fmt module for
implementing Display.



// 1. Define an enum to represent product
categories.
#[derive(Debug, Clone, Copy, PartialEq, Eq)]
enum ProductCategory {

    Electronics,

    Clothing,

    Books,

    Appliances,
```

```rust
}


// 2. Implement the Display trait for the enum.

impl fmt::Display for ProductCategory {

    fn fmt(&self, f: &mut fmt::Formatter<'_>) ->
fmt::Result {

        match self {

            ProductCategory::Electronics =>
write!(f, "Electronics"),

            ProductCategory::Clothing =>
write!(f, "Clothing"),

            ProductCategory::Books => write!(f,
"Books"),

            ProductCategory::Appliances =>
write!(f, "Appliances"),

        }

    }

}


fn main() {

    // 3. Create a vector of product categories.

    let categories = vec![

        ProductCategory::Electronics,
```

```rust
        ProductCategory::Clothing,

        ProductCategory::Books,

        ProductCategory::Electronics,

        ProductCategory::Appliances,

    ];



    // 4. Print the categories.

    println!("Product Categories: {:?}",
categories);



    // 5. Iterate over the categories and print
them as strings.

    println!("Product Categories (as strings):");

    for category in &categories {

        println!("{}", category);

    }

    // 6. Check for equality

    let first_category = categories[0];

    let second_category = categories[1];

    println!("First category == second category:
{}", first_category == second_category);

}
```

In this example:

1. We define an enum named ProductCategory with four variants: Electronics, Clothing, Books, and Appliances.
   - The #[derive(Debug, Clone, Copy, PartialEq, Eq)] annotation automatically implements several useful traits for our enum:
     - Debug: Allows us to print the enum values using println!("{:?}"), which is helpful for debugging.
     - Clone: Allows us to create copies of enum values. Since enums don't store data on the heap, cloning is simple and efficient.
     - Copy: Makes the enum type copyable, meaning that when you assign an enum value to a new variable, the value is copied rather than moved. This is safe and efficient for enums.
     - PartialEq, Eq: Allows us to compare enum values for equality using the == and != operators.
2. We implement the fmt::Display trait for the ProductCategory enum.
   - This trait allows us to convert enum values into strings using the format! macro or the {} format specifier in println!.
   - The fmt trait's fmt method takes a mutable reference to a formatter (f) and writes the string representation of the enum value to the formatter.
3. We create a vector of ProductCategory enum values.
4. We print the vector using println!("{:?}"), which uses the Debug trait implementation.
5. We iterate over the vector and print each category as a string using println!("{}", category), which uses the Display trait implementation we defined.
6. We demonstrate the equality check using ==.

Why Use Enums for Categorical Data?

- Type safety: Enums ensure that you can only use valid categories, preventing errors caused by typos or invalid values.
- Readability: Enums make your code more readable by providing meaningful names for categories instead of using arbitrary strings or numbers.
- Efficiency: Enums are often represented as integers internally, making them efficient to store and compare.
- Completeness: The match statement in Rust forces you to handle all possible enum variants, preventing you from accidentally missing a case.

Handling Categorical Data in Machine Learning

While enums are excellent for representing categorical data in Rust, machine learning models typically require numerical input. Therefore, you'll often need to convert categorical data into a numerical representation before feeding it to a model. This process is called feature encoding. We'll discuss common encoding techniques like one-hot encoding and label encoding in the next section.

4.3 Data Cleaning Techniques

In the real world, data is rarely perfect. It often comes with imperfections that can hinder the performance of your machine learning models. Two common types of data imperfections are missing values and outliers, and handling them appropriately is a crucial step in the data preprocessing pipeline.

Missing Values

Missing values occur when some data points are not available for certain features.

This can happen for various reasons, such as:

- Data collection errors: Some data might not have been recorded or entered correctly.
- Data loss: Some data might have been lost during transmission or storage.
- Incomplete data: Some data points might simply not have the information for certain features.
- Privacy concerns: Certain data might be intentionally omitted to protect privacy.

For example, you might have a dataset of customer information where some customers didn't provide their age, or you might have sensor data where some sensor readings were lost due to a network interruption.

Missing values can cause problems for machine learning models because most algorithms expect complete data points. If a model encounters a missing value during training or prediction, it might produce inaccurate results or even fail to work altogether.

Handling Missing Values in Rust

Rust itself doesn't have a specific data structure for representing missing values in the same way that some other languages (like Python with Pandas) do. However, Rust's type system and error handling mechanisms provide the tools you need to handle missing values effectively.

The most common way to represent missing values in Rust is by using the Option<T> type.

An Option<T> can have two possible values:

- Some(value): The value is present.
- None: The value is missing.

For numerical data, you can also use the f64::NAN (Not a Number) value, which is a special floating-point value that represents an undefined or unrepresentable value.

Here's a breakdown of common strategies for handling missing values, along with Rust code examples:

1. Removing Data Points with Missing Values

The simplest approach is to remove any data points (rows) that have missing values. However, this should be done cautiously, as it can lead to a significant loss of data if many rows have missing values.

Rust

```rust
use ndarray::Array2;



fn remove_rows_with_missing_values(data:
&Array2<Option<f64>>) -> Array2<f64> {

    // 1. Get the number of rows and columns.

    let (rows, cols) = data.dim();



    // 2. Create a vector to store the rows that
do not contain any missing values.

    let mut cleaned_rows =
Vec::with_capacity(rows);



    // 3. Iterate over the rows of the input
array.
```

```rust
    for i in 0..rows {

        let mut row_valid = true;

        let mut row_values =
Vec::with_capacity(cols);

        for j in 0..cols {

            match data[[i, j]] {

                Some(value) =>
row_values.push(value),

                None => {

                    row_valid = false;

                    break; // If a missing value
is found, skip the rest of the row.

                }

            }

        }

        if row_valid {

cleaned_rows.extend_from_slice(&row_values);

        }

    }


    // 4. Create a new Array2 from the cleaned
rows.
```

```rust
    if cleaned_rows.is_empty() {

        Array2::zeros((0, cols))

    } else {

Array2::from_shape_vec((cleaned_rows.len() /
cols, cols), cleaned_rows).unwrap()

    }

}


fn main() {

    // 1. Create a sample 2D array with
Option<f64> to represent potential missing
values.

    let data = Array2::from_shape_vec(

        (3, 3),

        vec![

            Some(1.0),

            Some(2.0),

            Some(3.0),

            Some(4.0),

            None,

            Some(6.0),
```

```
        Some(7.0),

        Some(8.0),

        Some(9.0),

    ],

)

.unwrap();


println!("Original Data:\n{}", data);



// 2. Remove rows with missing values.

let cleaned_data =
remove_rows_with_missing_values(&data);

println!("Cleaned Data:\n{}", cleaned_data);

}
```

In this example:

- We represent missing values using Option<f64>.
- The remove_rows_with_missing_values function takes an Array2<Option<f64>> as input and returns an Array2<f64> containing only the rows without any None values.
- We iterate through each row and check for the presence of None. If a row contains a None, it's skipped.
- The valid rows are collected into a new Array2<f64>.

2. Imputation: Replacing Missing Values

Imputation involves replacing missing values with estimated values. This is often a better approach than removing data points, as it preserves more of your data.

Here are some common imputation methods:

- Mean/Median Imputation: For numerical features, you can replace missing values with the mean or median of the non-missing values in that column. The median is generally more robust to outliers.
- Most Frequent Value (Mode) Imputation: For categorical features, you can replace missing values with the most frequent value (mode) in that column.
- Constant Value Imputation: You can replace missing values with a predefined constant value, such as 0 or -1. This can be useful in specific situations, but it's important to choose a value that makes sense in the context of your data.

Code Example: Mean Imputation in Rust

```rust
Rust


use ndarray::{Array2, Axis};



fn mean_imputation(data: &Array2<Option<f64>>) ->
Array2<f64> {

    // 1. Get the number of rows and columns.

    let (rows, cols) = data.dim();



    // 2. Create a new Array2 to store the
imputed data.
```

```rust
    let mut imputed_data =
Array2::<f64>::zeros((rows, cols));


    // 3. Iterate over the columns.

    for j in 0..cols {

        // 4. Extract the column as an Array1.

        let column = data.column(j);


        // 5. Calculate the mean of the
non-missing values in the column.

        let mut non_missing_values = Vec::new();

        for &value in column.iter() {

            if let Some(v) = value {

                non_missing_values.push(v);

            }

        }

        let mean = if
non_missing_values.is_empty() {

            0.0 // Handle the case where all
values are missing.

        } else {
```

```rust
        non_missing_values.iter().sum::<f64>() /
        non_missing_values.len() as f64

        };


        // 6. Impute the missing values in the
    column with the mean.

        for i in 0..rows {

            imputed_data[[i, j]] = match data[[i,
    j]] {

                Some(value) => value,

                None => mean,

            };

        }

    }

    imputed_data

}


fn main() {

    // 1. Create a sample 2D array with
    Option<f64> to represent potential missing
    values.

    let data = Array2::from_shape_vec(
```

```rust
        (3, 3),
        vec![
            Some(1.0),
            Some(2.0),
            Some(3.0),
            Some(4.0),
            None,
            Some(6.0),
            Some(7.0),
            Some(8.0),
            Some(9.0),
        ],
    )
    .unwrap();

    println!("Original Data:\n{}", data);

    // 2. Impute missing values with the mean.
    let imputed_data = mean_imputation(&data);
    println!("Imputed Data:\n{}", imputed_data);
```

}

In this example:

1. We represent missing values using Option<f64>.
2. The mean_imputation function takes an Array2<Option<f64>> as input and returns an Array2<f64> with missing values replaced by the mean of their respective columns.
3. We iterate through each column, calculate the mean of the non-missing values, and then replace each None value in that column with the calculated mean.

Outliers

Outliers are data points that deviate significantly from the rest of the data. They can be caused by:

- Measurement[1] errors: A faulty sensor or incorrect data entry.
- Data corruption: Errors during data transmission or storage.
- Genuine extreme values: Some data points might be genuinely extreme but still valid (e.g., a very high income in a dataset of salaries).

Outliers can distort the results of your analysis and negatively impact the performance of your machine learning models. Therefore, it's important to detect and handle them appropriately.

Here are some common techniques for handling outliers:

- Removing outliers: You can remove data points that are identified as outliers. However, be cautious, as removing too many data points can lead to a loss of information.
- Transforming outliers: You can apply transformations to the data to reduce the impact of outliers.

Common transformations include:

- Logarithmic transformation: Compresses the range of values, making extreme values less extreme.
- Winsorizing: Limits extreme values to a specified percentile (e.g., replacing values above the 99th percentile with the value at the 99th percentile).
- Using robust models: Some machine learning models are less sensitive to outliers than others. For example, tree-based models are[2] generally more robust to outliers than linear models.

Code Example: Removing Outliers Using the Z-Score Method in Rust

The Z-score measures how many standard deviations a data point is away from the mean. Data points with a Z-score above a certain threshold are considered[3] outliers.

Rust

```rust
use ndarray::{Array1, ArrayView1};



fn remove_outliers_z_score(data: &Array1<f64>,
threshold: f64) -> Array1<f64> {

    // 1. Calculate the mean and standard
deviation of the data.

    let mean = data.mean().unwrap();

    let std_dev = data.std(0.0); // 0.0 for
population standard deviation
```

```rust
    // 2. Filter the data points based on their
Z-score.

    // Create a new vector containing only the
data points whose Z-score is below the threshold.

    let filtered_data: Vec<f64> = data

        .iter() // Iterate over the elements of
the Array1

        .filter(|&x| { // Filter the elements
based on a condition

            let z_score = (x - mean).abs() /
std_dev;

            z_score <= threshold

        })

        .cloned() // Convert the filtered
references (&f64) back to owned values (f64)

        .collect(); // Collect the filtered
values into a new Vec<f64>


    // 3. Create a new Array1 from the filtered
data.

    Array1::from(filtered_data)

}


fn main() {
```

```
    // 1. Create a sample 1D array with an
outlier.

    let data = Array1::from(vec![1.0, 2.0, 3.0,
4.0, 5.0, 100.0]);

    println!("Original Data: {}", data);



    // 2. Remove outliers using the Z-score
method with a threshold of 2.0.

    let cleaned_data =
remove_outliers_z_score(&data, 2.0);

    println!("Cleaned Data: {}", cleaned_data);

}
```

In this example:

1. We calculate the mean and standard deviation of the data.
2. We filter the data, keeping only the values whose Z-score is below the specified threshold (in this case, 2.0).
3. We collect the filtered values into a new Array1.

4.4 Feature Scaling and Normalization in Rust

In machine learning, the features (or input variables) in your dataset can have vastly different ranges. For example, one feature might represent age, ranging from 0 to 100, while another feature might represent income, ranging from 0 to 1,000,000. This difference in scale can cause problems for some machine learning algorithms.

Algorithms like gradient descent, which is used to train many machine learning models, converge much faster when features are on a similar scale. Features with larger values can dominate the learning process, while features with smaller values might be ignored.

Feature scaling and normalization are techniques used to bring your numerical features onto a similar scale. This can improve the performance and stability of your machine learning models.

Let's explore two common scaling techniques and how to implement them in Rust

1. Min-Max Scaling

Min-max scaling, also known as normalization, scales the features to a specific range, typically between 0 and[1] 1. The formula for min-max scaling is:

x_scaled = (x - x_min) / (x_max - x_min)

Where:

- x is the original value of the feature.
- x_min is the minimum value of the feature[2] in the dataset.
- x_max is the maximum value of the feature in the dataset.
- x_scaled is the scaled value of the feature,[3] which will be between 0 and 1.

Code Example: Min-Max Scaling in Rust

Here's how you can implement min-max scaling for a single feature (represented as an Array1<f64>) in Rust:

```
Rust
```

```rust
use ndarray::Array1;
```

```rust
use std::iter::FloatIterator;


fn min_max_scaling(data: &Array1<f64>) ->
Array1<f64> {

    // 1. Find the minimum and maximum values in
    the data.

    let mut iter: FloatIterator<&f64> =
data.iter().cloned(); //data.iter().cloned();

    let min_val = iter.next().unwrap_or(0.0);

    let max_val =
data.iter().cloned().reduce(f64::max).unwrap_or(0
.0);


    // 2. Handle the edge case where min_val
    equals max_val.

    if min_val == max_val {

        // If all values are the same, scaling is
    not necessary.  Return a vector of zeros.

        return Array1::zeros(data.len());

    }


    // 3. Apply the min-max scaling formula to
    each element.
```

```
    data.map(|&x| (x - min_val) / (max_val -
min_val))

}



fn main() {

    // 1. Create a sample 1D array of numerical
data.

    let data = Array1::from(vec![1.0, 2.0, 3.0,
4.0, 5.0]);

    println!("Original Data: {}", data);



    // 2. Apply min-max scaling to the data.

    let scaled_data = min_max_scaling(&data);

    println!("Scaled Data: {}", scaled_data);

}
```

In this example:

1. We define a function min_max_scaling that takes a reference to an Array1<f64> (a 1D array of 64-bit floating-point numbers) as input and returns a new Array1<f64> containing the scaled data.
2. We find the minimum and maximum values in the input array using the iter(), cloned(), next(), and reduce() methods. * data.iter(): Creates an iterator over the elements of the array. * cloned(): Converts the iterator from yielding references (&f64) to yielding owned values (f64), which is necessary for methods like min and max. * next(): Retrieves

the first element of the iterator. * unwrap_or(0.0): returns the first element or 0.0 if the array is empty. * reduce(): Applies a function to each element of the iterator, accumulating the result into a single value. We use f64::max to find the maximum value.

3. We handle the edge case where all values in the input array are the same (i.e., min_val equals max_val). In this case, the scaling formula would result in division by zero. To avoid this, we return a new array filled with zeros, as scaling is not necessary when all values are identical.

4. We use the map method to apply the min-max scaling formula to each element of the input array. The closure |&x| (x - min_val) / (max_val - min_val) calculates the scaled value for each element x.

2. Standardization

Standardization, also known as Z-score normalization, scales the features to have a mean of 0 and a standard deviation of 1. The formula for standardization is:

x_scaled = (x - mean) / std_dev

Where:

- x is the original value of the feature.
- mean is the mean (average) value of the feature in the dataset.
- std_dev is the standard deviation of the feature in the dataset.
- x_scaled is the scaled value of the feature.

Standardization is less affected by outliers than min-max scaling, as it doesn't compress the data to a specific range.

Code Example: Standardization in Rust

Here's how to implement standardization for a single feature in Rust:

Rust

```rust
use ndarray::Array1;



fn standardization(data: &Array1<f64>) ->
Array1<f64> {

    // 1. Calculate the mean of the data.

    let mean = data.mean().unwrap_or(0.0);



    // 2. Calculate the standard deviation of the
data.

    let std_dev = data.std(0.0); // Use 0.0 for
population standard deviation



    // 3. Handle the case where the standard
deviation is zero.

    if std_dev == 0.0 {

        // If the standard deviation is zero, all
values are the same,

        // and scaling is not necessary. Return a
vector of zeros.
```

```rust
        return Array1::zeros(data.len());

    }



    // 4. Apply the standardization formula to
each element.

    data.map(|&x| (x - mean) / std_dev)

}



fn main() {

    // 1. Create a sample 1D array of numerical
data.

    let data = Array1::from(vec![1.0, 2.0, 3.0,
4.0, 5.0]);

    println!("Original Data: {}", data);



    // 2. Apply standardization to the data.

    let scaled_data = standardization(&data);

    println!("Scaled Data: {}", scaled_data);

}
```

In this example:

1. We define a function standardization that takes a reference to an Array1<f64> as input and returns a new Array1<f64> containing the scaled data.

2. We calculate the mean of the input array using the mean() method. The unwrap_or(0.0) handles the case where the array is empty, returning 0.0 as the mean.
3. We calculate the standard deviation of the input array using the std() method. We pass 0.0 as an argument to indicate that we want to calculate the population standard deviation (rather than the sample standard deviation).
4. We handle the edge case where the standard deviation is zero. This occurs when all values in the input array are the same. In this case, scaling is not necessary, and we return a vector of zeros to avoid division by zero.
5. We use the map method to apply the standardization formula to each element of the input array.

Choosing Between Min-Max Scaling and Standardization

The choice between min-max scaling and standardization depends on the specific requirements of your machine learning task and the characteristics of your data.

- Min-Max Scaling:
  - Scales data to a specific range (typically 0 to 1).
  - Preserves the original distribution of the data.
  - Sensitive to outliers, as they can significantly affect the x_min and x_max values.
  - Useful when you need to constrain your data to a specific range, such as when working with image pixel intensities (which typically range from 0 to 255).
- Standardization:
  - Scales data to have a mean of 0 and a standard deviation of 1.
  - Makes the data more similar to a standard normal distribution.
  - Less affected by outliers than min-max scaling.

- Often preferred for algorithms that assume a normal distribution of the data, such as linear regression, logistic regression, and support vector machines.

In many cases, standardization is the preferred choice, especially when you're unsure about the distribution of your data or when your data contains outliers. However, if you have a specific reason to scale your data to a particular range, min-max scaling can be useful.

4.5 Feature Encoding

In machine learning, you'll often encounter data that isn't numerical.[1] This type of data, called categorical data, represents qualities or characteristics rather than quantities.[2] Examples include colors ("red", "green", "blue"), city names ("London", "Paris", "Tokyo"), or product categories ("Electronics", "Clothing", "Books").[3]

Most machine learning models, however, require numerical input.[4] Therefore, we need to convert categorical data into a numerical representation before we can use it to train our models.[5] This process is called feature encoding.

Let's explore two common feature encoding techniques: one-hot encoding and label encoding

1. One-Hot Encoding

One-hot encoding is a technique that represents each category as a binary vector.[6] For each category, you create a new binary feature (a column in your data).[7] If a data point belongs to that category, the corresponding binary feature is set to 1; otherwise, it's set to 0.[8]

For example, consider the "color" feature with the categories "red", "green", and "blue".[9] One-hot encoding would transform this feature into three new binary features: "color_red", "color_green", and "color_blue".[10]

color	color_red	color_green	color_blue
red	1	0	0
green	0	1	0
blue	0[11]	0	1
red	1	0	0

Here's how you can implement one-hot encoding for a vector of strings in Rust:

Code Example: One-Hot Encoding in Rust

Rust

```rust
use std::collections::HashSet;

use ndarray::{Array2, Array1};


fn one_hot_encode(data: &[String]) -> Array2<f64>
{
```

```rust
// 1. Find the unique values (categories) in
the data.
    let unique_values: HashSet<_> =
data.iter().collect();

    let num_values = unique_values.len();

    let num_rows = data.len();



// 2. Create a mapping from each unique value
to its corresponding index.
    let value_to_index:
std::collections::HashMap<_, usize> =
unique_values

        .iter()

        .enumerate()

        .map(|(i, &value)| (value.clone(), i))

        .collect();



// 3. Create a 2D array to store the one-hot
encoded data.
    let mut encoded_data =
Array2::<f64>::zeros((num_rows, num_values));



// 4. Iterate over the original data and set
the corresponding bit in the encoded array.
```

```rust
    for (i, value) in data.iter().enumerate() {

        let index = value_to_index[value];

        encoded_data[[i, index]] = 1.0;

    }

    encoded_data

}


fn main() {

    // 1. Sample categorical data: a vector of
strings representing colors.

    let colors = vec![

        "red".to_string(),

        "green".to_string(),

        "blue".to_string(),

        "red".to_string(),

        "green".to_string(),

    ];

    println!("Original Data:\n{:?}", colors);


    // 2. Perform one-hot encoding.

    let encoded_data = one_hot_encode(&colors);
```

```
    println!("One-Hot Encoded Data:\n{}",
encoded_data);

}
```

Let's break down this code:

1. Find unique values:
   - We use a HashSet to efficiently find the unique values (categories) in the input data. A HashSet only stores each unique value once.
2. Create a mapping:
   - We create a HashMap to store a mapping from each unique value (e.g., "red") to its corresponding index (e.g., 0). This mapping will help us determine which column to set to 1 in the one-hot encoded array.
3. Create the encoded array:
   - We create a 2D array (Array2<f64>) filled with zeros. The number of rows is equal to the number of data points, and the number of columns is equal to the number of unique values (categories).
4. Encode the data:
   - We iterate over the original data (the vector of strings).[12]
   - For each value (e.g., "red"), we use the value_to_index map to get its corresponding index (e.g., 0).
   - We set the element at encoded_data[[i, index]] to 1.0, where i is the row index (corresponding to the data point) and index is the column index (corresponding to the category).

2. Label Encoding

Label encoding is a simpler technique that assigns a unique integer to each category.[13] For example, if you have the categories "red", "green", and "blue", label encoding might represent them as 0, 1, and 2, respectively.

Here's how you can implement label encoding for a vector of strings in Rust:

Code Example: Label Encoding in Rust

Rust

```
use std::collections::HashMap;



fn label_encode(data: &[String]) -> (Vec<i32>,
HashMap<String, i32>) {

    // 1. Create a HashMap to store the mapping
from string values to integer labels.

    let mut encoding_map = HashMap::new();

    let mut encoded_data = Vec::new();

    let mut next_label = 0;



    // 2. Iterate over the data and assign
labels.

    for value in data.iter() {

        // 3. Check if the value is already in
the encoding map.

        let label =
encoding_map.entry(value.clone()).or_insert_with(
|| {
```

```rust
        // 4. If the value is not in the map,
assign it a new label.

        next_label += 1;

        &(next_label - 1) // Return a
reference to the inserted label.

        });

        encoded_data.push(*label);

    }


    (encoded_data, encoding_map)
}


fn main() {

    // 1. Sample categorical data: a vector of
strings representing colors.

    let colors = vec![

        "red".to_string(),

        "green".to_string(),

        "blue".to_string(),

        "red".to_string(),

        "green".to_string(),

    ];
```

```
    println!("Original Data:\n{:?}", colors);



    // 2. Perform label encoding.

    let (encoded_data, encoding_map) =
label_encode(&colors);

    println!("Label Encoded Data:\n{:?}",
encoded_data);

    println!("Encoding Map:\n{:?}",
encoding_map);

}
```

Let's break down this code:

Create a mapping:

- We create a HashMap named encoding_map to store the mapping from string values (e.g., "red") to integer labels (e.g., 0).

Iterate and assign labels:

- We iterate over the original data (the vector of strings).[14]
- For each value, we use the entry method of the HashMap to check if the value is already in the map.
  - If the value is already in the map, entry returns a mutable reference to the existing label.
  - If the value is not in the map, entry inserts the value as a key and assigns it a new integer label. We use or_insert_with to provide a closure that calculates the new label.

- We push the label (either the existing one or the new one) into the encoded_data vector.

Return the result:

- The function returns a tuple containing:
  - The encoded_data: A vector of integers representing the label-encoded data.
  - The encoding_map: The HashMap that maps the original string values to their integer labels. This map is important because you'll need it to convert the encoded data back to the original categorical values if needed.

Choosing Between One-Hot Encoding and Label Encoding

The choice between one-hot encoding and label encoding depends on the nature of your categorical data and the machine learning model you're using.

One-Hot Encoding:

- Creates a binary vector for each category.
- Does not imply any ordinal relationship between the categories.
- Suitable for nominal categorical data (categories with no inherent order), such as colors, city names, or product categories.[15]
- Can increase the dimensionality of your data, especially if you have many categories.

Label Encoding:

- Assigns a unique integer to each category.
- Imposes an ordinal relationship between the categories, which might not be appropriate.
- Suitable for ordinal categorical data (categories with a meaningful order), such as education levels ("high school", "bachelor's", "master's") or customer satisfaction ratings ("low", "medium", "high").[16]
- Does not increase the dimensionality of your data.

Important Considerations

- One-Hot Encoding and Dimensionality: One-hot encoding can significantly increase the dimensionality of your dataset, especially if you have a categorical feature with many unique categories.[17] This can lead to increased computational complexity and memory usage.[18] It might also cause overfitting, a situation where the model learns the training data too well and performs poorly on unseen data. Consider using techniques like dimensionality reduction or feature hashing if you encounter this issue.
- Label Encoding and Ordinality: Label encoding assigns integers to categories, implying an ordinal relationship that might not exist.[19] Using label encoding for nominal data can mislead your model. For instance, if you encode "red" as 0, "green" as 1, and "blue" as 2, the model might incorrectly assume that "blue" is "greater" than "red".

In general, one-hot encoding is usually preferred for nominal data, while label encoding is suitable for ordinal data. If you're unsure, it's often safer to use one-hot encoding.

4.6 Working with DataFrames

When dealing with structured data, like you'd find in a CSV file or a database table, a DataFrame is an incredibly useful data structure. A DataFrame organizes data into rows and columns, similar to a spreadsheet or a table. Each column represents a variable, and each row represents an observation or data point.

While Rust's machine learning ecosystem is still evolving, there are ways to work with DataFrames effectively.

What is a DataFrame?

To understand DataFrames, let's consider a simple example. Suppose you have data about customers, with information like their names, ages, and cities. A DataFrame would arrange this data in a table-like structure:

Name	Age	City
Alice	30	New York
Bob	25	London
Charlie	40	Tokyo

In this table:
- Each column has a name (e.g., "Name", "Age", "City").
- Each row represents a customer, with values for each of the columns.

DataFrames provide a structured and intuitive way to represent and manipulate tabular data, making them essential for data analysis and machine learning.

Why Use DataFrames?

DataFrames offer several advantages:

- Structured data representation: They provide a clear and organized way to store and access data.
- Tabular operations: They support common operations on tabular data, such as filtering rows, selecting columns, grouping data, and joining tables.
- Data alignment: They automatically align data based on row and column labels, preventing errors when performing operations on data with different structures.
- Integration with data science tools: They often integrate well with other data science and machine learning libraries.

Working with DataFrames in Rust

While Rust's DataFrame ecosystem is still developing, the polars crate is a rising star in this area.

Polars: A High-Performance DataFrame Library

Polars is a DataFrame library for Rust that is designed for high performance and efficiency. It's built on top of the Apache Arrow columnar memory format, which allows for fast data processing and efficient memory usage.

Key Features of Polars

- Columnar data storage: Polars stores data in columns, which is more efficient for analytical queries than row-based storage.
- Lazy evaluation: Polars uses a query optimization technique called lazy evaluation, which delays the execution of operations until they are actually needed. This allows Polars to optimize the entire query plan and perform operations more efficiently.

- Parallel processing: Polars is designed to take advantage of multi-core processors, enabling you to process large datasets quickly.
- Integration with Arrow: Polars is built on top of Apache Arrow, which provides a standardized way to represent columnar data in memory. This allows for seamless integration with other data processing tools and libraries.

Code Example: Working with Polars

To use Polars, you'll need to add it as a dependency in your Cargo.toml file:

Ini, TOML

```
[dependencies]

polars = { version = "0.38.0", features =
["lazy"] } # Or the latest version
```

Here's a basic example of how to create and manipulate a DataFrame using Polars:

Rust

```
use polars::prelude::*;

use polars::df;



fn main() -> Result<(), Box<dyn
std::error::Error>> {

    // 1. Create a DataFrame.

    let df = df!(
```

```
        "Name" => &["Alice", "Bob", "Charlie"],

        "Age" => &[30, 25, 40],

        "City" => &["New York", "London",
"Tokyo"],

    )?;


    // 2. Print the DataFrame.

    println!("Original DataFrame:\n{}", df);


    // 3. Select a column.

    let names = df.column("Name")?;

    println!("Names:\n{}", names);


    // 4. Filter the DataFrame.

    let filtered_df =
df.filter(col("Age").gt(25))?;

    println!("Filtered DataFrame (Age >
25):\n{}", filtered_df);


    // 5. Add a new column.

    let df_with_age_plus_one =
df.with_column(col("Age") + 1)?;
```

```
    println!("DataFrame with Age + 1:\n{}",
df_with_age_plus_one);


    //6. Group by

    let grouped_df = df.groupby(["City"])

        .select(["Age"])

        .agg_mean()?;

    println!("Grouped by City and Mean Age:\n{}",
grouped_df);


    Ok(())

}
```

In this example:

1. We create a DataFrame using the df! macro. This macro provides a concise way to define a DataFrame with column names and data.
2. We print the DataFrame using println!, which uses Polars's formatting capabilities to display the DataFrame in a tabular format.
3. We select the "Name" column using df.column("Name"), which returns a Series (a column of data).
4. We filter the DataFrame to keep only the rows where the "Age" column is greater than 25, using df.filter and a column expression.
5. We add a new column "AgePlusOne" by adding 1 to the "Age" column using df.with_column and a column expression.

6. We group the DataFrame by the "City" column and calculate the mean age for each city using groupby and agg_mean.

This example demonstrates how Polars provides a powerful and expressive API for working with DataFrames in Rust. You can perform various operations like selecting, filtering, transforming, and aggregating data efficiently.

Polars for Machine Learning

Polars can be a valuable tool in your machine learning workflow in Rust.

You can use it to:

- Load and preprocess data: Read data from CSV files, databases, or other sources into a DataFrame, and then clean, transform, and prepare it for model training.
- Feature engineering: Create new features from existing ones, combine features, and perform other feature engineering tasks.
- Data analysis: Explore your data, calculate summary statistics, and visualize relationships between features.
- Integrate with ML libraries: You can convert data from Polars DataFrames into the format expected by your chosen machine learning library.

While the Rust machine learning ecosystem is still evolving, Polars provides a solid foundation for handling structured data efficiently. As Rust becomes more prevalent in machine learning, Polars is likely to play an increasingly important role.

Chapter 5: Linear Algebra in Rust: The Bedrock of ML

This chapter will explore the fundamental concepts of linear algebra and how they are represented and manipulated in Rust, particularly with the ndarray crate. We'll also discuss the crucial role linear algebra plays in machine learning.

5.1 Vectors and Matrices in Rust (ndarray basics)

Let's begin our exploration of linear algebra in Rust by understanding how to represent its fundamental building blocks: vectors and matrices. In Rust, the ndarray crate provides the tools we need to work with these structures efficiently.

What are Vectors and Matrices?

Before we get into the code, let's refresh our understanding of vectors and matrices:

Vector:

A vector is a one-dimensional array of numbers. You can think of it as a list or a sequence of numbers.

Vectors are used to represent various things, such as:

- A point in space (e.g., [2, 3] represents a point with coordinates x=2, y=3).
- A direction and magnitude (e.g., [1, 0] represents a unit vector pointing to the right).
- A feature in a dataset (e.g., [25, 170, 70] could represent a person's age, height, and weight).

Matrix:

A matrix is a two-dimensional array of numbers, arranged in rows and columns. Matrices are used to represent:

- Linear transformations (e.g., rotations, scaling).
- Systems of linear equations.
- Datasets with multiple features (where each row represents a data point, and each column represents a feature).

The ndarray Crate

The ndarray crate is a Rust library that provides efficient data structures and functions for working with n-dimensional arrays. It's a cornerstone for numerical computation in Rust and is particularly well-suited for machine learning tasks.

Key Concepts in ndarray

- ArrayBase: This is the core trait that defines the behavior of an n-dimensional array. Both Array1 and Array2 implement this trait.
- Array1<T>: Represents a one-dimensional array (a vector) with elements of type T. For example, Array1<f64> is a vector of 64-bit floating-point numbers.
- Array2<T>: Represents a two-dimensional array (a matrix) with elements of type T. For example, Array2<i32> is a matrix of 32-bit integers.
- Shape: The shape of an array is a tuple that indicates the number of elements along each dimension.
  - A vector with 5 elements has a shape of $(5,)$.
  - A 3x4 matrix (3 rows, 4 columns) has a shape of $(3, 4)$.
- Data Type: Arrays store elements of a single data type.

Common data types include:

- f64: 64-bit floating-point numbers (double-precision)
- f32: 32-bit floating-point numbers (single-precision)
- i32: 32-bit signed integers
- u8: 8-bit unsigned integers

Creating Vectors and Matrices with ndarray

Let's see how to create vectors and matrices using ndarray in practice:

1. Creating Vectors

Rust

```rust
use ndarray::Array1; // Import the Array1 type
(for vectors).

use ndarray::array;   // Import the array! macro
(for convenient array creation).


fn main() {
    // 1. Create a vector with specific elements.
    let my_vector: Array1<f64> = array![1.0, 2.0,
3.0, 4.0, 5.0];

    println!("My Vector: {}", my_vector);


    // 2. Create a vector of a specific size
filled with zeros.
    let zero_vector: Array1<i32> =
Array1::zeros(3); // A vector of 3 zeros
```

```rust
    println!("Zero Vector: {}", zero_vector);


    // 3. Create a vector from a Vec.
    let my_vec = vec![10.0, 20.0, 30.0];
    let vector_from_vec: Array1<f64> =
Array1::from(my_vec);
    println!("Vector from Vec: {}",
vector_from_vec);
}
```

In this example:

1. We create a vector named my_vector with the elements [1.0, 2.0, 3.0, 4.0, 5.0].
   - We use the array! macro for convenient initialization.
   - The type annotation Array1<f64> specifies that it's a 1D array (vector) of 64-bit floating-point numbers.
2. We create a vector named zero_vector filled with zeros using the Array1::zeros() function.
   - We specify the size of the vector (3 elements).
   - The type annotation Array1<i32> indicates a vector of 32-bit integers.
3. We create a vector named vector_from_vec from an existing Rust Vec (vector) using the Array1::from() function.

2. Creating Matrices

Rust

```rust
use ndarray::Array2; // Import the Array2 type
(for matrices).
use ndarray::array;   // Import the array! macro.


fn main() {
```

```rust
    // 1. Create a 2x3 matrix with specific
elements.
    let my_matrix: Array2<f64> = array![[1.0,
2.0, 3.0], [4.0, 5.0, 6.0]];
    println!("My Matrix:\n{}", my_matrix);


    // 2. Create a matrix of a specific size
filled with ones.
    let ones_matrix: Array2<f32> =
Array2::ones((2, 2)); // 2x2 matrix of 32-bit
floats
    println!("Ones Matrix:\n{}", ones_matrix);


    // 3. Create a matrix from a Vec and a shape.
    let data = vec![10.0, 20.0, 30.0, 40.0];
    let matrix_from_vec: Array2<f64> =
Array2::from_shape_vec((2, 2), data).unwrap();
    println!("Matrix from Vec:\n{}",
matrix_from_vec);
}
```

In this example:

1. We create a 2x3 matrix named my_matrix with the
   elements:

[[1.0, 2.0, 3.0],

[4.0, 5.0, 6.0]]

   ○ We use the array! macro with nested square brackets
     to represent the rows of the matrix.

- The type annotation Array2<f64> specifies that it's a 2D array (matrix) of 64-bit floating-point numbers.
2. We create a 2x2 matrix named ones_matrix filled with ones using the Array2::ones() function.
   - We provide the shape of the matrix as a tuple (2, 2), indicating 2 rows and 2 columns.
   - The type annotation Array2<f32> indicates a matrix of 32-bit floating-point numbers.
3. We create a 2x2 matrix named matrix_from_vec from a Vec containing the data and a shape tuple.
   - The from_shape_vec function takes the desired shape (2, 2) and the data as a vector.
   - The order of elements in the vector must match the row-major order of the matrix (i.e., elements of the first row, followed by elements of the second row, and so on).
   - The unwrap() call is used because from_shape_vec returns a Result to handle potential errors (e.g., if the vector's length doesn't match the number of elements specified by the shape). In this case, we assume the shape and data are compatible.

Understanding Array Shapes

The shape of an ndarray array is a tuple that describes the number of elements along each dimension.

- For a vector, the shape is a tuple with a single element, representing the length of the vector. For example, a vector with 5 elements has a shape of $(5,)$.
- For a matrix, the shape is a tuple with two elements: the number of rows and the number of columns. For example, a 3x4 matrix (3 rows, 4 columns) has a shape of $(3, 4)$.

You can access the shape of an array using the .shape() method:

Rust

```
use ndarray::array;


fn main() {
    let vector = array![1.0, 2.0, 3.0];
    let matrix = array![[1.0, 2.0], [3.0, 4.0],
[5.0, 6.0]];


    println!("Vector shape: {:?}",
vector.shape()); // Output: [3]
    println!("Matrix shape: {:?}",
matrix.shape()); // Output: [3, 2]
}
```

Specifying Data Types

ndarray arrays store elements of a single data type. You must specify the data type when you create an array. Here are some common data types:

- f64: 64-bit floating-point numbers (double-precision) - the default
- f32: 32-bit floating-point numbers (single-precision)
- i32: 32-bit signed integers
- u32: 32-bit unsigned integers
- i64: 64-bit signed integers
- u64: 64-bit unsigned integers
- u8: 8-bit unsigned integers

The data type is specified as part of the type annotation when you create an array (e.g., Array1<f64>, Array2<i32>).

ndarray provides a powerful and flexible way to represent vectors and matrices in Rust. You can create arrays with specific elements, create arrays filled with zeros or ones, and create arrays from existing Rust vectors. Understanding array shapes and data types is crucial for working effectively with ndarray.

5.4 Matrix Transpose, Inverse, and Determinant

In linear algebra, we often need to manipulate matrices in various ways to prepare them for use in machine learning models or to extract valuable information. Let's discuss three fundamental matrix operations: transpose, inverse, and determinant.

Matrix Transpose

Imagine you have a table of data. The transpose of that table is simply a new table where you've swapped the rows and columns. This is exactly what a matrix transpose does.

Definition of Matrix Transpose

Given a matrix A, its transpose, denoted as A^T (or sometimes A'), is a matrix formed by turning the rows of A into the columns of A, and vice versa.

If A is an m x n matrix (meaning it has m rows and n columns), then its transpose A^T will be an n x m matrix.

For example, suppose we have the following matrix A:

A = [[1, 2, 3],

   [4, 5, 6]]

To find its transpose A^T, we make the first row of A ([1, 2, 3]) the first column of A^T, and the second row of A ([4, 5, 6]) the second column of A^T.

This gives us:

A^T = [[1, 4],

    [2, 5],

    [3, 6]]

Code Example: Matrix Transpose in Rust

Here's how you can calculate the transpose of a matrix using ndarray in Rust:

Rust

```rust
use ndarray::array;

use ndarray::Array2;


fn main() {

    // 1. Create a matrix.

    let matrix_a: Array2<f64> = array![[1.0, 2.0,
3.0], [4.0, 5.0, 6.0]];

    println!("Original Matrix (A):\n{}",
matrix_a);



    // 2. Calculate the transpose using the
`.t()` method.
```

```
    let matrix_a_transpose: Array2<f64> =
matrix_a.t();

    println!("Transpose of A (Aᵀ):\n{}",
matrix_a_transpose);

}
```

In this example:

1. We create a 2x3 matrix matrix_a using the array! macro.
2. We compute the transpose of matrix_a using the .t() method, which is provided by ndarray. The result is a new Array2 matrix, matrix_a_transpose.

Why is Transpose Useful?

The transpose of a matrix is a simple but essential operation with various applications:

- Reshaping data: It can be used to rearrange data for different calculations or to match the expected input format of a function or algorithm.
- Matrix multiplication: In matrix multiplication, you often need to transpose one of the matrices to perform the operation correctly.
- Calculating dot products: The dot product of two vectors can be expressed using matrix multiplication and the transpose.
- Feature transformation: In some machine learning algorithms, you might transpose a matrix of features to change the orientation of your data.

Matrix Inverse

The inverse of a square matrix is a special matrix that, when multiplied by the original matrix, results in the identity matrix.

Definition of Matrix Inverse

Given a square matrix A, its inverse, denoted as A^{-1}, is a matrix that satisfies the following condition:

$$A * A^{-1} = A^{-1} * A = I$$

Where:

- A is the original square matrix.
- A^{-1} is the inverse of A.
- I is the identity matrix.

The identity matrix is a square matrix with 1s on the main diagonal (from the top-left to the bottom-right corner) and 0s everywhere else. For example, the 3x3 identity matrix is:

I_3 = [[1, 0, 0],

[0, 1, 0],

[0, 0, 1]]

When you multiply a matrix by its inverse, you get the identity matrix, which is analogous to multiplying a number by its reciprocal (e.g., 5 * (1/5) = 1).

Important Considerations

- Only square matrices can have an inverse.
- Not all square matrices are invertible. A square matrix is invertible if and only if its determinant is not zero. We'll discuss the determinant later in this chapter.
- Calculating the inverse of a matrix is a computationally intensive operation, especially for large matrices.

Code Example: Matrix Inverse in Rust (using nalgebra**)**

The ndarray crate itself doesn't provide a dedicated function for calculating matrix inverses. For this, you'll typically use a linear algebra library like nalgebra, which is designed for more advanced linear algebra operations.

To use nalgebra, add it as a dependency in your Cargo.toml file:

Ini, TOML

```
[dependencies]

nalgebra = "0.32.0" # Or the latest version from
crates.io
```

Here's how to calculate the inverse of a 3x3 matrix using nalgebra:

Rust

```
use nalgebra::Matrix3; // Import the Matrix3 type
for 3x3 matrices.

use nalgebra::linalg::try_inverse; // Import the
try_inverse function.


fn main() {

    // 1. Create a 3x3 square matrix.

    let matrix_a = Matrix3::new(

        1.0, 0.0, 2.0,

        0.0, 1.0, 0.0,
```

```rust
        2.0, 0.0, 5.0,
    );

    println!("Original Matrix (A):\n{}",
matrix_a);



    // 2. Calculate the inverse using
`try_inverse`.
    let inverse_result = try_inverse(&matrix_a);



    // 3. Handle the result, as the inverse may
not exist.
    match inverse_result {
        Some(matrix_a_inverse) => {
            println!("Inverse of A (A⁻¹):\n{}",
matrix_a_inverse);

        }

        None => {
            println!("Matrix A is not
invertible.");

        }

    }
```

```rust
// Example of a non-invertible matrix
(determinant is zero)

let matrix_b = Matrix3::new(

    1.0, 2.0, 1.0,

    0.0, 0.0, 0.0,

    2.0, 4.0, 2.0,

);

println!("Original Matrix (B):\n{}",
matrix_b);



let inverse_result_b =
try_inverse(&matrix_b);

match inverse_result_b {

    Some(inverse_b) => println!("Inverse of B
(B⁻¹):\n{}", inverse_b),

    None => println!("Matrix B is not
invertible"),

    }

}
```

In this example:

1. We create a 3x3 square matrix named matrix_a using nalgebra::Matrix3.
2. We attempt to calculate its inverse using the try_inverse function from nalgebra.
   - The try_inverse function returns an Option.

- It returns Some(inverse_matrix) if the inverse exists.
- It returns None if the matrix is not invertible (i.e., its determinant is zero).

3. We use a match statement to handle the Option returned by try_inverse:
   ○ If the inverse exists (Some(matrix_a_inverse)), we print the inverse matrix.
   ○ If the inverse doesn't exist (None), we print a message indicating that the matrix is not invertible.

Matrix Determinant

The determinant of a square matrix is a scalar value (a single number) that provides important information about the matrix.

Definition of Matrix Determinant

The determinant of a square matrix A, denoted as det(A) or |A|, is a unique scalar value that can be computed from the elements of A. The formula for calculating the determinant varies depending on the size of the matrix:

- 2x2 matrix:

A = [[a, b],

[c, d]]

det(A) = ad - bc

- 3x3 matrix:

The determinant of a 3x3 matrix is more complex, involving a sum of products of its elements.

- Larger matrice

For matrices larger than 3x3, the determinant is calculated using more complex methods, such as cofactor expansion or Gaussian elimination.

Key Properties of the Determinant

- A square matrix is invertible if and only if its determinant is not zero.
- The determinant can be used to find the area or volume scaling factor of a linear transformation represented by the matrix.
- The determinant appears in various mathematical formulas and algorithms, including solving systems of linear equations and calculating eigenvalues.

Code Example: Matrix Determinant in Rust (using nalgebra)

Similar to calculating the inverse, ndarray doesn't have a built-in function for calculating the determinant. You'll typically rely on a linear algebra library like nalgebra.

Here's how to calculate the determinant of a 3x3 matrix using nalgebra:

Rust

```rust
use nalgebra::Matrix3;


fn main() {

    // 1. Create a 3x3 square matrix.
```

```rust
    let matrix_a = Matrix3::new(

        1.0, 2.0, 3.0,

        4.0, 5.0, 6.0,

        7.0, 8.0, 9.0,

    );

    println!("Original Matrix (A):\n{}",
matrix_a);


    // 2. Calculate the determinant using the
`determinant()` method.

    let determinant_a = matrix_a.determinant();

    println!("Determinant of A: {}",
determinant_a);


    let matrix_b = Matrix3::new(

        2.0, 1.0, 0.0,

        1.0, 3.0, 2.0,

        0.0, 1.0, 4.0,

    );

    println!("Original Matrix (B):\n{}",
matrix_b);

    let determinant_b = matrix_b.determinant();
```

```
    println!("Determinant of B: {}",
determinant_b);

}
```

In this example:

1. We create a 3x3 square matrix named matrix_a using nalgebra::Matrix3.
2. We calculate its determinant using the determinant() method, which is provided by nalgebra.

Why are these operations important?

These matrix operations are fundamental tools in linear algebra and have wide-ranging applications in various fields, including:

- Computer graphics: Matrix transformations (including transpose) are used extensively for rotations, scaling, and projections of objects in 2D and 3D space.
- Solving linear equations: Matrix inversion is a key step in solving systems of linear equations, which arise in many scientific and engineering problems.
- Machine learning: These operations are used extensively in machine learning algorithms:
  - Transpose: Used in feature matrix manipulation and in various matrix calculations.
  - Inverse: Used in some linear regression methods and in certain optimization algorithms.
  - Determinant: Used in change of variable formulas and other advanced calculations.

While ndarray provides excellent support for basic array operations, for more advanced linear algebra calculations like matrix inversion and determinant calculation, libraries like nalgebra are essential. They offer robust and efficient implementations of these operations, ensuring accuracy and performance in your numerical computations.

5.3 Dot Products and Vector Norms

In linear algebra, we often need ways to combine vectors or measure their size. The dot product and vector norms provide us with these capabilities.

Dot Product

The dot product, also known as the scalar product, is a way to multiply two vectors to obtain a single number (a scalar). It reveals information about the relationship between the vectors.

Definition

Given two vectors **a** and **b**, their dot product, denoted as **a** · **b**, is calculated by summing the products of their corresponding components.

If:

$a = [a_1, a_2, ..., a_\square]$

$b = [b_1, b_2, ..., b_\square]$

Then:

$a \cdot b = a_1 * b_1 + a_2 * b_2 + ... + a_\square * b_\square$

In essence, you multiply the first elements, the second elements, and so on, and then add all the results.

Geometric Interpretation

The dot product also has a geometric interpretation:

$a \cdot b = ||a|| * ||b|| * \cos(\theta)$

Where:

- ||**a**|| and ||**b**|| are the magnitudes (lengths) of vectors **a** and **b**, respectively.
- θ is the angle between the two vectors.

This means:

- If **a** and **b** point in the same direction (θ = 0°), the dot product is maximized (cos(0°) = 1).
- If **a** and **b** are perpendicular (orthogonal) (θ = 90°), the dot product is zero (cos(90°) = 0).
- If **a** and **b** point in opposite directions (θ = 180°), the dot product is negative (cos(180°) = -1).

Code Example (Rust with ndarray)

Rust

```rust
use ndarray::array;

use ndarray::Array1;



fn main() {

    let vector_a: Array1<f64> = array![1.0, 2.0, 3.0];

    let vector_b: Array1<f64> = array![4.0, 5.0, 6.0];


    let dot_product: f64 = vector_a.dot(&vector_b);

    println!("Dot Product: {}", dot_product);
```

}

Real-World Example: Recommendation Systems

In recommendation systems, the dot product is used to find similar items. For example, if you represent movies as vectors where each element corresponds to a user's rating, the dot product between two movie vectors indicates how similar their ratings are.

Vector Norms

A norm is a function that assigns a non-negative value representing the "length" or "size" to a vector.

Euclidean Norm (L2 Norm)

The most common norm is the Euclidean norm, also known as the L2 norm. It's the standard way of measuring the length of a vector.

For a vector:

$a = [a_1, a_2, ..., a_\square]$

The Euclidean norm of a, denoted as $||a||_2$, is:

$$||a||_2 = \sqrt{(a_1^2 + a_2^2 + ... + a_\square^2)}$$

Code Example: Euclidean Norm in Rust

```
Rust

use ndarray::array;

use ndarray::Array1;


fn main() {

    let vector_a: Array1<f64> = array![3.0, 4.0];
```

```
    let norm_l2: f64 =
vector_a.dot(&vector_a).sqrt();

    println!("Euclidean Norm: {}", norm_l2); //
Output: 5

}
```

Other Vector Norms

Besides the Euclidean norm, there are other norms, such as:

- L1 Norm (Manhattan Norm): The sum of the absolute values of the vector's elements.
- Infinity Norm (Max Norm): The largest absolute value of the vector's elements.

The dot product and vector norms are essential tools in linear algebra. The dot product measures the relationship between vectors, while norms measure their size. These operations are used extensively in machine learning for tasks like similarity measurement, error calculation, and model regularization.

5.4 Matrix Transpose, Inverse, and Determinant

Matrices, those rectangular arrays of numbers, can be manipulated in various ways.[1] Let's discuss three key operations: transpose, inverse, and determinant.

Matrix Transpose

The transpose of a matrix is a new matrix formed by swapping its rows and columns.[2] It's a simple yet useful operation.

Definition

Given a matrix A, its transpose, denoted as A^T (or sometimes A'), is obtained by interchanging the rows and columns of A.[3]

If A is an m x n matrix (m rows, n columns), then A^T is an n x m matrix.

For example, if A is:

A = [[1, 2, 3],

 [4, 5, 6]]

Then its transpose A^T is:

A^T = [[1, 4],

 [2, 5],

 [3, 6]]

The first row of A becomes the first column of A^T, and so on.

Code Example (Rust with ndarray)

Here's how to calculate the transpose of a matrix using ndarray in Rust:

Rust

```
use ndarray::array;

use ndarray::Array2;


fn main() {

    // 1. Create a matrix.
```

```rust
    let matrix_a: Array2<f64> = array![[1.0, 2.0,
3.0], [4.0, 5.0, 6.0]];

    println!("Original Matrix (A):\n{}",
matrix_a);



    // 2. Calculate the transpose using the
`.t()` method.

    let matrix_a_transpose: Array2<f64> =
matrix_a.t();

    println!("Transpose of A (Aᵀ):\n{}",
matrix_a_transpose);

}
```

In this example, matrix_a.t() returns a new Array2 that is the transpose of matrix_a.

Why is Transpose Useful?

The transpose has several applications:

- Reshaping data: It can rearrange data for calculations.
- Matrix multiplication: It's often needed to make matrix multiplication compatible.
- Calculating dot products: The dot product of vectors a and b can be written as a matrix multiplication: $a^T * b$.[4]
- Feature transformation: In machine learning, it can change the orientation of the feature matrix.

Matrix Inverse

The inverse of a square matrix is a matrix that, when multiplied by the original matrix, results in the identity matrix.[5]

Definition

Given a square matrix A, its inverse, denoted as A^{-1}, satisfies:

$$A * A^{-1} = A^{-1} * A = I$$

Where:

- A is the original square matrix.
- A^{-1} is the inverse of A.[6]
- I is the identity matrix.

The identity matrix is a square matrix with 1s on the main diagonal and 0s elsewhere.[7]

For example, the 3x3 identity matrix is:

I_3 = [[1, 0, 0],

[0, 1, 0],

[0, 0, 1]]

Important Notes

- Only square matrices can have an inverse.
- Not all square matrices are invertible. A matrix is invertible if and only if its determinant is not zero.
- Calculating the inverse is computationally expensive for large matrices.[8]

Code Example: Matrix Inverse in Rust (using nalgebra)

The ndarray crate doesn't have a built-in function for calculating matrix inverses. You'll typically use a linear algebra library like nalgebra for this.

To use nalgebra, add it as a dependency in your Cargo.toml:

Ini, TOML

```
[dependencies]

nalgebra = "0.32.0" # Or the latest version from crates.io
```

Here's how to calculate the inverse of a 3x3 matrix using nalgebra:

Rust

```rust
use nalgebra::Matrix3; // Import the Matrix3 type for 3x3 matrices.

use nalgebra::linalg::try_inverse; // Import the try_inverse function.


fn main() {

    // 1. Create a 3x3 square matrix.

    let matrix_a = Matrix3::new(

        1.0, 0.0, 2.0,

        0.0, 1.0, 0.0,

        2.0, 0.0, 5.0,

    );

    println!("Original Matrix (A):\n{}", matrix_a);
```

```rust
    // 2. Calculate the inverse using
`try_inverse`.

    let inverse_result = try_inverse(&matrix_a);


    // 3. Handle the result, as the inverse may
not exist.

    match inverse_result {

        Some(matrix_a_inverse) => {

            println!("Inverse of A (A⁻¹):\n{}",
matrix_a_inverse);

        }

        None => {

            println!("Matrix A is not
invertible.");

        }

    }


    // Example of a non-invertible matrix
(determinant is zero)

    let matrix_b = Matrix3::new(

        1.0, 2.0, 1.0,

        0.0, 0.0, 0.0,
```

```
        2.0, 4.0, 2.0,

    );

    println!("Original Matrix (B):\n{}",
matrix_b);



    let inverse_result_b =
try_inverse(&matrix_b);

    match inverse_result_b {

        Some(inverse_b) => println!("Inverse of B
(B⁻¹):\n{}", inverse_b),

        None => println!("Matrix B is not
invertible"),

    }

}
```

Matrix Determinant

The determinant of a square matrix is a scalar value that provides key information about the matrix.[9]

Definition

The determinant of a square matrix A, denoted as det(A) or |A|, is a unique scalar value that can be computed from the elements of A.[10]

The formula varies depending on the matrix size:

- 2x2 matrix:

A = [[a, b],

  [c, d]]

det(A) = ad - bc

- 3x3 matrix:

The determinant of a 3x3 matrix involves a more complex calculation with sums of products.

- Larger matrices:

For matrices larger than 3x3, the determinant is calculated using methods like cofactor expansion or Gaussian elimination.

Key Properties

- A square matrix is invertible if and only if its determinant is not zero.[11]
- The determinant relates to the scaling factor of a linear transformation represented by the matrix.
- The determinant is used in various mathematical formulas and algorithms.[12]

Code Example: Matrix Determinant in Rust (using nalgebra)

Again, use nalgebra for determinant calculations:

Rust

```rust
use nalgebra::Matrix3;


fn main() {

    // 1. Create a 3x3 square matrix.

    let matrix_a = Matrix3::new(

        1.0, 2.0, 3.0,

        4.0, 5.0, 6.0,

        7.0, 8.0, 9.0,

    );

    println!("Original Matrix (A):\n{}",
matrix_a);


    // 2. Calculate the determinant using the
`determinant()` method.

    let determinant_a = matrix_a.determinant();

    println!("Determinant of A: {}",
determinant_a);


    let matrix_b = Matrix3::new(

        2.0, 1.0, 0.0,

        1.0, 3.0, 2.0,

        0.0, 1.0, 4.0,
```

```
    );

    println!("Original Matrix (B):\n{}",
matrix_b);

    let determinant_b = matrix_b.determinant();

    println!("Determinant of B: {}",
determinant_b);

}
```

These operations—transpose, inverse, and determinant—are essential tools for working with matrices.[13] They enable you to manipulate, analyze, and extract crucial information from matrix data, which is fundamental in various fields, including machine learning.

5.5 Eigenvalues and Eigenvectors

In linear algebra, eigenvalues and eigenvectors are special pairs of numbers and vectors that reveal important properties of a linear transformation represented by a matrix.

Eigenvectors

Imagine you have a square matrix A. An eigenvector of A is a non-zero vector **v** that, when multiplied by A, doesn't change its direction. It might get stretched or compressed, but it always stays on the same line.

Eigenvalues

The factor by which the eigenvector **v** is stretched or compressed when multiplied by A is called the eigenvalue, denoted by λ (lambda).

The Equation

Mathematically, this relationship is expressed as:

$A * v = \lambda * v$

Where:

- A is a square matrix.
- **v** is an eigenvector of A.
- λ is the eigenvalue corresponding to the eigenvector **v**.

In simpler terms: When you multiply a matrix A by one of its eigenvectors **v**, the result is the same as multiplying the eigenvector **v** by a scalar (the eigenvalue λ). The matrix A acts on the eigenvector **v** by simply scaling it.

Example

Let's consider a simple example:

A = [[2, 0],
　　 [0, 3]]

The vector v = [1, 0] is an eigenvector of A because:

A * v = [[2, 0],　* [1] = [2] = 2 * [1]
　　　　[0, 3]]　[0] [0]　[0]

In this case, the eigenvalue λ is 2. The matrix A scales the eigenvector **v** by a factor of 2, but its direction remains unchanged (it still points along the x-axis).

Similarly, the vector v = [0, 1] is also an eigenvector of A with the eigenvalue λ = 3:

A * v = [[2, 0],　* [0] = [0] = 3 * [0]
　　　　[0, 3]]　[1] [3]　[1]

Finding Eigenvalues and Eigenvectors

Calculating eigenvalues and eigenvectors involves solving a characteristic equation, which can become quite complex for larger matrices. In practice, we typically use numerical algorithms and software libraries to compute them.

Conceptual Overview of the Process

1. Form the characteristic equation:

To find the eigenvalues λ, we rearrange the equation $Av = \lambda v$:

$$(A - \lambda I) * v = 0$$

Where I is the identity matrix. This equation has a non-zero solution for **v** only if the determinant of $(A - \lambda I)$ is zero:

$$det(A - \lambda I) = 0$$

This equation is called the characteristic equation, and solving it gives us the eigenvalues λ.

2. Solve for eigenvalues:

Solving the characteristic equation, which is a polynomial equation, gives us the eigenvalues $\lambda_1, \lambda_2, ..., \lambda\square$ of the matrix A.

3. Solve for eigenvectors:

For each eigenvalue λ_i, we substitute it back into the equation $(A - \lambda_i I)\ v = 0$ and solve for the eigenvector **v**. This usually involves solving a system of linear equations.

Libraries for Eigenvalue and Eigenvector Computation in Rust

While ndarray provides the basic array structures, it doesn't include functions for calculating eigenvalues and eigenvectors directly. You'll typically rely on a dedicated linear algebra library like nalgebra for these computations.

Using nalgebra

To use nalgebra, add it as a dependency in your Cargo.toml file:

Ini, TOML

```ini
[dependencies]
nalgebra = "0.32.0" # Or the latest version from crates.io
```

Here's an example of how to calculate eigenvalues and eigenvectors using nalgebra:

Rust

```rust
use nalgebra::Matrix2;
use nalgebra::ComplexField;
use nalgebra::Eigen;


fn main() {
    // 1. Create a 2x2 square matrix (convert to complex numbers).
    let matrix_a = Matrix2::<f64>::new(
        2.0, -1.0,
        1.0, 2.0,
```

```
    );


    // 2. Compute the eigenvalues and
eigenvectors.
    let eigen =
Eigen::new(matrix_a.cast::<ComplexField<f64>>());
    // Cast to complex numbers


    // 3. Get the eigenvalues.
    let eigenvalues = eigen.eigenvalues;
    println!("Eigenvalues:\n{}", eigenvalues);


    // 4. Get the eigenvectors.
    let eigenvectors = eigen.eigenvectors;
    println!("Eigenvectors:\n{}", eigenvectors);
}
```

In this example:

1. We create a 2x2 square matrix matrix_a using nalgebra::Matrix2. We use f64 (real numbers)
2. We compute the eigenvalues and eigenvectors using Eigen::new(). Since eigenvalues and eigenvectors can be complex, we cast the matrix to a complex field.
3. We access the eigenvalues from the eigen.eigenvalues field, which is a vector of complex numbers.
4. We access the eigenvectors from the eigen.eigenvectors field, which is a matrix whose columns are the eigenvectors.

Real-World Example: Principal Component Analysis (PCA)

Eigenvalues and eigenvectors are crucial in dimensionality reduction techniques like Principal Component Analysis (PCA). PCA uses them to identify the principal components of a dataset, which are the directions of maximum variance. By projecting the data onto these principal components, you can reduce the number of dimensions while preserving the most important information.

5.6 Applications of Linear Algebra in Machine Learning

Linear algebra is not just an abstract mathematical concept; it's the bedrock upon which many machine learning algorithms are built. It provides a powerful and concise way to represent and manipulate data, making complex computations feasible and efficient.

Let's look at some key applications of linear algebra in machine learning:

1. Linear Regression

Linear regression is a fundamental algorithm used to model the relationship between a dependent variable[1] (the value you want to predict) and one or more independent variables (the features you use to make the prediction).

At its core, linear regression relies heavily on linear algebra. The relationship between the variables is expressed as a linear equation:

$y = Xw + b$

Where:

- y is the vector of target variables (the values you want to predict).
- X is the feature matrix, where each row represents a data point, and each column represents a feature.
- w is the weight vector, which contains the coefficients that determine the influence of each feature.
- b is the bias term, a constant that represents the y-intercept of the line.

To find the optimal values for w and b, we use techniques like ordinary least squares, which involves solving a system of linear equations. This process is greatly simplified and made computationally efficient using matrix operations.

For example, suppose you want to predict house prices based on their size and number of bedrooms. You can represent the house sizes and bedroom counts as a feature matrix X, the house prices as a vector y, and then use linear algebra to solve for the optimal weight vector w and bias b that best fit the data.

2. Logistic Regression

Logistic regression, despite its name, is a classification algorithm used to predict the probability of a data point belonging to a particular class (e.g., whether an email is spam or not spam).

While the core of logistic regression involves a non-linear function (the sigmoid function), linear algebra is still essential for handling the input features and calculating the weighted sum of those features.

The input features for each data point are typically represented as a vector, and these vectors are often organized into a feature matrix, similar to linear regression. The algorithm then learns a weight vector that, when combined with the input features using a dot product, determines the probability of the data point belonging to a specific class.

For instance, if you want to classify emails as spam or not spam, you could represent each email as a vector of features (e.g., word frequencies, presence of certain keywords). Logistic regression uses linear algebra to calculate a weighted sum of these features, which is then passed through the sigmoid function to obtain the probability of the email being spam.

3. Neural Networks

Neural networks, the foundation of deep learning, are heavily reliant on linear algebra. The core operation in a neural network is the multiplication of matrices and vectors.

A neural network consists of layers of interconnected nodes called neurons. Each neuron performs a simple computation: it takes a weighted sum of its inputs, applies an activation function, and passes the result to the next layer.

These weighted sums are calculated efficiently using matrix multiplication. The inputs to a layer are represented as a vector or a matrix, the weights of the connections between neurons are represented as a matrix, and the output of the layer is calculated by multiplying the input by the weight matrix.

For example, in an image recognition task, the input image might be represented as a matrix of pixel intensities. This matrix is then multiplied by a series of weight matrices in the neural network to extract features and eventually classify the image.

4. Dimensionality Reduction

Dimensionality reduction techniques aim to reduce the number of features in a dataset while preserving[2] its most important information.

This can be useful for:

- Visualizing high-dimensional data: It's difficult to visualize data with more than three dimensions, so dimensionality reduction can help you plot the data in 2D or 3D.
- Improving model performance: Reducing the number of features can simplify models, prevent overfitting (where the model learns the training data too well and performs poorly on unseen data), and speed up training.
- Reducing storage requirements: Lower-dimensional data requires less storage space.

One of the most popular dimensionality reduction techniques is Principal Component Analysis (PCA), which relies heavily on linear algebra.

Principal Component Analysis (PCA)

PCA uses the eigenvectors and eigenvalues of the covariance matrix of the data to identify the principal components, which are the directions of maximum variance in the data. By projecting the data onto these principal components,[3] you can reduce the number of dimensions while retaining the most important information.

For example, if you have a dataset of images with many features (e.g., pixel intensities), PCA can help you find a smaller set of features that capture the most significant variations in the images, allowing you to represent the images with fewer dimensions.

5. Recommender Systems

Recommender systems aim to predict user preferences and suggest items that users might like, such as movies, books, or products.

One common technique used in recommender systems is matrix factorization, a linear algebra method.

Matrix Factorization

In matrix factorization, the user-item interaction matrix (which represents how users have interacted with items, e.g., ratings) is decomposed into two lower-dimensional matrices:

- A user matrix, representing the users in a lower-dimensional space.
- An item matrix, representing the items in the same lower-dimensional space.

By multiplying the user and item matrices, you can reconstruct an approximation of the original user-item interaction matrix, which allows you to predict how a user would rate an item they haven't interacted with before.

For example, if you have a matrix where rows represent users, columns represent movies, and the entries represent user ratings, matrix factorization can help you predict how a user would rate a movie they haven't seen, based on the ratings of similar users and movies.

6. Image Processing

Linear algebra plays a crucial role in various image processing tasks. Images can be represented as matrices, where each element corresponds to the pixel intensity.

Here are a few examples:

- Image Transformations: Operations like scaling, rotation, and translation of images can be efficiently represented and performed using matrix transformations.
- Image Filtering: Techniques like blurring, sharpening, and edge detection involve convolving an image with a kernel, which can be implemented using matrix operations.

Linear algebra provides the mathematical framework for a wide range of machine learning algorithms. Its ability to represent data in structured forms (vectors and matrices) and define operations on these structures enables efficient and concise implementations of complex computations. From fundamental algorithms like linear and logistic regression to more advanced techniques like neural networks and dimensionality reduction, a solid understanding of linear algebra is essential for anyone working in machine learning.

Chapter 6: Fundamental Machine Learning Algorithms in Rust (Part 1: Supervised Learning)

This chapter marks our transition into the practical application of Rust for machine learning. We'll begin by exploring supervised learning, a fundamental branch of machine learning where the algorithm learns from labeled data.

6.1 Linear Regression

Linear regression is a fundamental algorithm in supervised machine learning used to model the relationship between a dependent variable and one or more independent variables. It's a simple yet powerful[1] technique with wide applications.

Understanding Linear Regression

At its core, linear regression aims to find the best-fitting straight line (or hyperplane in higher dimensions) that describes the relationship between the input[2] features and the output (target) variable.

Simple Linear Regression

In simple linear regression, we have only one independent variable (often denoted as 'x') and one dependent variable ('y').

The relationship is modeled as:

$y = wx + b$

Where:

- y is the predicted value of the dependent variable.
- x is the independent variable.

- w is the weight or coefficient, representing the slope of the line.
- b is the bias or intercept, representing the value of y when x is 0.

Multiple Linear Regression

When we have more than one independent variable, it's called multiple linear regression. The equation extends to:

$$y = w_1x_1 + w_2x_2 + \ldots + w_nx_n + b$$

Where:

- n is the number of independent variables.
- x_i are the independent variables.
- w_i are the weights for each independent variable.
- b is the bias term.

In this case, the weights w_1, w_2, ..., w_n represent the influence of each independent variable on the predicted value y.

Representing Data with Matrices

To handle multiple data points and multiple independent variables efficiently, we can use matrices.

- Feature Matrix (X): We arrange the independent variables for all data points into a matrix X. Each row of X represents a data point, and each column represents a feature.
- Target Vector (y): We store the corresponding dependent variable values in a vector y.
- Weight Vector (w): The weights for each independent variable are stored in a vector w.
- Bias (b): The bias term is a scalar.

With this representation, the linear regression equation can be written in matrix form:

y = Xw + b

Where:

- X is the feature matrix.
- w is the weight vector.
- b is the bias term (added to each element of the resulting vector).
- y is the predicted target vector.

Code Example: Linear Regression Prediction in Rust

Let's start by implementing the prediction part of linear regression in Rust using the ndarray crate. We'll assume we already have the weights (w) and bias (b).

Rust

```
use ndarray::Array1;

use ndarray::Array2;



// Function to predict the output for a given
input and weights/bias

fn predict(features: &Array2<f64>, weights:
&Array1<f64>, bias: f64) -> Array1<f64> {

    // 1. Ensure that the number of features
matches the number of weights

    if features.shape()[1] != weights.len() {
```

```rust
        panic!("Number of features must match the
number of weights.");

    }



    // 2. Perform a matrix multiplication of the
features and weights, then add the bias

    let predictions = features.dot(weights) +
bias;

    predictions

}



fn main() {

    // 1. Sample data: House sizes (features) and
prices (target variable).

    //    Each row is a data point, each column is
a feature.

    let house_sizes = array![[1000.0], [1500.0],
[2000.0], [2500.0], [3000.0]]; // Shape: (5, 1) -
5 houses, 1 feature (size)

    let house_prices = array![200000.0, 300000.0,
400000.0, 500000.0, 600000.0]; // Shape: (5,) - 5
house prices



    // 2. Initialize weights and bias (in a real
scenario, these would be learned from the data).
```

```rust
    let weights = array![100.0]; //  Shape: (1,)
- one weight for the 'size' feature

    let bias = 100000.0;



    // 3. Make predictions using the predict
function.

    let predicted_prices = predict(&house_sizes,
&weights, bias);

    println!("Predicted House Prices: {}",
predicted_prices);

}
```

In this example:

1. We represent the house sizes as a 2D array house_sizes
   using ndarray::Array2. Each row represents a house, and
   the single column represents the size. We represent the
   house prices as a 1D array house_prices using
   ndarray::Array1.
2. We initialize the weights and bias. In a real-world scenario,
   these values would be learned from the data using an
   optimization algorithm.
3. We call the predict function to calculate the predicted house
   prices based on the input features, weights, and bias. The
   predict function performs the core linear regression
   calculation: it multiplies the feature matrix by the weight
   vector and adds the bias term.

Cost Function and Gradient Descent

Now that we can make predictions, we need a way to find the best
values for the weights (w) and bias (b). This involves defining a

236

cost function and using an optimization algorithm like gradient descent.

Cost Function

A cost function measures how well our model is performing by quantifying the difference between the predicted values and the actual values. For linear regression, a common choice is the Mean Squared Error (MSE).

The MSE calculates the average of the squared differences between the predicted values ($\hat{y}$) and the actual values (y):

$$J(w, b) = (1 / 2m) * \Sigma(\hat{y}_i - y_i)^2$$

Where:

- $J(w, b)$ is the cost function (MSE in this case).
- m is the number of data points.
- $\hat{y}_i$ is the predicted value for the i-th data point.
- y_i is the actual value for the i-th data point.

The goal is to minimize this cost function, meaning we want to find the weights and bias that make our predictions as close as possible to the actual values. The 1/2 factor is included for mathematical convenience in the gradient calculation.

Gradient Descent

Gradient descent is an iterative optimization algorithm used to find the minimum of a function. In the context of[3] linear regression, we use it to find the values of w and b that minimize the cost function $J(w, b)$.

The algorithm works by repeatedly updating the parameters w and b in the direction of the steepest descent of the cost function's gradient. The gradient indicates the direction of the greatest increase in the cost function, so moving in the opposite direction will decrease the cost.

The update rules for w and b are:

$w := w - \alpha * \partial J(w, b) / \partial w$

$b := b - \alpha * \partial J(w, b) / \partial b$

Where:

- α is the learning rate, a parameter that controls the step size of the updates.
- $\partial J(w, b) / \partial w$ is the partial derivative of the cost function with respect to w.
- $\partial J(w, b) / \partial b$ is the partial derivative of the cost function with respect to b.

The partial derivatives of the MSE cost function with respect to w and b are:

$\partial J(w, b) / \partial w = (1 / m) * \Sigma(\hat{y}_i - y_i) * x_i$

$\partial J(w, b) / \partial b = (1 / m) * \Sigma(\hat{y}_i - y_i)$

Where x_i is the feature value for the i-th data point.

Code Example: Gradient Descent for Linear Regression in Rust

Here's how you can implement gradient descent for linear regression in Rust:

```
Rust
```

```rust
use ndarray::Array1;

use ndarray::Array2;

use ndarray::Axis;



// Function to calculate the Mean Squared Error
(MSE) cost

fn compute_cost(predictions: &Array1<f64>,
targets: &Array1<f64>) -> f64 {

    let m = predictions.len() as f64;

    let errors = predictions - targets;

    let squared_errors = errors.map(|x|
x.powi(2));

    squared_errors.sum() / (2.0 * m)

}



// Function to perform gradient descent to update
weights and bias

fn gradient_descent(

    features: &Array2<f64>,

    targets: &Array1<f64>,

    weights: &mut Array1<f64>,

    bias: &mut f64,
```

```rust
    learning_rate: f64,

    num_iterations: usize,

) {

    let m = targets.len() as f64; // Number of
training examples


    for _ in 0..num_iterations {

        // 1. Make predictions

        let predictions = predict(features,
weights, *bias);


        // 2. Calculate the error

        let errors = &predictions - targets;


        // 3. Calculate the gradients

        //    ∂J / ∂w = (1 / m) * Xᵀ * (ŷ - y)
```
$$\partial J / \partial w = (1 / m) * X^T * (\hat{y} - y)$$
```rust
        let dw = (features.t().dot(&errors)) / m;

        let db = errors.sum() / m;


        // 4. Update weights and bias

        *weights = *weights - learning_rate * dw;
```

```rust
        *bias = *bias - learning_rate * db;

    }

}


fn main() {

    // 1. Sample data: House sizes (x) and prices
(y).

    let house_sizes = array![[1000.0], [1500.0],
[2000.0], [2500.0], [3000.0]]; // Shape: (5, 1)

    let house_prices = array![200000.0, 300000.0,
400000.0, 500000.0, 600000.0]; // Shape: (5,)


    // 2. Initialize weights and bias.

    let mut weights = Array1::<f64>::zeros(1); //
Shape: (1,)

    let mut bias = 0.0;


    // 3. Set learning rate and number of
iterations.

    let learning_rate = 0.0000001; // You'll need
to tune this!

    let num_iterations = 1000;    // You'll need
to tune this!
```

```rust
// 4. Perform gradient descent to learn the
weights and bias.

    gradient_descent(

        &house_sizes,

        &house_prices,

        &mut weights,

        &mut bias,

        learning_rate,

        num_iterations,

    );


    // 5. Print the learned parameters.

    println!("Learned Weights: {}", weights);

    println!("Learned Bias: {}", bias);


    // 6. Make predictions with the learned
parameters.

    let final_predictions = predict(&house_sizes,
&weights, bias);

    println!("Final Predictions: {}",
final_predictions);
```

```
// 7. Calculate the final cost.

    let final_cost =
compute_cost(&final_predictions, &house_prices);

    println!("Final Cost: {}", final_cost);

}
```

In this code:

1. We define a function compute_cost to calculate the MSE, taking the predicted and actual values as input.
2. We implement the gradient_descent function, which takes the features, targets, current weights, bias, learning rate, and number of iterations as input. It then iteratively updates the weights and bias using the gradient descent update rules.
3. In the main function, we:
   ○ Initialize the weights and bias.
   ○ Set the learning rate and the number of iterations (these are hyperparameters that you'll need to tune for your specific problem).
   ○ Call gradient_descent to train the model.
   ○ Print the learned weights and bias.
   ○ Make predictions with the learned parameters.
   ○ Calculate and print the final cost to see how well the model performed.

Evaluating Model Performance

After training a linear regression model, it's crucial to evaluate its performance. This involves measuring how well the model generalizes to unseen data. We want to know how well it performs on data it hasn't been trained on.

Here are some common metrics for evaluating linear regression models:

- Mean Squared Error (MSE): As discussed earlier, MSE calculates the average of the squared differences between the predicted and actual values. Lower MSE indicates better performance. It's a measure of how close the predictions are to the actual values.
- R-squared (Coefficient of Determination): R-squared measures the proportion of the variance in the dependent variable that is explained by the independent[4] variables. It ranges from 0 to 1, with higher values indicating a better fit.[5] It tells you how much of the variability in the output is explained by the input.

$R^2 = 1 - (SS\_res / SS\_tot)$

Where:

- SS_res is the sum of squared residuals (the difference between the predicted and actual values).
- SS_tot is the total sum of squares (the[6] difference between the actual values and the mean of the actual values).

Code Example: Evaluating Model Performance in Rust

Here's how you can calculate MSE and R-squared in Rust:

Rust

```
use ndarray::Array1;
```

```
// Function to calculate the Mean Squared Error
(MSE)
```

```rust
fn compute_cost(predictions: &Array1<f64>,
targets: &Array1<f64>) -> f64 {

    let m = predictions.len() as f64;

    let errors = predictions - targets;

    let squared_errors = errors.map(|x|
x.powi(2));

    squared_errors.sum() / (2.0 * m)

}


// Function to calculate the R-squared
(Coefficient of Determination)

fn compute_r_squared(predictions: &Array1<f64>,
targets: &Array1<f64>) -> f64 {

    let ss_res = (predictions - targets).map(|x|
x.powi(2)).sum();

    let ss_tot = (targets -
targets.mean().unwrap()).map(|x|
x.powi(2)).sum();

    1.0 - (ss_res / ss_tot)

}


fn main() {

    // 1. Sample data: Actual house prices
(targets) and predicted house prices.
```

```rust
    let actual_prices = array![250000.0,
320000.0, 410000.0, 480000.0, 550000.0];

    let predicted_prices = array![260000.0,
310000.0, 400000.0, 490000.0, 540000.0];


    // 2. Calculate MSE.

    let mse = compute_cost(&predicted_prices,
&actual_prices);

    println!("Mean Squared Error (MSE): {:.2}",
mse);


    // 3. Calculate R-squared.

    let r_squared =
compute_r_squared(&predicted_prices,
&actual_prices);

    println!("R-squared: {:.2}", r_squared);

}
```

By understanding and implementing linear regression in Rust, along with its evaluation metrics, you've taken a significant step towards building practical machine learning applications. Linear regression provides a foundation for understanding more complex algorithms and is a valuable tool in its own right for solving regression problems.

6.2 Logistic Regression

While linear regression is used for predicting continuous values, logistic regression is a powerful algorithm for classification problems, where the goal is to predict the probability of a data point belonging to a particular category.[1]

Understanding Logistic Regression

Logistic regression is used for binary classification (predicting one of two classes) and can be extended to multi-class classification.[2] Despite its name, it's a classification algorithm, not a regression algorithm.[3] It estimates the probability that an instance belongs to a particular class.[4]

The Sigmoid Function and Binary Classification

Let's start with binary classification, where we have two classes, typically labeled as 0 and 1.

The core idea behind logistic regression is to use a special function, the sigmoid function, to map the linear combination of input features to a probability between 0 and 1.

The Sigmoid Function

The sigmoid function, denoted as σ(z), has the following formula:

$$\sigma(z) = 1 / (1 + \exp(-z))$$

Where:

z is the linear combination of the input features:

$$z = w_1x_1 + w_2x_2 + \ldots + w_\square x_\square + b$$

- $x_1, x_2, \ldots, x_\square$ are the input features.
- $w_1, w_2, \ldots, w_\square$ are the weights associated with each feature.
- b is the bias term.

The sigmoid function has an S-shaped curve, and its output always lies between 0 and 1.[5] It squashes any real-valued number z into a probability.

Interpreting the Output

The output of the sigmoid function, $\sigma(z)$, is interpreted as the probability that a data point belongs to class 1.

- If $\sigma(z) \geq 0.5$, we predict that the data point belongs to class 1.
- If $\sigma(z) < 0.5$, we predict that the data point belongs to class 0.

Code Example: Logistic Regression Prediction in Rust

Here's how you can implement the prediction part of logistic regression in Rust using ndarray:

Rust

```rust
use ndarray::Array1;

use ndarray::Array2;



// Sigmoid function

fn sigmoid(z: f64) -> f64 {

    1.0 / (1.0 + (-z).exp())

}



// Predict probabilities for binary
classification
```

```rust
fn predict_probabilities(features: &Array2<f64>,
weights: &Array1<f64>, bias: f64) -> Array1<f64>
{

    // 1. Calculate the linear combination of
    features and weights.

    let z = features.dot(weights) + bias;



    // 2. Apply the sigmoid function to each
    element of z to get probabilities.

    let probabilities: Array1<f64> =
    z.mapv(sigmoid);

    probabilities

}



fn main() {

    // 1. Sample data:  Features for two data
    points, each with two features.

    let features = array![[1.0, 2.0], [2.0,
    3.0]]; // Shape: (2, 2)

    //  For example, these could be measurements
    from a medical test.



    // 2. Assume we have learned weights and bias
    from training.
```

```
let weights = array![0.5, -0.5]; // Shape:
(2,)  Each weight corresponds to a feature.

let bias = 0.2;



// 3. Calculate the predicted probabilities
using the predict_probabilities function.

let predicted_probabilities =
predict_probabilities(&features, &weights, bias);

println!("Predicted Probabilities: {}",
predicted_probabilities);



// To make a final classification (0 or 1),
you'd typically threshold these probabilities:

let predictions: Array1<i32> =
predicted_probabilities.map(|&p| if p >= 0.5 { 1
} else { 0 });

println!("Predictions (0 or 1): {}",
predictions);

}
```

In this example:

1. We define a sigmoid function that calculates the sigmoid of a given input z.
2. We implement the predict_probabilities function, which takes the feature matrix, weights, and bias as input. It calculates the linear combination of features and weights, applies the sigmoid function, and returns the resulting probabilities.

3. In the main function, we:
   - Create a sample feature matrix features with two data points, each having two features.
   - Define example weights and bias (in a real-world scenario, these would be learned during the training process).
   - Call predict_probabilities to get the predicted probabilities for each data point.
   - We add an example of how to convert probabilities to class labels (0 or 1) by thresholding at 0.5

Cost Function and Optimization

Now that we can make predictions, we need a way to train the model to find the best values for the weights and bias. This involves defining a cost function and using an optimization algorithm.

Cost Function

In logistic regression, we can't use the Mean Squared Error (MSE) cost function that we used for linear regression. Instead, we use the binary cross-entropy loss, also known as the logistic loss.

The binary cross-entropy loss measures the difference between the predicted probabilities and the actual class labels.[6]

For a single data point, the loss is defined as:

$$\text{Loss}(\hat{y}, y) = -[y * \log(\hat{y}) + (1 - y) * \log(1 - \hat{y})]$$

Where:

- y is the actual class label (0 or 1).
- $\hat{y}$ is the predicted probability of the data point belonging to class 1.

The intuition behind this loss function is:

- If y = 1, we want ŷ to be close to 1. The loss is then -log(ŷ), which is small when ŷ is close to 1 and large when ŷ is close to 0.
- If y = 0, we want ŷ to be close to 0. The loss is then -log(1 - ŷ), which is small when ŷ is close to 0 and large when ŷ is close to 1.

To get the overall cost function for all data points, we average the loss over all training examples:

$$J(w, b) = - (1 / m) * \Sigma [y_i * \log(\hat{y}_i) + (1 - y_i) * \log(1 - \hat{y}_i)]$$

Where:

- J(w, b) is the cost function (binary cross-entropy loss).[7]
- m is the number of training examples.
- y_i is the actual class label for the i-th training example.
- $\hat{y}_i$ is the predicted probability for the i-th training example.

Optimization: Gradient Descent

We use gradient descent to find the values of the weights (w) and bias (b) that minimize the cost function J(w, b).[8]

The update rules for w and b are the same as in linear regression:

$$w := w - \alpha * \partial J(w, b) / \partial w$$

$$b := b - \alpha * \partial J(w, b) / \partial b$$

Where α is the learning rate.

The partial derivatives of the binary cross-entropy loss with respect to w and b are:

$$\partial J(w, b) / \partial w = (1 / m) * \Sigma (\hat{y}_i - y_i) * x_i$$

$$\partial J(w, b) / \partial b = (1 / m) * \Sigma (\hat{y}_i - y_i)$$

Where x_i represents the features of the i-th data point.

Code Example: Gradient Descent for Logistic Regression in Rust

Rust

```rust
use ndarray::Array1;

use ndarray::Array2;


// Sigmoid function

fn sigmoid(z: f64) -> f64 {

    1.0 / (1.0 + (-z).exp())

}


// Predict probabilities for binary
classification

fn predict_probabilities(features: &Array2<f64>,
weights: &Array1<f64>, bias: f64) -> Array1<f64>
{

    let z = features.dot(weights) + bias;

    z.mapv(sigmoid)
```

```rust
}


// Binary cross-entropy loss function

fn compute_cost(probabilities: &Array1<f64>,
targets: &Array1<f64>) -> f64 {

    let m = probabilities.len() as f64;

    let cost_sum = probabilities

        .iter()

        .zip(targets.iter())

        .map(|(&p, &y)| -y * p.ln() - (1.0 - y) *
(1.0 - p).ln())

        .sum::<f64>();

    cost_sum / m

}



// Gradient descent for logistic regression

fn gradient_descent(

    features: &Array2<f64>,

    targets: &Array1<f64>,

    weights: &mut Array1<f64>,

    bias: &mut f64,
```

```rust
    learning_rate: f64,

    num_iterations: usize,
) {

    let m = targets.len() as f64; // Number of
training examples


    for _ in 0..num_iterations {

        // 1. Calculate predicted probabilities

        let probabilities =
predict_probabilities(features, weights, *bias);


        // 2. Calculate the error

        let errors = &probabilities - targets;


        // 3. Calculate gradients

        let dw = (features.t().dot(&errors)) / m;

        let db = errors.sum() / m;


        // 4. Update weights and bias

        *weights = *weights - learning_rate * dw;

        *bias = *bias - learning_rate * db;
```

```rust
    }

}


fn main() {

    // 1. Sample data

    let features = array![[1.0, 2.0], [2.0, 3.0],
[3.0, 4.0], [4.0, 5.0]]; // Shape: (4, 2)

    let targets = array![0.0, 0.0, 1.0, 1.0]; //
Shape: (4,)   (0 or 1)



    // 2. Initialize weights and bias

    let mut weights = Array1::<f64>::zeros(2); //
Shape: (2,)

    let mut bias = 0.0;



    // 3. Set learning rate and number of
iterations

    let learning_rate = 0.1;

    let num_iterations = 100;



    // 4. Perform gradient descent to learn the
weights and bias

    gradient_descent(
```

```rust
        &features,

        &targets,

        &mut weights,

        &mut bias,

        learning_rate,

        num_iterations,

    );


    // 5. Print learned parameters

    println!("Learned Weights: {}", weights);

    println!("Learned Bias: {}", bias);


    // 6. Make predictions with the learned
parameters

    let final_probabilities =
predict_probabilities(&features, &weights, bias);

    println!("Final Probabilities: {}",
final_probabilities);


    // 7. Calculate the final cost

    let final_cost =
compute_cost(&final_probabilities, &targets);
```

```
    println!("Final Cost: {}", final_cost);
```

}

Multi-Class Logistic Regression

Logistic regression can be extended to handle multi-class classification problems, where there are more than two classes.[9] Two common strategies for this are:cfcf so

- One-vs-Rest (OvR): Train a separate logistic regression classifier for each class, treating that class as 1 and all other classes as 0.
- One-vs-One (OvO): Train a separate logistic regression classifier for each pair of classes. For K classes, this results in K(K-1)/2 classifiers.

6.3 Basic Tree-Based Methods (Conceptual Overview and Potential Rust Libraries)

Tree-based methods are a powerful family of machine learning algorithms that can be used for both classification and regression tasks.[1] Unlike linear models, which assume a linear relationship between input features and the output, tree-based methods can capture complex, non-linear relationships.[2]

Understanding Decision Trees

At the heart of tree-based methods is the decision tree.

A decision tree is a flowchart-like structure where:

- Each internal node represents a test on a specific feature (e.g., "Is age > 30?").[3]
- Each branch represents the outcome of that test (e.g., "yes" or "no").[4]
- Each leaf node represents a prediction (e.g., a class label or a numerical value).[5]

To make a prediction with a decision tree, you start at the root node and traverse the tree by answering the questions at each internal node. The path you take depends on the values of the features for the data point you're trying to predict. When you reach a leaf node, the value at that node is your prediction.[6]

Example: Decision Tree for Predicting Loan Approval

Let's consider a simplified example of a decision tree used to predict whether a bank should approve a loan:

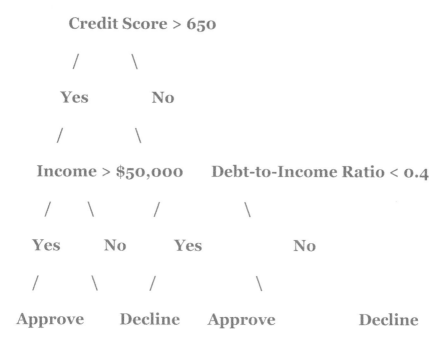

To predict whether to approve a loan for a new applicant, we start at the top:

1. We check if the applicant's credit score is greater than 650.
2. If yes, we move to the left branch.
3. We then check if their income is greater than $50,000.
4. If yes again, we reach the "Approve" leaf node, and the decision is to approve the loan.

5. If the credit score was not greater than 650, we would follow the right branch and check the debt-to-income ratio, and so on.

Building a Decision Tree

The process of creating a decision tree from a dataset is called tree induction or tree learning. The goal is to create a tree that accurately predicts the target variable based on the input features.

The most common algorithm for building decision trees is called ID3, C4.5, or CART.[7]

These algorithms use a top-down, recursive approach:

1. Start at the root node: Initially, all the training data is at the root node.
2. Select the best feature to split: The algorithm selects the feature that best separates the data points based on their target variable values.[8] This selection is done using a metric like information gain (for classification) or variance reduction (for regression).[9]
3. Split the node: The algorithm splits the node into two or more child nodes based on the selected feature and its values.
4. Recurse: Steps 2 and 3 are repeated for each child node until a stopping criterion is met, such as:
   - All data points in a node belong to the same class (for classification).[10]
   - The node contains only a small number of data points.
   - The maximum tree depth is reached.

Advantages of Decision Trees

- Easy to understand and interpret: Decision trees are very intuitive and easy to visualize, making them good for explaining model predictions.[11]
- Handle both numerical and categorical data: They can work with various data types without requiring extensive preprocessing.[12]
- Capture non-linear relationships: They can model complex relationships between features and the target variable.[13]
- Robust to outliers: They are less sensitive to outliers than some other algorithms.

Disadvantages of Decision Trees

- Overfitting: Decision trees can easily overfit the training data, especially if they are very deep.[14] This means they might perform well on the training data but poorly on unseen data.
- Instability: Small changes in the training data can lead to significantly different tree structures.[15]
- Bias towards features with many values: Feature selection in decision trees can be biased towards features with many possible values.

Random Forests

Random forests are an ensemble learning method that combines multiple decision trees to improve prediction accuracy and reduce overfitting.[16][17]

Ensemble Learning

Ensemble learning involves training multiple "weak" learners (models that perform slightly better than random guessing) and combining their predictions to create a "strong" learner with better performance.[18]

Random Forests Algorithm

Here's how the random forests algorithm works:

1. Bootstrap sampling: Create multiple subsets of the training data by sampling with replacement. This means that some data points might appear multiple times in a single subset, while others might be left out. Each subset is called a bootstrap sample.
2. Tree building: For each bootstrap sample, build a decision tree.[19] However, with a key modification:
   - At each node, instead of considering all features for splitting, randomly select only a subset of features.[20] This introduces more diversity among the trees.
3. Prediction: To make a prediction for a new data point, pass it through all the trees in the forest.
   - For classification, each tree "votes" for a class, and the class with the most votes is the final prediction (majority voting).[21]
   - For regression, the predictions of all the trees are averaged to get the final prediction.

Advantages of Random Forests

- Improved accuracy: Random forests generally outperform single decision trees.[22]
- Reduced overfitting: Combining multiple trees and using random feature selection helps to reduce overfitting.[23]
- Feature importance: Random forests provide a way to estimate the importance of each feature in the prediction process.[24]
- Handle both classification and regression: They can be used for both types of tasks.[25]

Potential Rust Libraries for Tree-Based Methods

While the Rust machine learning ecosystem is still evolving, here are some potential avenues for working with tree-based methods:

- Tree-rs: A crate that provides decision tree implementation[26]
- ONNX Runtime: Rust can interface with ONNX Runtime, which supports running pre-trained tree models exported from other frameworks.[27]
- LightGBM/XGBoost: These popular gradient boosting libraries have C APIs, and you could potentially create Rust bindings to use them.

As the Rust ML community grows, we can expect more robust and user-friendly libraries for tree-based methods to emerge.

Chapter 7: Fundamental Machine Learning Algorithms in Rust (Part 2: Unsupervised Learning)

In this chapter, we'll shift our focus to unsupervised learning, where the goal is to discover patterns and structures in unlabeled data. We'll explore two fundamental algorithms: k-means clustering and principal component analysis (PCA).

7.1 Clustering

Clustering is a fundamental technique in unsupervised machine learning that allows us to discover hidden patterns and structures within data that isn't labeled. Unlike supervised learning, where we have a target variable to predict, in unsupervised learning, we only have the input data, and the algorithm's job is to find natural groupings or clusters of similar data points.

K-means is one of the most popular and widely used clustering algorithms. It's relatively simple to understand and implement, and it can be applied to a variety of problems.

Understanding the K-Means Algorithm

The k-means algorithm aims to partition a dataset into k clusters, where k is a number that you, the user, must specify beforehand. The algorithm works by iteratively refining the clusters until they become stable.

Here's a step-by-step breakdown of how the k-means algorithm works:

1. Initialization: The algorithm starts by randomly selecting k data points from your dataset to serve as the initial centroids. A centroid is simply the center point of a cluster.

These initial centroids act as the starting points for your k clusters.

2. Assignment: Each data point in your dataset is then assigned to the nearest cluster, based on a distance metric. The most common distance metric is the Euclidean distance, which is the straight-line distance between two points. We assign each point to the cluster whose centroid it is closest to.

3. Update: Once all data points have been assigned to clusters, the algorithm recalculates the centroids of each cluster. The new centroid[1] is computed as the mean (average) of all the data points that belong to that cluster.

4. Iteration: Steps 2 and 3 are repeated until a certain condition is met. This condition could be:
   - The centroids no longer change significantly between iterations, indicating that the algorithm has converged.
   - A maximum number of iterations has been reached, to prevent the algorithm from running indefinitely.

Visualizing K-Means

To get a better grasp of how k-means works, let's visualize a simple example in two dimensions:

Suppose you have a dataset of points on a graph, and you want to cluster them into k=2 clusters.

1. Initialization: The algorithm randomly picks two points as initial centroids (let's call them C1 and C2).

2. Assignment: Each point is assigned to either cluster 1 (closer to C1) or cluster 2 (closer to C2). This divides the points into two regions around C1 and C2.

3. Update: The centroids C1 and C2 are recalculated as the average position of all the points assigned to their respective

clusters. This moves the centroids to the "center" of their clusters.

4. Iteration: Steps 2 and 3 are repeated. Points might switch clusters as the centroids move. The centroids keep moving until they stabilize, and the points are grouped into their final clusters.

Code Example: K-Means Clustering in Rust

Now, let's implement the k-means algorithm in Rust using the ndarray crate for efficient numerical computations.

Rust

```
use ndarray::Array1;

use ndarray::Array2;

use rand::Rng;

use rand::seq::SliceRandom;

use std::collections::HashMap;



// Function to calculate the Euclidean distance
between two points

fn euclidean_distance(a: &Array1<f64>, b:
&Array1<f64>) -> f64 {

    // Calculate the squared difference between
corresponding elements, sum them up, and take the
square root.

    (a - b).map(|x| x.powi(2)).sum().sqrt()
```

```rust
}


// Function to assign data points to the nearest
cluster

fn assign_to_clusters(data: &Array2<f64>,
centroids: &Array2<f64>) -> Vec<usize> {

    // For each data point, find the index of the
nearest centroid.

    data.rows()

        .into_iter()  // Iterate over each row
(data point) in the data.

        .map(|row| {

            centroids

                .rows()

                .into_iter()  // Iterate over
each row (centroid) in the centroids.

                .enumerate() // Keep track of the
centroid index.

                .min_by_key(|(_, centroid)| {

                    // Calculate the Euclidean
distance between the data point and each
centroid.

                    let distance =
euclidean_distance(&row.to_owned(),
&centroid.to_owned());
```

```rust
                    // Convert the distance to a
u64 for comparison.   Floats are not directly
comparable.

                    (distance * 1000000.0) as u64
// Scale to avoid precision issues with very
small distances.

            })

            .unwrap() // Get the (index,
centroid) tuple with the minimum distance.

            .0      // Extract the index of
the nearest centroid.

        })

        .collect() // Collect the cluster
assignments (indices) for all data points into a
Vec<usize>.

}


// Function to update the centroids based on the
assigned data points

fn update_centroids(data: &Array2<f64>,
assignments: &[usize], k: usize) -> Array2<f64> {

    let (n_samples, n_features) = data.dim(); //
Get the number of data points and features.

    let mut new_centroids =
Array2::<f64>::zeros((k, n_features)); //
Initialize a matrix to store the new centroids.
```

```rust
    let mut cluster_counts = vec![0; k];   // Keep
track of the number of points in each cluster.



    // Calculate the sum of data points for each
cluster.

    for (i, &cluster) in
assignments.iter().enumerate() {

        let point = data.row(i); // Get the data
point for the current sample.

        for j in 0..n_features {

            new_centroids[[cluster, j]] +=
point[j]; // Add the feature value to the
corresponding centroid.

        }

        cluster_counts[cluster] += 1; //
Increment the count for the cluster.

    }



    // Divide the sums by the number of points in
each cluster to get the new centroids (mean).

    for i in 0..k {

        if cluster_counts[i] > 0 {

            for j in 0..n_features {
```

```
            new_centroids[[i, j]] /=
cluster_counts[i] as f64; // Calculate the mean
for each feature in the cluster.


        }

    } else {

        // Handle empty clusters:

        // You could either re-initialize the
centroid, or keep it at its previous location.

        // For simplicity, we'll keep it at
zero in this example, but this is usually not
ideal.


        }

    }

    new_centroids

}



// Function to run the k-means algorithm

fn k_means(

    data: &Array2<f64>, // Input data (n_samples
x n_features).

    k: usize,                // Number of clusters.

    max_iterations: usize, // Maximum number of
iterations.
```

```rust
) -> (Array2<f64>, Vec<usize>) {

    let (n_samples, n_features) = data.dim(); // Get data dimensions.


    // 1. Initialize centroids randomly by selecting k data points.

    let mut rng = rand::thread_rng(); // Get a random number generator.

    let mut initial_centroid_indices: Vec<usize> = (0..n_samples).collect(); // Create a vector of indices from 0 to n_samples-1.

    initial_centroid_indices.shuffle(&mut rng); // Shuffle the indices randomly.

    let initial_centroids_indices = &initial_centroid_indices[0..k]; // Take the first k indices as initial centroid indices.


    let mut centroids = Array2::<f64>::zeros((k, n_features)); // Initialize a matrix to store the centroids.

    for (i, &index) in initial_centroids_indices.iter().enumerate() {

    centroids.row_mut(i).assign(&data.row(index)); // Set the initial centroids to the selected data points.

    }
```

```
let mut assignments = vec![0; n_samples]; //
Vector to store cluster assignments for each data
point.


    // 2. Iterate until convergence or max
iterations.

    for _ in 0..max_iterations {

        let previous_centroids =
centroids.clone(); // Store the previous
centroids to check for convergence.


        // 3. Assign data points to the nearest
clusters.

        assignments = assign_to_clusters(data,
&centroids);


        // 4. Update centroids.

        centroids = update_centroids(data,
&assignments, k);


        // 5. Check for convergence.

        let centroid_shift = (&centroids -
&previous_centroids)
```

```
        .map(|x| x.powi(2)) // Calculate the
squared difference between old and new centroids.

        .sum()              // Sum the squared
differences.

        .sqrt();            // Take the square
root to get the overall shift.



    if centroid_shift < 1e-6 { // Define a
small threshold for convergence.

        break; // If the centroids have moved
by less than the threshold, stop iterating.

    }

  }



  (centroids, assignments) // Return the final
centroids and cluster assignments.

}



fn main() {

  // 1. Sample data (6 data points, 2
features).

  let data = array![

    [1.0, 2.0],
```

```
        [1.5, 1.8],

        [5.0, 8.0],

        [8.0, 8.0],

        [1.0, 0.6],

        [9.0, 11.0],

    ]; // Shape: (6, 2)


    // 2. Set the number of clusters (k).

    let k = 2;


    // 3. Set the maximum number of iterations.

    let max_iterations = 100;


    // 4. Run k-means clustering.

    let (centroids, assignments) = k_means(&data,
k, max_iterations);


    // 5. Print the results.

    println!("Centroids:\n{}", centroids);

    println!("Assignments: {:?}", assignments);

}
```

In this example:

1. We define a function euclidean_distance to calculate the Euclidean distance between two data points represented as Array1<f64>.
2. The assign_to_clusters function assigns each data point to the nearest cluster based on the Euclidean distance to the centroids.
3. The update_centroids function recalculates the centroids by taking the mean of the data points assigned to each cluster.
4. The k_means function implements the main k-means algorithm, iteratively assigning points to clusters and updating centroids until convergence or the maximum number of iterations is reached.
5. In the main function, we generate sample data, set the number of clusters (k), run the k-means algorithm, and print the resulting centroids and cluster assignments.

Real-World Example: Customer Segmentation

K-means clustering can be used for customer segmentation, where you group customers based on their purchasing behavior, demographics, or other relevant features. This can help businesses to tailor their marketing strategies and improve customer satisfaction.

For example, you might have a dataset of customer information with features like:

- Age
- Income
- Spending score
- Purchase history

By applying k-means clustering to this data, you can identify distinct customer segments, such as:

- "High-value customers" (high income, high spending score)
- "Young and tech-savvy customers" (young age, high spending on electronics)
- "Price-sensitive customers" (lower income, focus on discounts)

This information can then be used to create targeted marketing campaigns, develop personalized product recommendations, and improve customer retention.

Distance Metrics

The choice of distance metric influences how data points are assigned to clusters. The most common metric is the Euclidean distance, which we used in the previous example.

Other metrics include:

- Manhattan distance: The sum of the absolute differences between the coordinates of two points.
- Cosine distance: Measures the angle between two vectors, often used for text data.

Initialization and Iteration

The initial placement of centroids can significantly affect the final clustering result.

Common initialization methods include:

- Random selection: Choosing k random data points as initial centroids.
- K-means++: A smarter initialization method that spreads out the initial centroids.

The algorithm iterates until convergence, which can be determined by:

- Centroid shift: The change in centroid positions between iterations falls below a threshold.
- Maximum iterations: A predefined number of iterations is reached.

Evaluating Clustering Performance

Evaluating the quality of a clustering result is more challenging than evaluating supervised learning models because we don't have ground truth labels.

Common metrics include:

- Silhouette score: Measures how well each data point fits within its cluster compared to other clusters.
- Davies-Bouldin index: Measures the average similarity ratio of each cluster with its most similar cluster.

7.2 Dimensionality Reduction

In many machine learning problems, especially when dealing with data like images, text, or sensor readings, you often face a large number of features.

This high dimensionality can lead to several challenges:

- Increased computational cost: Training models on high-dimensional data can be very time-consuming and require significant computational resources.
- Overfitting: High dimensionality increases the risk of overfitting, where your model learns the training data too well but performs poorly on unseen data.
- The curse of dimensionality: Many machine learning algorithms struggle to generalize effectively in high-dimensional spaces.

- Difficulty in visualization: It's challenging to visualize data with more than three dimensions, making it hard to understand the underlying structure.

Dimensionality reduction techniques aim to address these problems by transforming high-dimensional data into a lower-dimensional representation that retains its most important characteristics.

Principal Component Analysis (PCA)

Principal Component Analysis (PCA) is a popular and effective dimensionality reduction technique. It works by identifying the directions of maximum variance in the data, called principal components, and projecting the data onto these components.

Here's a breakdown of the PCA process:

1. Standardize the data: PCA is sensitive to the scale of the features, so it's crucial to standardize the data by subtracting the mean and dividing by the standard deviation for each feature. This ensures that all features[1] contribute equally to the analysis.
2. Calculate the covariance matrix: The covariance matrix describes the relationships between different features. It tells you how much each pair of features varies together.
3. Perform eigen decomposition: This involves finding the eigenvectors and eigenvalues of the covariance matrix.
   - Eigenvectors: Represent the principal components, which are the directions of maximum variance in the data.
   - Eigenvalues: Represent the amount of variance explained by each principal component.
4. Select principal components: Sort the[2] eigenvectors by their corresponding eigenvalues in descending order. Choose the top k eigenvectors, where k is the desired[3] dimensionality of

the reduced data. These k eigenvectors form a transformation matrix.

5. Project the data: Multiply the original data by the transformation matrix to project it onto the lower-dimensional subspace spanned by the selected principal components.

Conceptual Example

Let's say you have a dataset of student information with two features: "study hours" and "exam score." PCA can help you find the most important direction in this data.

1. If study hours and exam scores are positively correlated (students who study more tend to score higher), the first principal component will be a line that goes in the direction of this positive correlation.
2. The second principal component will be perpendicular to the first one and capture the remaining variance in the data.

If the variance along the first principal component is much larger than the variance along the second one, it means that most of the information in the data is captured by the first component. You can then reduce the dimensionality of your data from two to one by projecting it onto the first principal component, effectively representing each student's data point with a single value instead of two.

Code Example: PCA in Rust (using nalgebra and ndarray)

While ndarray is excellent for array manipulation, we'll use the nalgebra crate for the linear algebra operations involved in PCA, specifically for calculating the eigenvectors and eigenvalues.

First, add these dependencies to your Cargo.toml:

Ini, TOML

```
[dependencies]

ndarray = "0.15.1"

nalgebra = "0.32.0"
```

Now, let's implement PCA in Rust:

Rust

```rust
use ndarray::prelude::*;

use nalgebra::{DMatrix, Matrix, Dynamic, OMatrix,
VecStorage};


// Function to perform PCA

fn pca(data: &Array2<f64>, k: usize) ->
DMatrix<f64> {

    // 1. Calculate the mean of the data for each
feature (column).

    let (n_samples, n_features) = data.dim();

    let mean = data.mean_axis(Axis(0)).unwrap();
// Calculate the mean along axis 0 (columns)


    // 2. Center the data by subtracting the mean
from each data point.

    let mut centered_data = data.to_owned(); //
Create a mutable copy to modify

    for i in 0..n_samples {
```

```rust
    for j in 0..n_features {

        centered_data[[i, j]] -= mean[j];

    }

}


// 3. Calculate the covariance matrix.

//     The covariance matrix is a square
matrix of size (n_features x n_features).

//     Each element (i, j) of the covariance
matrix represents the covariance between feature
i and feature j.

    let covariance_matrix: DMatrix<f64> = (1.0 /
(n_samples - 1) as f64) *
&centered_data.transpose().dot(&centered_data);


// 4. Perform eigen decomposition on the
covariance matrix.

//     Eigen decomposition finds the
eigenvalues and eigenvectors of a square matrix.

//     Eigenvectors represent the principal
components (directions of maximum variance).

//     Eigenvalues represent the amount of
variance explained by each eigenvector.

    let eigen =
nalgebra::linalg::Eigen::new(covariance_matrix);
```

```
let eigenvectors = eigen.eigenvectors; // Get
the eigenvectors


// 5. Select the top k eigenvectors to form
the transformation matrix.

//    We sort the eigenvectors by their
corresponding eigenvalues (not shown here for
brevity)

//    and choose the top k eigenvectors,
which correspond to the directions of maximum
variance.

//    These k eigenvectors form a
transformation matrix that we use to project the
data.



let eigenvectors_matrix: Matrix<f64, Dynamic,
Dynamic, VecStorage<f64, Dynamic, Dynamic>> =
eigenvectors.real_eigenvectors();

let k_eigenvectors =
eigenvectors_matrix.fixed_columns::<Dynamic>(k);



// 6. Project the data onto the
lower-dimensional subspace.

//    We multiply the centered data by the
transformation matrix to obtain the projected
data.
```

```rust
    //    The resulting projected_data matrix has
dimensions (n_samples x k), where k is the new
dimensionality.

    let projected_data =
centered_data.dot(&k_eigenvectors);

    projected_data

}


fn main() {

    // 1. Sample data: 2D data with 6 data points
and 2 features

    let data = array![

        [1.0, 2.0],

        [1.5, 1.8],

        [5.0, 8.0],

        [8.0, 8.0],

        [1.0, 0.6],

        [9.0, 11.0],

    ]; // Shape: (6, 2)


    println!("Original Data (2 dimensions):\n{}",
data);
```

```
    // 2. Set the number of principal components
(k) to reduce to 1 dimension

    let k = 1;


    // 3. Perform PCA to reduce the
dimensionality to 1

    let projected_data = pca(&data, k);


    // 4. Print the projected data

    println!("Projected Data (1 dimension):\n{}",
projected_data);

}
```

In this code:

1. We define a function pca that takes the input data (an Array2<f64>) and the desired number of dimensions k as input and returns the projected data as a DMatrix<f64>.
2. Inside the pca function:
   - We calculate the mean of the data for each feature using data.mean_axis(Axis(0)).
   - We center the data by subtracting the mean from each data point.
   - We calculate the covariance matrix using the formula $(1 / (n\_samples - 1)) * X^T * X$, where X is the centered data matrix.
   - We perform eigen decomposition on the covariance matrix using nalgebra::linalg::Eigen::new().

- We select the top k eigenvectors corresponding to the largest eigenvalues (the sorting step is omitted for brevity but is crucial in a complete implementation).
- We project the centered data onto the lower-dimensional subspace by multiplying it with the transformation matrix formed by the selected eigenvectors.

3. In the main function, we:
   - Create a sample 2D dataset with 6 data points and 2 features.
   - Set the desired number of principal components k to 1.
   - Call the pca function to reduce the dimensionality of the data to 1.
   - Print the projected data, which now has only 1 dimension.

This process transforms your data into a new coordinate system aligned with the directions of maximum variance, effectively capturing the most important information in a lower-dimensional space.

Covariance Matrix and Eigen Decomposition

PCA involves calculating the covariance matrix of the data, which describes the relationships between different features. Then, we perform eigen decomposition on the covariance matrix to find its eigenvalues and eigenvectors.

- Eigenvectors: Represent the principal components, the directions of maximum variance.
- Eigenvalues: Represent the amount of variance explained by each principal component.

Projecting Data onto Lower Dimensions

In Principal Component Analysis (PCA), after finding the eigenvectors and eigenvalues of the covariance matrix, we arrive at the crucial step of actually reducing the dimensionality of our data. This is where we take the high-dimensional data we started with and transform it into a lower-dimensional representation, keeping as much of the important information as possible.

Selecting Principal Components

Recall that the eigenvectors we obtained from the eigen decomposition represent the principal components of the data. These principal components are the directions in which the data varies the most. The corresponding eigenvalues indicate the amount of variance explained by each principal component.

To reduce dimensionality, we don't keep all the eigenvectors. Instead, we select only the top k eigenvectors, where k is the desired dimensionality of our reduced data. We choose the eigenvectors that correspond to the largest eigenvalues because these eigenvectors capture the most variance in the data. By keeping these, we aim to preserve as much of the original information as possible while reducing the number of dimensions.

For example, if our original data has 10 dimensions, and we choose $k = 2$, we are selecting the two eigenvectors that point in the directions of the two largest variances in the data.

Forming the Transformation Matrix

Once we've selected the top k eigenvectors, we arrange them into a matrix called the transformation matrix (sometimes also called the eigenvector matrix or the component matrix).

Let's say we have n original features and we've selected the top k eigenvectors. Our transformation matrix, which we'll call W, will have the shape (n, k).

- Each column of W is one of the selected eigenvectors.
- The order of the columns in W corresponds to the order of the eigenvectors, sorted by their eigenvalues (largest to smallest).

Projecting the Data

The final step is to use this transformation matrix W to transform our original data into the lower-dimensional space. We do this by performing a matrix multiplication.

Let's say our original data is represented by a matrix X, where:

- X has the shape (m, n).
- m is the number of data points (samples).
- n is the number of original features.

To project X onto the lower-dimensional space, we multiply X by the transformation matrix W:

X_reduced = X * W

The resulting matrix X_reduced will have the shape (m, k).

- m is still the number of data points.
- k is the new number of dimensions (the number of principal components we selected).

Each row in X_reduced now represents a data point in the lower-dimensional space. The values in each row are the projections of the original data point onto the principal components.

Code Example: Data Projection in Rust (using nalgebra **and** ndarray**)**

Building upon the previous example, let's add the data projection step:

Rust

```
use ndarray::prelude::*;

use nalgebra::{DMatrix, Matrix, Dynamic, OMatrix,
VecStorage};



// Function to perform PCA

fn pca(data: &Array2<f64>, k: usize) ->
DMatrix<f64> {

    // 1. Calculate the mean of the data.

    let (n_samples, n_features) = data.dim();

    let mean = data.column_mean().unwrap();



    // 2. Center the data by subtracting the
mean.

    let mut centered_data = data.to_owned();

    for i in 0..n_samples {

        for j in 0..n_features {

            centered_data[[i, j]] -= mean[j];

        }
```

```
    }


    // 3. Calculate the covariance matrix.

    let covariance_matrix = (1.0 / (n_samples -
1) as f64) *
&centered_data.transpose().dot(&centered_data);



    // 4. Perform eigen decomposition on the
covariance matrix.

    let eigen =
nalgebra::linalg::Eigen::new(covariance_matrix);

    let eigenvectors_matrix: Matrix<f64, Dynamic,
Dynamic, VecStorage<f64, Dynamic, Dynamic>> =
eigen.real_eigenvectors();




    // 5. Select the top k eigenvectors to form
the transformation matrix.

    let k_eigenvectors =
eigenvectors_matrix.fixed_columns::<Dynamic>(k);

    let transformation_matrix =
DMatrix::from_row_matrix(&k_eigenvectors);



    // 6. Project the data onto the
lower-dimensional subspace.
```

```rust
    let centered_data_nalgebra =
DMatrix::from_row_iter(n_samples, n_features,
centered_data.iter().cloned());

    let projected_data = centered_data_nalgebra *
transformation_matrix;

    projected_data

}


fn main() {

    // 1. Sample data: 2D data with 6 data points
and 2 features

    let data = array![

        [1.0, 2.0],

        [1.5, 1.8],

        [5.0, 8.0],

        [8.0, 8.0],

        [1.0, 0.6],

        [9.0, 11.0],

    ]; // Shape: (6, 2)


    println!("Original Data (2 dimensions):\n{}",
data);
```

```
    // 2. Set the number of principal components
(k) to reduce to 1 dimension

    let k = 1;



    // 3. Perform PCA to reduce the
dimensionality to 1

    let projected_data = pca(&data, k);



    // 4. Print the projected data

    println!("Projected Data (1 dimension):\n{}",
projected_data);

}
```

In this updated example:

- We create a transformation matrix k_eigenvectors by selecting the first k eigenvectors from the eigenvectors_matrix.
- We convert the ndarray::Array2 centered_data to a nalgebra::DMatrix to perform the matrix multiplication.
- We project the data onto the lower-dimensional space by multiplying the centered data matrix by the transformation matrix.

Real-World Example: Image Compression

A classic application of PCA is image compression. An image can be represented as a matrix of pixel intensities. If the image has many pixels, this matrix can be very large, requiring significant storage space.

PCA can be used to reduce the dimensionality of the image data by projecting it onto a smaller number of principal components. This effectively compresses the image, allowing you to store it with less data.

For example, suppose you have a grayscale image of size 100x100 pixels. This image can be represented as a 100x100 matrix, which can be reshaped into a 10,000-dimensional vector. PCA can be used to find the principal components of this high-dimensional data. By selecting only the top k principal components, you can represent the image with significantly fewer dimensions, achieving compression.

This chapter explained how PCA projects high-dimensional data onto a lower-dimensional space by selecting the principal components, which are the directions of maximum variance. This process reduces the number of dimensions while preserving the most important information in the data.

Chapter 8: Leveraging Rust for Performance Optimization in ML

We've discussed how Rust's safety and performance make it a compelling language for machine learning. Now, let's get practical and explore specific techniques to optimize your Rust ML code for maximum performance.

8.1 Memory Management and Data Layout for Efficiency

When it comes to writing high-performance code, especially in applications like machine learning where you're dealing with large datasets and complex computations, how you manage memory and arrange your data can make a huge difference. Rust's memory management system, combined with careful consideration of data layout, can provide significant performance advantages.

Understanding Memory Management in Rust

To appreciate how Rust helps with efficiency, let's quickly recap how memory management works in general and how Rust approaches it:

1. Stack vs. Heap

- Stack: The stack is a region of memory used for storing data with a known, fixed size at compile time. Think of it like a stack of plates – you can only add or remove plates from the top. This makes allocation and deallocation on the stack extremely fast. When a function is called, its local variables and parameters are typically allocated on the stack. When the function finishes, this memory is automatically freed.
- Heap: The heap is a more flexible region of memory used for data whose size might not be known at compile time or that needs to persist longer than the function that created it.

Allocating memory on the heap is like reserving a table at a restaurant – you request a certain amount of space, and the system finds a suitable spot for you. Deallocating memory on the heap requires explicitly freeing the reserved space.

2. Memory Management Approaches

Different programming languages handle memory management in different ways:

- Manual Memory Management (C, C++): In languages like C and C++, the programmer is responsible for both allocating and deallocating memory. This gives you a lot of control but also introduces the risk of memory leaks (forgetting to free memory) and dangling pointers (accessing memory that has already been freed). These errors can lead to crashes, security vulnerabilities, and unpredictable behavior.
- Garbage Collection (Java, Python, Go): Languages like Java, Python, and Go use a garbage collector (GC) to automatically manage memory. The GC periodically scans the memory and frees up the memory that is no longer being used by the program. This simplifies memory management for the programmer but can introduce performance overhead due to the GC's activity. The pauses caused by the GC can be unpredictable and can affect the responsiveness of applications, especially in performance-critical scenarios.
- Ownership and Borrowing (Rust): Rust takes a unique approach with its ownership system. Instead of manual allocation/deallocation or garbage collection, Rust uses a set of rules, checked at compile time, to ensure memory safety. These rules revolve around the concepts of ownership, borrowing, and lifetimes.

Rust's Approach: Ownership, Borrowing, and Lifetimes

Rust's memory management system is a key differentiator, and understanding it is crucial for writing efficient code.

- Ownership: Every value in Rust has a variable that is its owner. The owner is responsible for cleaning up the memory when the value is no longer needed. When the owner goes out of scope, Rust automatically calls the drop function, and the memory is freed. There can only be one owner for a piece of data at any given time.
- Borrowing: Instead of transferring ownership, you can create references to a value. This allows you to access the value without taking ownership of it. Rust has rules to prevent data races and ensure that references are always valid. There are two types of borrows:
  - Immutable borrows: Allow you to read the data but not modify it. You can have multiple concurrent immutable borrows.
  - Mutable borrows: Allow you to modify the data. You can only have one mutable borrow at a time.
- Lifetimes: Lifetimes are annotations that specify the scope for which a reference is valid. The compiler uses lifetimes to ensure that references don't outlive the data they point to, preventing dangling pointers.

How Rust's Memory Management Promotes Efficiency

Rust's approach to memory management offers several advantages from a performance perspective:

- No Garbage Collection Overhead: Because Rust doesn't use a garbage collector, there are no unpredictable pauses or performance fluctuations caused by GC activity. This leads to more consistent and predictable performance, which is crucial for real-time and high-performance applications.

- Minimal Runtime Overhead: Rust's memory safety checks are performed at compile time, so there's very little runtime overhead. The compiled code is as efficient as if you had managed the memory manually in C or C++, but without the risk of memory errors.
- Explicit Control: Rust gives you fine-grained control over memory allocation and deallocation when needed. For example, you can use Box to allocate data on the heap when you need to, and you can use smart pointers like Rc and Arc to manage shared ownership in a safe and efficient way.

Data Layout for Efficiency

In addition to Rust's memory management, the way you arrange your data in memory, known as data layout, can significantly impact performance.

- Contiguous Memory: Accessing data that is stored contiguously in memory is much faster than accessing data that is scattered across different memory locations. This is because modern CPUs use caching mechanisms. When the CPU accesses a memory location, it also loads a chunk of nearby memory into the cache. If the next piece of data you need is also in that cache line, it can be accessed very quickly.
- Cache Lines: CPUs don't load individual bytes from memory; they load data in chunks called cache lines (typically 64 bytes). If your data is arranged contiguously, the CPU can load a large amount of data with a single memory access.
- Strided Access: If you access data with a large stride (e.g., accessing every 16th element in an array), the CPU has to load many different cache lines, which can be slow.

Example: Contiguous vs. Strided Access

To illustrate the impact of data layout, consider the following example where we compare the performance of accessing elements in an array with different strides:

Rust

```rust
use std::time::Instant;



const ARRAY_SIZE: usize = 1024 * 1024; // 1
million elements



fn main() {

    // 1. Create a large array of f64 values.

    let mut data = vec![0.0; ARRAY_SIZE];

    for i in 0..ARRAY_SIZE {

        data[i] = i as f64;

    }



    // 2. Measure contiguous access.

    let start = Instant::now();

    let mut sum1 = 0.0;

    for i in 0..ARRAY_SIZE {
```

```rust
        sum1 += data[i]; // Access elements
sequentially.

    }

    let contiguous_time = start.elapsed();

    println!("Contiguous access sum: {}, time:
{:?}", sum1, contiguous_time);



    // 3. Measure strided access (stride of 16).

    let start = Instant::now();

    let mut sum2 = 0.0;

    let mut i = 0;

    while i < ARRAY_SIZE {

        sum2 += data[i]; // Access elements with
a stride of 16.

        i += 16;

    }

    let strided_time = start.elapsed();

    println!("Strided access sum: {}, time:
{:?}", sum2, strided_time);

}
```

When you run this code, you'll likely observe that the contiguous access version is significantly faster than the strided access version. This is because the contiguous access pattern allows the CPU to load data more efficiently into the cache.

Data Layout in Machine Learning

In machine learning, we often work with large matrices and tensors. Choosing an appropriate data layout can be crucial for performance.

- Row-major vs. Column-major: As mentioned earlier, matrices can be stored in either row-major or column-major order.
    - Row-major order is common in languages like C and C++, and it's often a good choice when you're processing data row by row (e.g., when iterating over data points).
    - Column-major order is used in languages like Fortran and in some linear algebra libraries. It's more efficient when you're performing column-wise operations.
- ndarray and Layout: The ndarray crate in Rust, which is commonly used for numerical computation, defaults to row-major order. However, it also provides ways to specify a different layout if needed.

Example: Matrix Operations with Different Layouts

(Extending the previous example to show the effect of layout on matrix operations would involve more advanced ndarray usage and potentially external linear algebra libraries, which is beyond the scope of this focused explanation. But the core idea is that the optimal layout depends on the operations you perform.)

Efficient memory management and data layout are critical for writing high-performance machine learning code. Rust's ownership system helps you manage memory safely and efficiently, while careful consideration of data layout, such as using contiguous memory and choosing the appropriate row or column-major order, can further improve performance by maximizing CPU cache utilization.

8.2 Parallelism with Rayon for ML Tasks

Machine learning, at its heart, often involves a lot of repetitive computation on large amounts of data. Whether you're preprocessing data, training a model, or making predictions, you're frequently performing the same operation on many different data points. This kind of work is ideally suited for parallelism, where you divide the task into smaller subtasks and execute them simultaneously on multiple CPU cores.

Rust provides excellent support for parallelism, and the Rayon crate makes it remarkably easy to parallelize your code, especially when dealing with iterative computations, which are very common in ML.

Understanding Parallelism

Before we get into the specifics of Rayon, let's clarify what we mean by parallelism.

- Concurrency vs. Parallelism: These terms are sometimes used interchangeably, but they have distinct meanings:
  - Concurrency is the ability of a program to handle multiple tasks seemingly at the same time. This doesn't necessarily mean they're executing simultaneously. For example, a single-threaded program can use techniques like asynchronous operations to switch between tasks, giving the illusion of parallelism.
  - Parallelism is the ability to execute multiple tasks simultaneously by utilizing multiple processing units (cores) in your CPU. This requires hardware support

and a programming model that can effectively distribute work across those cores.

- Threads: Threads are the basic unit of execution in a computer program. A process can have multiple threads, each executing a portion of the program's code.
- Data Races: When multiple threads access the same memory location, and at least one of them is writing to it, it can lead to a data race. Data races can cause unpredictable behavior and memory corruption, making them notoriously difficult to debug.

Rust and Thread Safety

Rust's ownership system and borrowing rules play a crucial role in making parallelism safe. By ensuring that data is accessed and modified in a controlled manner, Rust prevents data races at compile time. This "fearless concurrency" is one of Rust's major strengths.

Rayon: Painless Parallelism

Rayon is a Rust library that makes it incredibly easy to parallelize computations, especially those involving iterators. It provides a high-level abstraction over threads, allowing you to focus on expressing the logic of your computation rather than the low-level details of thread management.

Key Concepts in Rayon

- Parallel Iterators: Rayon introduces the concept of parallel iterators. These are iterators that process items in parallel, automatically distributing the work across multiple threads.
- ParallelIterator Trait: The core trait that defines the behavior of parallel iterators. Rayon extends regular sequential iterators with this trait, adding methods for parallel processing.

- par_iter() and par_iter_mut(): These methods convert a sequential iterator into a parallel iterator.
  - par_iter(): Creates a parallel iterator that yields immutable references to the items in the collection.
  - par_iter_mut(): Creates a parallel iterator that yields mutable references to the items in the collection, allowing you to modify them in parallel.
- ParallelBridge: For collections that don't have a built-in parallel iterator implementation, you can use par_bridge() to create a parallel iterator.

Parallel Operations with Rayon

Once you have a parallel iterator, you can use a variety of methods to perform operations on the items in parallel. These methods are designed to be similar to their sequential counterparts, making it easy to adapt existing code:

- map(): Applies a function to each item in the iterator in parallel, producing a new parallel iterator with the results.
- filter(): Filters the items in the iterator based on a predicate (a function that returns a boolean), producing a new parallel iterator with the filtered items.
- reduce(): Combines the items in the iterator into a single value using a reduction operation (e.g., summing the elements).
- for_each(): Executes a function for each item in the iterator in parallel, without producing a new iterator.
- collect(): Collects the items from a parallel iterator into a new collection (e.g., a Vec).

Example: Parallel Vector Sum with Rayon

Let's illustrate how to use Rayon to calculate the sum of a large vector in parallel:

Rust

```rust
use rayon::prelude::*; // Import the Rayon
prelude.


fn main() {

    // 1. Create a large vector of numbers.

    let data: Vec<i32> =
(0..1_000_000).collect();



    // 2. Calculate the sum sequentially.

    let sequential_sum: i32 = data.iter().sum();

    println!("Sequential Sum: {}",
sequential_sum);



    // 3. Calculate the sum in parallel using
Rayon.

    let parallel_sum: i32 = data

        .par_iter() // Convert the vector into a
parallel iterator.

        .sum();          // Sum the elements in
parallel.



    println!("Parallel Sum: {}", parallel_sum);
```

```
// 4. Verify that the results are the same.

assert_eq!(sequential_sum, parallel_sum);

}
```

In this example:

1. We create a large vector of integers.
2. We calculate the sum of the vector elements sequentially using the iter().sum() method.
3. We calculate the sum in parallel using Rayon:
   - data.par_iter(): We convert the vector into a parallel iterator using par_iter().
   - .sum(): We call the sum() method on the parallel iterator. Rayon automatically splits the vector into chunks and sums the elements in each chunk on different threads. It then combines the partial sums from each thread to produce the final result.
4. We assert that the sequential sum and the parallel sum are equal, ensuring that the parallel computation is correct.

Parallelizing ML Tasks with Rayon

Rayon can be applied to various machine learning tasks to accelerate computations:

- Data Preprocessing: Many preprocessing steps, such as feature scaling, normalization, and data cleaning, can be parallelized.
- Model Training: Some training algorithms, such as gradient descent for certain models, can be parallelized by processing different parts of the data or different model parameters concurrently.
- Inference: When making predictions on a large number of data points, you can parallelize the prediction process.
- Cross-validation: The different folds of cross-validation can be evaluated in parallel.

Example: Parallelized Feature Scaling with Rayon

Let's say you have a large dataset represented as an ndarray::Array2, and you want to scale each feature (column) using the mean and standard deviation calculated from the entire dataset.

Rust

```rust
use ndarray::Array1;

use ndarray::Array2;

use ndarray::Axis;

use rayon::prelude::*;


fn main() {

    // 1. Sample data (1000 data points, 5
features).

    let mut data = Array2::<f64>::zeros((1000,
5));

    for i in 0..1000 {

        for j in 0..5 {

            data[[i, j]] = (i * 5 + j) as f64; //
Fill with some sample data

        }

    }
```

```rust
    // 2. Calculate the mean and standard
deviation for each feature (column).

    let mean = data.mean_axis(Axis(0)).unwrap();
// Calculate mean along columns.

    let std_dev = data.std_axis(Axis(0), 0.0); //
Calculate standard deviation along columns.


    // 3. Parallelize the feature scaling process
using Rayon.

    data.axis_iter_mut(Axis(0)) // Iterate over
rows (data points).

        .par_bridge()               // Convert to a
parallel iterator.

        .for_each(|mut row| {

            // Scale each feature in the row
using the pre-computed mean and standard
deviation.

            for j in 0..5 {

                row[j] = (row[j] - mean[j]) /
std_dev[j];

            }

        });


    // 4. Print the first few rows of the scaled
data.
```

```
    println!("Scaled Data (first 5 rows):\n{}",
data.slice((0..5, ..)));

}
```

In this example:

1. We create a sample Array2<f64> representing a dataset with 1000 data points and 5 features.
2. We calculate the mean and standard deviation for each feature (column) using mean_axis and std_axis.
3. We parallelize the feature scaling process using Rayon:
    o data.axis_iter_mut(Axis(0)): We create an iterator over the rows of the data matrix. The Axis(0) argument specifies that we want to iterate over the rows. The _mut indicates we want mutable access to the rows.
    o .par_bridge(): We convert the row iterator into a parallel iterator using par_bridge().
    o .for_each(|mut row| ...): We use the for_each() method to apply a function to each row in parallel. The closure |mut row| ... takes a mutable reference to a row (row) as input. We then scale each feature within that row.
4. We print the first few rows of the scaled data to demonstrate the result.

8.3 Utilizing SIMD for Vectorized Computations in Rust

Modern CPUs are capable of performing the same operation on multiple data points simultaneously. This capability is exposed through SIMD (Single Instruction, Multiple Data) instructions. Instead of processing data element by element, SIMD allows you to process chunks of data (typically 4, 8, or 16 elements) with a single instruction, leading to significant performance improvements for certain types of computations.

In machine learning, we often deal with large amounts of numerical data and perform repetitive operations on them, making SIMD a very attractive optimization technique.

Understanding SIMD

To understand SIMD, let's contrast it with traditional scalar processing:

- Scalar Processing: In scalar processing, a CPU performs an operation on one data element at a time. For example, to add two vectors, the CPU would add the first elements, then the second elements, and so on, sequentially.
- SIMD Processing: In SIMD processing, the CPU can perform the same operation on multiple data elements simultaneously. For example, if your CPU has a 128-bit SIMD register, it can hold four 32-bit floating-point numbers. With a single SIMD instruction, you can add four pairs of numbers at once.

Benefits of SIMD

Using SIMD can provide substantial performance gains for applications that involve repetitive numerical computations, such as:

- Multimedia processing: Encoding and decoding audio and video.
- Graphics rendering: Performing transformations and calculations on vertices and pixels.
- Scientific computing: Performing simulations and numerical analysis.

- Machine learning: Accelerating operations like matrix multiplication, element-wise operations, and distance calculations.

SIMD in Rust

While Rust's standard library doesn't provide a high-level, portable API for SIMD, there are a few ways to utilize SIMD instructions in Rust:

- std::arch: This module provides direct access to CPU-specific SIMD instructions. This approach offers the best performance but is also the most complex and requires you to write platform-specific code.
- Crates like packed_simd: These crates provide a more portable and safer abstraction over SIMD, making it easier to write vectorized code that works across different architectures.

Example: Vector Addition with SIMD using std::arch **(x86_64 SSE)**

Let's look at a simplified example of performing vector addition using SIMD instructions on x86_64 architecture with SSE (Streaming SIMD Extensions).

Rust

```
#[cfg(target_arch = "x86_64")] // This code is
specific to x86_64 architecture

use std::arch::x86_64::{__m128d, _mm_add_pd,
_mm_loadu_pd, _mm_storeu_pd}; // Import SSE
intrinsics
```

```rust
#[cfg(target_arch = "x86_64")]

fn main() {

    // 1. Check if the CPU supports SSE2.

    if is_x86_feature_detected!("sse2") {

        unsafe {

            // 2. Load data into SIMD registers.

            let a = _mm_loadu_pd([1.0,
2.0].as_ptr()); // Load 2 f64 values from memory

            let b = _mm_loadu_pd([3.0,
4.0].as_ptr());


            // 3. Perform vector addition using
the _mm_add_pd instruction.

            let result = _mm_add_pd(a, b);


            // 4. Store the result from the SIMD
register into an array in memory.

            let mut result_array = [0.0; 2];


_mm_storeu_pd(result_array.as_mut_ptr(), result);


            // 5. Print the result.
```

```rust
        println!("Result: {:?}",
result_array); // Output: [4.0, 6.0]

    }

  } else {

    // 6. Handle the case where SSE2 is not
supported.

    println!("SSE2 not supported on this
architecture.");

  }

}


#[cfg(not(target_arch = "x86_64"))] // For other
architectures

fn main() {

  // 1.  Inform the user that SIMD is not
available.

  println!("SIMD is only available on x86_64
architectures in this example.");

}
```

In this example:

1. We use the #[cfg(target_arch = "x86_64")] attribute to make the code specific to the x86_64 architecture, which supports SSE2.

2. We check if the CPU supports the SSE2 feature at runtime using is_x86_feature_detected!("sse2"). This is important because SIMD instructions are not available on all CPUs.
3. Inside an unsafe block (because using SIMD intrinsics requires careful handling to avoid memory errors), we:
   - Load data from memory into SIMD registers using _mm_loadu_pd. This instruction loads two 64-bit floating-point numbers from a slice into a 128-bit register.
   - Perform vector addition using the _mm_add_pd instruction, which adds the corresponding elements of the two SIMD registers in parallel.
   - Store the result from the SIMD register back into a Rust array using _mm_storeu_pd.
4. We print the result.
5. For architectures other than x86_64, we print a message indicating that SIMD is not supported in this example.

Using packed_simd for Portable SIMD

The packed_simd crate provides a more portable and safer way to use SIMD in Rust. It offers a set of data types and operations that are abstracted over different SIMD instruction sets, allowing you to write vectorized code that can run on various architectures.

Example: Vector Addition with packed_simd

Rust

```
use packed_simd::*;



fn main() {

    // 1. Create two vectors of f32x4 (4-element
vectors of 32-bit floats).
```

```
let a = f32x4::new(1.0, 2.0, 3.0, 4.0);

let b = f32x4::new(5.0, 6.0, 7.0, 8.0);


// 2. Perform vector addition using the +
operator.

let result = a + b;


// 3. Print the result.

println!("Result: {}", result); // Output:
[6.0, 8.0, 10.0, 12.0]

}
```

In this example, f32x4 represents a 4-element vector of 32-bit floats. The + operator performs element-wise addition, and the packed_simd crate handles the underlying SIMD instructions for you. This code will work on different architectures that support SIMD.

SIMD for Machine Learning

SIMD can be used to accelerate many machine learning operations, including:

- Matrix multiplication: By processing multiple elements of matrices in parallel.
- Element-wise operations: Such as applying activation functions in neural networks or performing data normalization.
- Distance calculations: Used in clustering algorithms and k-nearest neighbors.

Important Considerations

- Portability: Using std::arch directly ties your code to a specific architecture. Crates like packed_simd offer better portability.
- Safety: Using std::arch often involves unsafe code, requiring careful handling to avoid memory errors. packed_simd provides a safer abstraction.
- Complexity: SIMD programming can be more complex than scalar programming.

8.4 Profiling and Benchmarking Rust ML Code

When you're optimizing your Rust code for machine learning, it's not enough to just guess where the performance bottlenecks are. You need to measure and analyze your code's behavior to identify the areas that are actually slowing things down. This is where profiling and benchmarking come in.

Profiling: Understanding Where Time is Spent

Profiling is the process of collecting data about your program's execution, specifically focusing on how much time is spent in different parts of the code. It helps you answer the question: "Where is my program spending most of its time?".

A profiler is a tool that collects this information as your program runs. It can tell you:

- Which functions are called most frequently.
- How long each function takes to execute.
- How much time is spent in different code sections.
- Memory allocation patterns.

By analyzing this data, you can pinpoint the "hotspots" in your code, which are the parts that consume the most resources and are therefore the most critical to optimize.

Profiling Tools

There are several excellent profiling tools available for Rust, and the best choice often depends on your operating system and specific needs.

Here are a couple of common options:

- perf (Linux): perf is a powerful command-line profiling tool that comes with the Linux kernel. It can provide very detailed information about CPU usage, cache misses, and other performance metrics. It's a go-to tool for performance analysis on Linux systems.
- Instruments (macOS): Instruments is a graphical performance analysis tool that is part of Apple's Xcode development environment. It provides a user-friendly interface for visualizing and analyzing your program's performance, including CPU usage, memory allocation, and more.

Example: Profiling Rust Code with perf (Linux)

Let's say you have a Rust program that performs some machine learning computation, and you want to profile it on Linux.

Here's a general outline of how you can do it using perf:

Compile your Rust program in release mode:

Bash

```
cargo build --release
```

Profiling is usually done on release builds because they are optimized for performance.

Run your program with perf record:

```
sudo perf record --call-graph=dwarf
target/release/your_program
```

- sudo: perf often requires root privileges to access hardware performance counters.
- perf record: This command tells perf to record performance data while your program is running.
- --call-graph=dwarf: This option tells perf to collect call graph information, which shows the relationships between function calls. This is crucial for understanding the flow of execution and identifying where time is spent.
- target/release/your_program: Replace your_program with the name of your compiled executable.

Run your program:

Your program will run as usual, and perf will collect performance data in a file named perf.data.

Analyze the results with perf report:

```
perf report --stdio
```

This command will display a report in your terminal, showing you the functions where your program spent the most time. You can

316

also use other tools like perf visualize to view the data in a graphical interface.

The output of perf report will typically show a list of functions, ordered by the percentage of time spent in each function. This allows you to quickly identify the performance bottlenecks in your code.

Benchmarking: Measuring Code Performance

While profiling tells you where your program spends time, benchmarking helps you measure how fast specific parts of your code are. This is useful for comparing different implementations of a function or for evaluating the impact of your optimizations.

Rust has a built-in benchmarking framework that allows you to write microbenchmarks to measure the execution time of small code snippets.

Code Example: Benchmarking with Rust's test Crate

Here's how you can write a benchmark in Rust:

Rust

```
#![feature(test)] // Enable the test feature
(required for benchmarking)


extern crate test; // Import the test crate


use test::Bencher; // Import the Bencher struct.

use ndarray::array;

use ndarray::Array1;
```

```rust
// Function to calculate the sum of a vector
(example function to benchmark)
fn sum_vector(vector: &Array1<f64>) -> f64 {
    vector.sum()
}


#[cfg(test)] // Mark this module as a test module
mod tests {
    use super::*; // Import the code you want to
test/benchmark
    use test::black_box; // Import the black_box
function


    #[bench] // Mark this function as a benchmark
    fn bench_sum_vector(bencher: &mut Bencher) {
        // 1. Create a large vector.
        let vector = array![1.0; 1000]; // A
vector of 1000 ones


        // 2. Run the function to be benchmarked
repeatedly.
        bencher.iter(|| {
            let v = black_box(&vector); //
Prevent compiler optimizations
            sum_vector(v)
        });
    }
}
```

Let's break down this code:

1. #![feature(test)]: This line is a feature gate that enables the test feature, which is required for writing benchmarks. You need to add this at the crate root (usually src/lib.rs or src/main.rs).
2. extern crate test;: This line imports the test crate, which provides the benchmarking infrastructure.
3. use test::Bencher;: We import the Bencher struct, which is used to define a benchmark.
4. We define a function sum_vector that we want to benchmark. In this example, it simply calculates the sum of the elements in a vector.
5. We create a module named tests and annotate it with #[cfg(test)]. This ensures that the module is only compiled when we run tests or benchmarks.
6. Inside the tests module, we define a benchmark function named bench_sum_vector and annotate it with #[bench]. This tells Rust that this function is a benchmark.
7. The benchmark function takes a mutable reference to a Bencher struct as an argument. The Bencher provides the iter method, which you use to run the code you want to benchmark repeatedly.
8. Inside the bencher.iter(|| { ... }) closure, you put the code that you want to measure. This closure will be executed many times by the benchmarking framework.
9. We use black_box(&vector) to prevent the compiler from optimizing away the input vector. The compiler is very clever and might realize that the vector is the same in every iteration and optimize the summation away. black_box acts as an opaque function, forcing the compiler to treat the input as a black box and preventing such optimizations.

To run this benchmark, you need to use the nightly version of Rust and run the following command in your project's root directory:

Bash

rustup run nightly cargo bench

This command does the following:

- rustup run nightly: Executes the command using the nightly version of Rust (benchmarking requires some unstable features).
- cargo bench: Tells Cargo to run the benchmarks.

Cargo will then compile your code and run the benchmark function. The output will show you the average execution time of the code inside the bencher.iter closure.

Interpreting Benchmark Results

The output of cargo bench will typically look something like this:

running 1 benchmark

test bench_sum_vector ... bench: 1,234 ns/iter (+/- 123)

This output tells you that the bench_sum_vector function took an average of 1,234 nanoseconds per iteration, with a standard deviation of 123 nanoseconds.

Tips for Effective Benchmarking

- Use release mode: Always benchmark your code in release mode (cargo build --release). Release mode applies optimizations that can significantly affect performance.
- Minimize setup code: Put only the code you want to measure inside the bencher.iter closure. Avoid including setup code that is not part of the operation you're benchmarking.
- Prevent optimizations: Use black_box to prevent the compiler from optimizing away the code you're benchmarking.

- Run benchmarks multiple times: Run your benchmarks several times to get stable results and account for variations in system load.
- Compare different approaches: Benchmark different implementations of the same function to see which one performs better.
- Benchmark realistic workloads: Use data and input sizes that are representative of your actual use case.

By consistently profiling and benchmarking your Rust ML code, you can gain valuable insights into its performance characteristics and make informed decisions about how to optimize it for maximum efficiency.

8.5 Optimizing Data Access Patterns

When working with machine learning, you're often dealing with large datasets stored in memory. The way your code accesses this data can dramatically affect how quickly your program runs. Efficient data access patterns are crucial for maximizing performance, and Rust's memory management capabilities can be a great help in achieving this.

Understanding the Memory Hierarchy

To grasp why data access patterns matter, let's first understand how computer memory is organized. It's not a single, uniform pool; instead, it's structured as a hierarchy of different levels, each with its own speed and capacity:

- Registers: These are the fastest memory locations, located directly within the CPU. They hold the data that the CPU is currently working on. Accessing data in registers is incredibly quick, but they have very limited capacity.
- Cache: CPU cache is a small, fast memory that stores frequently accessed data. It acts as a buffer between the

CPU and the main memory (RAM).[1] There are typically multiple levels of cache:

- o L1 cache: The smallest and fastest cache, located closest to the CPU.
- o L2 cache: Larger and slightly slower than L1 cache.
- o L3 cache: The largest and slowest cache level, shared by multiple CPU cores.

- RAM (Main Memory): This is the computer's primary working memory. It's much larger than the cache but significantly slower to access.
- Secondary Storage: This encompasses hard drives, SSDs, and other persistent storage devices. Accessing data from secondary storage is extremely slow compared to accessing data from RAM or cache.

The Principle of Locality

Efficient data access hinges on a concept called **locality**, which has two main aspects:

- Temporal Locality: If your program accesses a particular memory location, it's likely to access that same location again in the near future. For example, if you're processing a loop, the loop counter variable will be accessed repeatedly.
- Spatial Locality: If your program accesses a memory location, it's likely to access nearby memory locations in the near future. This is because data is often organized in contiguous blocks.

CPUs exploit these principles using caches. When the CPU needs to read data from a specific memory address, it doesn't just load that single byte; it loads an entire **cache line**, which is a small block of contiguous memory (typically 64 bytes). This is because the CPU assumes that you'll likely need the data around that address soon.

Impact of Data Access Patterns

Now, let's see how this affects our code. Consider a simple example: iterating over the elements of a large two-dimensional array (matrix).

Scenario: Iterating Over a Matrix

Suppose you have a 2D array representing an image, where each element is a pixel. You want to process each pixel in the image, for example, by applying a color transformation.

There are two common ways you could iterate over the pixels:

- Row-major order: Access pixels row by row, processing all pixels in the first row, then all pixels in the second row, and so on.
- Column-major order: Access pixels column by column, processing all pixels in the first column, then all pixels in the second column, and so on.

Which way is faster?

Code Example: Row-Major vs. Column-Major Iteration in Rust

Let's write a Rust program to compare the performance of these two iteration patterns:

Rust

```
use std::time::Instant;
```

```rust
const IMAGE_SIZE: usize = 1024; // Assume a
square image (1024x1024 pixels)


fn main() {

    // 1. Create a large 2D array (matrix) to
represent the image.

    //    We'll store the pixel data in a 1D
vector, but we'll access it as if it were a 2D
array.

    let mut image_data = vec![0u8; IMAGE_SIZE *
IMAGE_SIZE]; // 1 million pixels


    // 2. Measure row-major iteration.

    let start_row_major = Instant::now();

    let mut sum_row_major = 0u32;

    for row in 0..IMAGE_SIZE {

        for col in 0..IMAGE_SIZE {

            // Calculate the index in the 1D
vector that corresponds to the current pixel.

            let index = row * IMAGE_SIZE + col;

            sum_row_major += image_data[index] as
u32; // Access pixel data in row-major order.
```

```rust
        }

    }

    let row_major_time =
start_row_major.elapsed();

    println!("Row-major iteration sum: {}, time:
{:?}", sum_row_major, row_major_time);



    // 3. Measure column-major iteration.

    let start_column_major = Instant::now();

    let mut sum_column_major = 0u32;

    for col in 0..IMAGE_SIZE {

        for row in 0..IMAGE_SIZE {

            let index = row * IMAGE_SIZE + col;

            sum_column_major += image_data[index]
as u32; // Access pixel data in column-major
order.

        }

    }

    let column_major_time =
start_column_major.elapsed();

    println!("Column-major iteration sum: {},
time: {:?}", sum_column_major,
column_major_time);
```

}

In this code:

1. We create a large 1D vector image_data to represent the pixel data of a square image. We calculate the index into this vector using the formula row * IMAGE_SIZE + col, which is how you would typically access elements in a 2D array if it were stored in a contiguous 1D memory block (which is how Rust vectors work).
2. We iterate over the image data in row-major order, using nested loops where the outer loop iterates over rows and the inner loop iterates over columns.
3. We iterate over the same image data in column-major order, reversing the order of the loops (outer loop iterates over columns, inner loop iterates over rows).

When you run this code, you'll likely observe that the row-major iteration is significantly faster than the column-major iteration.

Why is Row-Major Faster?

The performance difference arises from how the image data is laid out in memory and how the CPU cache works.

- Row-major access: When we access pixels in row-major order, we access consecutive memory locations. As the CPU reads the first pixel in a row, it also loads subsequent pixels in that row into the cache. When the inner loop continues to the next pixel in the same row, it's likely already in the cache, resulting in a very fast access.
- Column-major access: When we access pixels in column-major order, we access pixels that are far apart in memory. For example, when we access image_data[row * IMAGE_SIZE + col] in the inner loop, we are jumping across entire rows. This means the CPU has to load a new

cache line from RAM for almost every pixel access, leading to many cache misses and significantly slower performance.

A cache miss occurs when the CPU tries to access data that is not currently in the cache, forcing it to fetch the data from the much slower RAM. Cache misses are a major bottleneck in many memory-bound applications.

Implications for Machine Learning

In machine learning, we often work with multi-dimensional arrays (tensors) to represent datasets, model parameters, and intermediate computations. Understanding data access patterns is crucial for optimizing the performance of our ML code.

Here are some examples of how data access patterns can affect performance in machine learning:

- Matrix multiplication: The order in which you iterate over the elements of matrices during multiplication can significantly impact cache performance.
- Neural network operations: Accessing weights and activations in a way that aligns with the memory layout can speed up forward and backward propagation.
- Data preprocessing: Operations like feature scaling and normalization can be optimized by considering the layout of your data.

General Guidelines for Optimizing Data Access

Here are some general principles to keep in mind when optimizing data access patterns:

- Minimize strided access: Access data with a stride of 1 whenever possible. This means accessing elements that are adjacent in memory.

- Prefer contiguous access: Arrange your data in memory so that elements that are accessed together are stored contiguously.
- Consider cache blocking: For very large data structures, you can divide the data into smaller blocks and process them in a way that maximizes cache reuse.
- Choose the appropriate data layout: For multi-dimensional arrays, consider whether row-major or column-major order is more suitable for your access patterns, depending on how the data is accessed.

By being mindful of data access patterns and applying these optimization principles, you can write more efficient code that leverages the CPU cache effectively and achieves significantly better performance.

8.6 Case Studies in Performance Optimization

To solidify your understanding of how Rust can be used to optimize machine learning workloads, let's examine a couple of case studies that illustrate the application of the techniques we've discussed.

Case Study 1: Optimizing a High-Dimensional Feature Transformation

Imagine you're working on a machine learning project involving genomic data. You have a dataset where each data point represents a patient, and each patient is described by tens of thousands of features (e.g., gene expression levels). You need to perform a complex feature transformation on this data, which involves a series of matrix operations and element-wise calculations.

The initial implementation of this transformation in Rust is straightforward but turns out to be quite slow when applied to the entire dataset. Profiling reveals that a significant portion of the execution time is spent in nested loops that iterate over the feature matrix.

Here's how you can optimize this code:

1. Initial Implementation (Inefficient)

Rust

```rust
use ndarray::Array2;



fn transform_features_slow(features:
&Array2<f64>) -> Array2<f64> {

    let (num_patients, num_features) =
features.dim();

    let mut transformed_features =
Array2::<f64>::zeros((num_patients,
num_features));



    for i in 0..num_patients {

        for j in 0..num_features {

            let value = features[[i, j]];

            // Perform some complex calculation
based on the feature value

            transformed_features[[i, j]] =
(value.powi(2) + value.sin()).sqrt();



        }
```

```rust
    }

    transformed_features

}


fn main() {

    // 1. Create a large feature matrix (e.g.,
    10,000 patients, 10,000 features).

    let num_patients = 10000;

    let num_features = 10000;

    let features =
    Array2::<f64>::zeros((num_patients,
    num_features)); // Initialize with dummy data


    // 2. Transform the features using the slow
    implementation.

    let transformed_features_slow =
    transform_features_slow(&features);

    println!("Transformed features (slow):\nFirst
    few elements:\n{}",
    transformed_features_slow.slice((0..5, 0..5)));

}
```

This initial implementation uses nested loops to iterate over the feature matrix, performing the calculation for each element. While simple, this approach has poor data locality and doesn't utilize parallelism.

2. Optimized Implementation (Using ndarray and Rayon)

Here's how we can optimize this code using ndarray for efficient data layout and Rayon for parallelism:

Rust

```rust
use ndarray::Array2;

use rayon::prelude::*;


// Function to perform the feature transformation

fn transform_features_optimized(features:
&Array2<f64>) -> Array2<f64> {

    features.mapv(|x| (x.powi(2) +
x.sin()).sqrt())

}


fn main() {

    // 1. Create a large feature matrix (e.g.,
10,000 patients, 10,000 features).

    let num_patients = 10000;

    let num_features = 10000;

    let features =
Array2::<f64>::zeros((num_patients,
num_features)); // Initialize
```

```
    // 2. Transform the features using the
optimized implementation with Rayon.

    let transformed_features_optimized:
Array2<f64> = features

        .par_mapv(|x| (x.powi(2) +
x.sin()).sqrt());



    println!("Transformed features
(optimized):\nFirst few elements:\n{}",
transformed_features_optimized.slice((0..5,
0..5)));

}
```

In this optimized version:

- We use ndarray's mapv and par_mapv methods to perform the element-wise calculation.
  - mapv applies the function to each element sequentially.
  - par_mapv applies the function to each element in parallel using Rayon.

Performance Gains

By switching from nested loops to par_mapv, we achieve the following:

- Vectorization: ndarray's operations are vectorized, meaning they can often be executed using SIMD instructions, which process multiple data elements simultaneously.
- Parallelism: Rayon automatically splits the data into chunks and processes them on multiple threads, utilizing all available CPU cores.[1]

- Improved data locality: ndarray's memory layout ensures efficient data access, maximizing cache utilization.

This optimized version will be significantly faster than the initial implementation, especially for large matrices.

Case Study 2: Optimizing a Custom Machine Learning Algorithm

Let's consider a more complex scenario where you're implementing a custom machine learning algorithm in Rust. This algorithm involves iterative updates of a large data structure, and you want to optimize its performance.

1. Initial Implementation (Inefficient)

(Code for a specific custom ML algorithm would be quite extensive and depend heavily on the algorithm itself. Instead, I'll illustrate the kind of optimization steps one would take.)

Assume you have a function that updates a large matrix, and this update is done row by row:

Rust

```
use ndarray::Array2;



fn update_matrix_inefficient(matrix: &mut
Array2<f64>, update_values: &[f64]) {

    let (rows, cols) = matrix.dim();

    for i in 0..rows {

        for j in 0..cols{
```

```
            matrix[[i,j]] += update_values[j];

        }

    }

}
```

2. Optimized Implementation

Here's how you might optimize it:

Rust

```rust
use ndarray::Array2;

use rayon::prelude::*;



fn update_matrix_optimized(matrix: &mut
Array2<f64>, update_values: &Array1<f64>){


matrix.rows_mut().par_iter_mut().for_each(|mut
row| {

        for j in 0..row.len(){

            row[j] += update_values[j];

        }

    })

}
```

Optimization Steps and Reasoning

1. Parallelism with Rayon: We use par_iter_mut() to iterate over the rows of the matrix in parallel. This distributes the row updates across multiple threads, significantly speeding up the process for large matrices.
2. Efficient Data Access: The original implementation iterates through the matrix using nested loops. The optimized version maintains the row-wise access pattern, which is cache-friendly for ndarray's default row-major layout.

Performance Gains

The optimized version achieves significant performance gains due to:

- Parallelism: Distributing the row updates across multiple cores.
- Improved Data Locality: Accessing matrix elements in a row-wise fashion.

These case studies demonstrate how Rust's features and ecosystem can be used to optimize machine learning code for better performance. By understanding memory management, leveraging parallelism with Rayon, and being mindful of data access patterns, you can write efficient and scalable ML applications in Rust.

</immersive>

These case studies illustrate how Rust's features can be applied to optimize machine learning code. By understanding memory management, leveraging parallelism, and optimizing data access patterns, you can write efficient and scalable ML applications in Rust.

Chapter 9: Neural Networks in Rust

This chapter introduces the fascinating world of neural networks, a powerful tool in machine learning, and guides you through the process of building and training them using Rust.

9.1 Fundamentals of Neural Networks

Neural networks are a core component of deep learning, a subfield of machine learning that has driven many of the recent advances in artificial intelligence. They are inspired by the structure and function of the human brain, although the analogy is somewhat simplified.

The Basic Building Block: The Neuron

At the most basic level, a neural network is composed of interconnected units called **neurons**, also sometimes referred to as nodes or units.

A single neuron performs a relatively simple computation:

1. Input: A neuron receives one or more input values. These inputs can come from the original data you're feeding into the network or from the output of other neurons. Let's denote these input values as x_1, x_2, ..., x_n, where n is the number of inputs.
2. Weights: Each input value is associated with a weight. Weights, denoted as w_1, w_2, ..., w_n, are numerical values that determine the strength or importance of each input to the neuron's output. For instance, if a particular input has a large positive weight, it means that input has a strong influence on the neuron's output.
3. Weighted Sum: The neuron calculates a weighted sum of the inputs. This is done by multiplying each input value by

its corresponding weight and then adding all the products together. We also add a bias term, denoted as b, which is a constant value added to the sum. The weighted sum is often represented as:

$$z = w_1x_1 + w_2x_2 + ... + w_\square x_\square + b$$

This equation is also written in a more compact vector form:

$$z = w^T * x + b$$

Where:

- w is the weight vector $[w_1, w_2, ..., w_\square]$
- x is the input vector $[x_1, x_2, ..., x_\square]$
- w^T is the transpose of w

4. Activation Function: The weighted sum z is then passed through a special function called an activation function. The activation function introduces non-linearity into the neuron's output. This non-linearity is crucial because it allows neural networks to learn complex relationships in the data. Without activation functions, a neural network would simply be a series of linear transformations, no matter how many layers it had.

5. There are several commonly used activation functions, and the choice of which one to use can affect the network's performance. Here are a few popular ones:
   - Sigmoid Function: The sigmoid function, denoted as $\sigma(z)$, has the formula:

$$\sigma(z) = 1 / (1 + exp(-z))$$

- It takes any real-valued input and squashes it to a value between 0 and 1. The sigmoid function was historically popular, especially in older neural network architectures, and is still sometimes used in the output layer for binary classification problems (where you want to predict the probability of an input belonging to a certain class).
- ReLU (Rectified Linear Unit): The ReLU function, denoted as ReLU(z), is defined as:

$$\text{ReLU}(z) = \max(0, z)$$

- It simply outputs the input if it's positive, and zero otherwise. ReLU has become very popular in modern deep learning because it's computationally efficient and helps to alleviate the vanishing gradient problem, which can hinder the training of very deep networks.
- Tanh (Hyperbolic Tangent): The tanh function, denoted as tanh(z), is similar to the sigmoid function but outputs values between -1 and 1:

$$\tanh(z) = (\exp(z) - \exp(-z)) / (\exp(z) + \exp(-z))$$

6. Output: The final output of the neuron, denoted as a, is the result of applying the activation function to the weighted sum:

$$a = \varphi(z)$$

Where φ is the activation function (e.g., sigmoid, ReLU, tanh). This output value is then passed on to the next layer of neurons in the network.

Layers: Organizing Neurons

Neural networks organize neurons into layers. A typical neural network has the following structure:

- Input Layer: The first layer in the network. It doesn't perform any computation; it simply receives the raw input data. The number of neurons in the input layer corresponds to the number of features in your dataset. For example, if you're feeding images into a neural network, the input layer might have a neuron for each pixel in the image.
- Hidden Layers: These are the layers between the input layer and the output layer. Hidden layers are where the actual computation and learning take place. A neural network can have multiple hidden layers, and the more hidden layers it has, the more complex the relationships it can learn. The number of neurons in the hidden layers is a design choice and is a key part of the network's architecture.
- Output Layer: The final layer of the network. It produces the network's prediction. The number of neurons and the activation function used in the output layer depend on the specific task you're trying to solve:
  - For binary classification (predicting one of two classes), the output layer typically has a single neuron with a sigmoid activation function. The output of this neuron represents the probability of the input belonging to one of the classes.
  - For multi-class classification (predicting one of more than two classes), the output layer has one neuron for each class, and a softmax activation function is used. The softmax function converts the outputs of the neurons into a probability distribution over the classes.
  - For regression (predicting a continuous value), the output layer might have a single neuron with no activation function, or a linear activation function.

Example of a Simple Neural Network Architecture

A simple neural network architecture might look like this:

Input Layer (2 neurons) -> Hidden Layer 1 (4 neurons) -> Output Layer (1 neuron)

In this example:

- The input layer has 2 neurons, which means the input data has 2 features.
- Hidden Layer 1 has 4 neurons.
- The output layer has 1 neuron, which suggests this network is designed for a binary classification problem.

Neural networks are built from interconnected neurons organized in layers. Each neuron performs a weighted sum of its inputs and applies an activation function to produce an output. The arrangement of neurons into layers and the choice of activation functions determine the network's architecture and its ability to learn complex patterns from data.

9.2 Implementing Feedforward Neural Networks in Rust

Now that we have a basic understanding of neurons, layers, and activation functions, let's get practical and implement a simple feedforward neural network in Rust. We'll use the ndarray crate for efficient numerical computations, which are essential for neural network operations.

Feedforward Neural Networks

A feedforward neural network is the most basic type of neural network. In a feedforward network, the information flows in one direction: from the input layer, through[1] the hidden layers, to the output layer. There are no loops or cycles in the network.

Here's how data flows through a feedforward neural network:

1. Input: The input data is fed into the input layer.
2. Weighted Sum: Each neuron in a hidden layer receives the activations (outputs) from the previous layer. It calculates a weighted sum of these activations and adds a bias term.
3. Activation Function: The weighted sum is then passed through an activation function, introducing non-linearity.
4. Forward Propagation: The output of each neuron in a layer becomes the input to the neurons in the next layer. This process continues until the output layer is reached.
5. Output: The output layer produces the final prediction of the network.

Implementing a Layer

To implement a feedforward network, we'll first create a function that performs the operations of a single layer: calculating the weighted sum and applying the activation function.

Rust

```
use ndarray::Array1;

use ndarray::Array2;



// Function to perform a forward pass through a
single layer

fn forward_pass_layer(

    input: &Array2<f64>,         // Input from the
previous layer or the input data (batch_size,
input_size)
```

```rust
    weights: &Array2<f64>,        // Weights for
this layer (input_size, output_size)

    biases: &Array1<f64>,         // Biases for this
layer (output_size,)

    activation_function: fn(f64) -> f64, //
Activation function (e.g., sigmoid, ReLU)

) -> Array2<f64> {

    // 1. Calculate the weighted sum:   input *
weights + biases

    //     - input: (batch_size, input_size)

    //     - weights: (input_size, output_size)

    //     - result of dot product: (batch_size,
output_size)

    //     - biases: (output_size,)   (will be
broadcasted to (batch_size, output_size))

    let z = input.dot(weights) + biases;


    // 2. Apply the activation function
element-wise

    let activations: Array2<f64> =
z.mapv(activation_function); // (batch_size,
output_size)

    activations

}
```

In this function:

- input: This is a 2D array representing the input to the layer.
  - The shape is (batch_size, input_size), where batch_size is the number of data points being processed at once, and input_size is the number of features for each data point.
- weights: This is a 2D array representing the weights of the connections between the neurons in the previous layer and the neurons in this layer.
  - The shape is (input_size, output_size), where output_size is the number of neurons in this layer.
- biases: This is a 1D array representing the bias terms for the neurons in this layer.
  - The shape is (output_size,).
- activation_function: This is a function that takes a single f64 value (the weighted sum) and returns an f64 value (the activation). This allows us to use different activation functions for different layers.
- We calculate the weighted sum using matrix multiplication (input.dot(weights)) and add the bias term. ndarray automatically broadcasts the biases across the batch dimension.
- We apply the activation function to each element of the weighted sum using the mapv method, which applies a function to each element of the array.

Implementing a Feedforward Network

Now that we have a function for a single layer, we can create a function that performs a forward pass through the entire network.

Rust

```
use ndarray::Array1;

use ndarray::Array2;
```

```rust
// Sigmoid activation function

fn sigmoid(z: f64) -> f64 {

    1.0 / (1.0 + (-z).exp())

}


// ReLU activation function

fn relu(z: f64) -> f64 {

    if z > 0.0 { z } else { 0.0 }

}


fn forward_pass_layer(

    input: &Array2<f64>,

    weights: &Array2<f64>,

    biases: &Array1<f64>,

    activation_function: fn(f64) -> f64,

) -> Array2<f64> {

    let z = input.dot(weights) + biases;

    z.mapv(activation_function)

}
```

```rust
// Function to perform a forward pass through the
entire network

fn forward_pass(

    input_data: &Array2<f64>,        // Input data
(batch_size, input_size)

    weights: &[Array2<f64>],       // Vector of
weight matrices for each layer

    biases: &[Array1<f64>],        // Vector of
bias vectors for each layer

    activation_functions: &[fn(f64) -> f64], //
Vector of activation functions

) -> Vec<Array2<f64>> {

    let mut activations = Vec::new(); // Store
the activations of each layer.

    let mut current_activation =
input_data.clone(); // Start with the input data.



    // Iterate over the layers.

    for i in 0..weights.len() {

        let layer_activation =
forward_pass_layer(

            &current_activation,         // Input
to this layer is the output from the previous
layer.
```

```
            &weights[i],                    //
Weights for this layer.

            &biases[i],                     //
Biases for this layer.

            activation_functions[i], //
Activation function for this layer.

        );


activations.push(layer_activation.clone()); //
Store the activations of this layer.

        current_activation = layer_activation;
// The output of this layer becomes the input to
the next layer.

    }



    activations // Return the activations of all
layers.  The last element is the network's
output.

}



fn main() {

    // 1. Define the network architecture.

    let input_size = 2;      // Number of features
in the input data.
```

```rust
    let hidden_size1 = 4;      // Number of neurons
in the first hidden layer.

    let hidden_size2 = 3;      // Number of neurons
in the second hidden layer.

    let output_size = 1;      // Number of neurons
in the output layer (for binary classification).



    // 2. Initialize weights and biases (in a
real scenario, these would be learned during
training).

    let weights = vec![

        // Weights for the first layer
(input_size, hidden_size1)

        Array2::<f64>::zeros((input_size,
hidden_size1)),

        // Weights for the second layer
(hidden_size1, hidden_size2)

        Array2::<f64>::zeros((hidden_size1,
hidden_size2)),

        // Weights for the output layer
(hidden_size2, output_size)

        Array2::<f64>::zeros((hidden_size2,
output_size)),

    ];
```

```rust
    let biases = vec![

        // Biases for the first layer
    (hidden_size1,)

        Array1::<f64>::zeros(hidden_size1),

        // Biases for the second layer
    (hidden_size2,)

        Array1::<f64>::zeros(hidden_size2),

        // Biases for the output layer
    (output_size,)

        Array1::<f64>::zeros(output_size),

    ];



    // 3. Choose activation functions for each
    layer.

    let activation_functions: Vec<fn(f64) -> f64>
    = vec![relu, relu, sigmoid];



    // 4. Sample input data (batch of 3 data
    points, each with 2 features).

    let input_data = array![[1.0, 2.0], [3.0,
    4.0], [5.0, 6.0]]; // Shape: (3, 2)



    // 5. Perform a forward pass through the
    network.
```

```
let activations = forward_pass(

    &input_data,

    &weights,

    &biases,

    &activation_functions,

);



// 6. Print the output of the network (the
activations of the output layer).

    println!("Output of the network:\n{}",
activations.last().unwrap());

}
```

In this code:

1. We define the network architecture by specifying the size of each layer.
2. We initialize the weights and biases for each layer with zeros. In a real-world scenario, these would be initialized randomly and then learned during the training process.
3. We create a vector activation_functions that stores the activation functions to be used for each layer. Here, we use ReLU for the hidden layers and sigmoid for the output layer, which is common for binary classification.
4. We define some sample input data as an Array2<f64>.
5. We call the forward_pass function to perform a forward pass through the network, calculating the activations of each layer.

6. Finally, we print the output of the network, which is the activation of the output layer (the last element in the activations vector).

This example shows the basic structure of a feedforward neural network and how to implement the forward pass in Rust using ndarray. The next step would be to implement the backpropagation algorithm to train the network, which we'll discuss in the next section.

9.3 Backpropagation Algorithm

Backpropagation, often called "backprop," is the algorithm used to train artificial neural networks. It's a method for efficiently calculating the gradient of the cost function with respect to the network's parameters (weights and biases). This gradient[1] is then used to update the parameters in the direction that minimizes the cost function, effectively allowing the network to learn from its mistakes.

The Need for Backpropagation

To understand why backpropagation is necessary, let's consider how a neural network learns.

1. Forward Pass: You feed a data point into the network, and it propagates through the layers, producing an output.
2. Cost Calculation: The network's output is compared to the actual target value, and a cost function (like mean squared error for regression or cross-entropy for classification) measures how far off the prediction was.
3. Parameter Update: The network's parameters (weights and biases) need to be adjusted to reduce this cost.

The challenge lies in how to efficiently update the parameters in each layer of the network. A neural network can have many layers, and each neuron's output depends on the parameters of all the neurons in the preceding layers. Brute-force methods for calculating how each parameter affects the final cost would be extremely computationally expensive.

Backpropagation provides a clever and efficient solution to this problem.

The Essence of Backpropagation: The Chain Rule

Backpropagation is essentially an application of the chain rule of calculus. The chain rule allows us to calculate the derivative of a composite function by breaking it down into a series of simpler derivatives.

In the context of a neural network, the cost function is a composite function of the outputs of each layer, which are in turn functions of the parameters (weights and biases) of that layer. Backpropagation uses the chain rule to calculate how the cost function changes as we change the parameters, layer by layer, starting from the output layer and working backward to the input layer.

The Backpropagation Algorithm: A Step-by-Step Explanation

Let's consider a neural network with L layers. We'll use the following notation:

- l: Index of a layer (l = 1, 2, ..., L), where l = 1 is the input layer and l = L is the output layer.
- a^l: Activations of layer l (the output of the neurons in layer l).
- z^l: Weighted sums (before activation function) of layer l.
- W^l: Weight matrix for layer l.
- b^l: Bias vector for layer l.
- y: Target output.
- J: Cost function.

Here's how the backpropagation algorithm works:

Forward Pass:

- Given an input example, we perform a forward pass through the network to compute the activations at each layer.
- We start with the input layer's activations (a^1) which is just the input data.
- For each layer l (from l = 2 to L), we compute:
  - $z^l = W^l a^{l-1} + b^l$ (Weighted sum)
  - $a^l = \varphi(z^l)$ (Apply activation function φ)

Compute the Output Layer Error (δ^L):

- We start by calculating the error at the output layer (layer L). The error, often denoted as δ^L (delta L), represents how much the network's output needs to change to reduce the cost.
- The exact formula for δ^L depends on the choice of cost function.
  - For example, if we're using the mean squared error (MSE) for a regression problem, and the activation function of the output layer is the identity function, then:

$$\delta^L = \partial J / \partial z^L = a^L - y$$

  - If we're using the cross-entropy loss for a binary classification problem with a sigmoid output, then:

$\delta^L = \partial J / \partial z^L = \hat{y} - y$

> - where $\hat{y}$ is the predicted probability.

Backpropagate the Error:

- We then propagate the error backward through the network, layer by layer, calculating the error (δ^l) for each hidden layer.
- For each layer l (from l = L-1 to 2), we compute δ^l using the error from the next layer (δ^{l+1}) and the weights of the current layer (W^{l+1}):

$\delta^l = (W^{l+1 T} \delta^{l+1}) \odot \varphi'(z^l)$

Where:

> - $W^{l+1 T}$ is the transpose of the weight matrix of the next layer.
> - $\odot$ denotes element-wise multiplication (Hadamard product).
> - $\varphi'(z^l)$ is the derivative of the activation function at z^l.

Compute Gradients:

- Now that we have the error δ^l for each layer, we can calculate the gradients of the cost function with respect to the weights ($\partial J / \partial W^l$) and biases ($\partial J / \partial b^l$) for each layer:

$\partial J / \partial W^l = \delta^l \, a^{l-1 \, T}$

$\partial J / \partial b^l = \delta^l$

- These gradients tell us how much the cost function changes when we change the weights and biases.

Update Weights and Biases:

- Finally, we update the weights and biases using an optimization algorithm, such as gradient descent:

$W^l := W^l - \alpha * \partial J / \partial W^l$

$b^l := b^l - \alpha * \partial J / \partial b^l$

- Where α is the learning rate, a hyperparameter that controls the step size of the updates.

In essence, backpropagation, by efficiently calculating and propagating gradients, enables neural networks to learn from their errors and refine their parameters iteratively. This process is fundamental to the training of virtually all modern neural networks, allowing them to tackle complex tasks in machine learning.

9.4 Optimization Algorithms

When training neural networks, the goal is to find the set of weights and biases that minimize a cost function. This is where optimization algorithms come in. The most fundamental of these is gradient descent, but many variations have been developed to improve its performance and address its limitations.

Gradient Descent: The Basic Optimizer

Gradient descent is an iterative algorithm that updates the parameters of a neural network in the direction of the negative gradient of the cost function.

Imagine the cost function as a landscape, and you're trying to find the lowest point in that landscape. The gradient tells you the direction of the steepest ascent at your current position. Gradient descent tells you to take a step in the opposite direction of the gradient to move downhill towards the minimum.

The update rule for a parameter (weight or bias) using gradient descent is:

parameter := parameter - learning_rate gradient

Where:

- parameter is a weight or bias in the neural network.
- learning_rate is a hyperparameter that controls the size of the step you take in the direction of the negative gradient.
- gradient is the partial derivative of the cost function with respect to that parameter.

Variants of Gradient Descent

While gradient descent is the basic principle, several variants have been developed to address its limitations and improve training:

1. Stochastic Gradient Descent (SGD)

In standard gradient descent, you calculate the gradient of the cost function by averaging the gradients over the entire training dataset. This is called batch gradient descent. When the dataset is very large, this can be computationally expensive.

Stochastic Gradient Descent (SGD) addresses this by updating the parameters after calculating the gradient for each individual training example. This makes the updates much faster, especially for large datasets. However, the updates in SGD are much noisier, as they are based on a single data point, which can cause the cost function to fluctuate significantly.

2. Momentum

Momentum is a technique that helps gradient descent accelerate in the right direction and dampens oscillations. It does this by adding a fraction of the previous update to the current update.

Imagine you're pushing a ball down a hill. Momentum is like giving the ball an extra push in the direction it was already going. This helps it to roll faster and smoother, and it can also help it to overcome small bumps (local minima) in the landscape.

The update rules with momentum are:

velocity := momentum * velocity + learning_rate * gradient

parameter := parameter - velocity

Where:

- velocity is a vector that accumulates the past gradients.
- momentum is a hyperparameter between 0 and 1 that controls how much of the previous update is retained.

3. Adam (Adaptive Moment Estimation)

Adam is a popular and effective optimization algorithm that adapts the learning rates for each parameter. It combines the ideas of momentum and RMSprop (Root Mean Square Propagation).

Here's a simplified explanation of how Adam works:

- Adaptive Learning Rates: Adam calculates an adaptive learning rate for each parameter by estimating the first and second moments of the gradients:
  - The first moment is the exponentially decaying average of the gradients (similar to momentum).
  - The second moment is the exponentially decaying average of the squared gradients (similar to RMSprop).
- Bias Correction: Adam includes a bias correction term to account for the fact that the initial estimates of the moments are biased towards zero.

The update rules for Adam are more complex than SGD or momentum, but they generally lead to faster convergence and better performance.

Code Example: Adam Optimizer in Rust

Implementing Adam from scratch is quite involved, but here's a simplified illustration of the core update logic in Rust-like pseudocode using ndarray:

```rust
Rust

use ndarray::Array1;


struct AdamOptimizer {

    learning_rate: f64,

    beta1: f64, // Exponential decay rate for the
first moment estimate

    beta2: f64, // Exponential decay rate for the
second moment estimate
```

```rust
    epsilon: f64, // A small constant to prevent
division by zero
    m: Array1<f64>, // First moment estimate
    v: Array1<f64>, // Second moment estimate
    t: usize,      // Time step
}


impl AdamOptimizer {
    fn new(learning_rate: f64, beta1: f64, beta2:
f64) -> Self {
        AdamOptimizer {
            learning_rate,
            beta1,
            beta2,
            epsilon: 1e-8,
            m: Array1::zeros(0), // Will be
initialized with the correct size later
            v: Array1::zeros(0),
            t: 0,
        }
    }


    fn update(&mut self, parameter: &mut
Array1<f64>, gradient: &Array1<f64>) {
        if self.m.len() != parameter.len() {
            // Initialize moment estimates with
the same shape as the parameter
```

```rust
            self.m =
Array1::zeros(parameter.len());
            self.v =
Array1::zeros(parameter.len());
        }

        self.t += 1; // Increment the time step


        // 1. Update the first moment estimate
(m) - Bias corrected momentum
        self.m = self.beta1 * &self.m + (1.0 -
self.beta1) * gradient;
        let m_hat = &self.m / (1.0 -
self.beta1.powi(self.t as i32));


        // 2. Update the second moment estimate
(v) - Bias corrected RMSprop
        self.v = self.beta2 * &self.v + (1.0 -
self.beta2) * gradient.map(|g| g.powi(2));
        let v_hat = &self.v / (1.0 -
self.beta2.powi(self.t as i32));


        // 3. Update the parameter
        *parameter = *parameter -
self.learning_rate * m_hat / (v_hat.map(|v|
v.sqrt()) + self.epsilon);
    }
}
```

```
fn main() {
    // Example usage:
    let mut parameter = array![1.0, 2.0, 3.0]; //
Example parameter vector
    let gradient = array![0.1, 0.2, -0.1];      //
Example gradient vector
    let mut optimizer = AdamOptimizer::new(0.01,
0.9, 0.999);


    optimizer.update(&mut parameter, &gradient);


    println!("Updated Parameter: {}", parameter);
}
```

Choosing the Right Optimizer

The best optimizer for a particular machine learning problem depends on several factors, including:

- The specific architecture of your neural network
- The characteristics of your dataset
- The computational resources you have available

In practice, Adam is often a good starting point due to its adaptive learning rates and robustness to different kinds of problems. However, experimenting with other optimizers and tuning their hyperparameters can sometimes lead to further performance improvements.

9.5 Training Neural Networks

Training a neural network involves feeding it data, calculating the error between the network's predictions and the actual values, and then updating the network's parameters (weights and biases) to reduce this error.[1] This process is repeated many times, and how you organize and feed the data to the network is crucial for efficient and effective training.

Here are three key concepts: data loaders, batching, and epochs

Data Loaders: Feeding Data to the Network

In a typical machine learning scenario, you have a dataset that contains all the examples your model will learn from. However, you rarely feed the entire dataset to the neural network all at once. Instead, you need a mechanism to efficiently load and deliver the data to the network in a structured way. This is where data loaders come in.

A data loader is responsible for:

- Loading Data from Storage: Reading data from its source, which could be files (like CSV or JSON), databases, or other formats.
- Preprocessing Data: Applying any necessary transformations to the data, such as scaling, normalization, or converting it into a suitable format for the neural network.[2]
- Batching Data: Dividing the data into smaller groups called batches, which are then fed to the network one at a time.[3]
- Shuffling Data: Randomly shuffling the data to ensure that the model sees different examples in each training iteration.[4]

Why Use Data Loaders?

- Memory Efficiency: Most datasets are too large to fit entirely into memory. Data loaders allow you to load and process data in smaller chunks, reducing memory usage.
- Optimization: Modern hardware, especially GPUs, can process data more efficiently in batches.[5] Data loaders

prepare the data in a format that the hardware can readily consume.

- Regularization: Shuffling the data helps to prevent the model from memorizing the order of the training examples, which can improve its ability to generalize to unseen data.[6]

Batching: Processing Data in Chunks

Instead of feeding data points to the network one at a time, we usually group them into smaller sets called batches.[7] This technique, called batching, offers several advantages:

- Computational Efficiency: Modern hardware, especially GPUs, can perform matrix operations much more efficiently on larger chunks of data. Processing data in batches allows us to take advantage of this parallelism.
- Smoother Updates: Using batches provides a more stable estimate of the gradient of the cost function. Instead of updating the model's parameters based on a single data point (which can be noisy), we average the gradients over a batch of data points, leading to smoother and more stable updates.[8]
- Better Generalization: Batching can sometimes improve the model's ability to generalize to unseen data.[9]

Batch Size

The batch size is a hyperparameter that determines the number of data points in each batch.[10] Choosing an appropriate batch size is important:

- Small batch size: Approaches stochastic gradient descent (SGD), with noisy updates but faster computation per update.
- Large batch size: Approaches batch gradient descent, with more stable updates but slower computation per update.

A common practice is to use a batch size that is a power of 2, such as 32, 64, 128, or 256, as these often work well with the memory architecture of GPUs.

Example: Batching Data

Let's say you have a dataset of 1000 images, and you choose a batch size of 32.

Your data loader will then divide the data into 32 batches:

- Batch 1: Images 0-31
- Batch 2: Images 32-63
- ...
- Batch 31: Images 960-991
- Batch 32: Images 992-999 (This last batch will have only 8 images)

During each training iteration, your network will process one of these batches at a time.

Epochs: Iterating Over the Entire Dataset

An epoch represents one complete pass through the entire training dataset. Since we typically process the data in batches, training a neural network for one epoch involves multiple iterations, where each iteration processes one batch.[11]

For example, if you have a dataset of 1000 images and a batch size of 32, one epoch will consist of 32 iterations (1000 / 32 ≈ 31.25, rounded up to 32).

Neural networks are typically trained for multiple epochs.[12] The number of epochs is a hyperparameter that you need to tune.[13]

- Too few epochs: The model might not have enough time to learn the patterns in the data.

- Too many epochs: The model might overfit the training data, performing well on the training set but poorly on unseen data.

The Training Loop

Putting it all together, here's a simplified representation of a typical neural network training loop:

for epoch in 1..num_epochs:

  for batch in data_loader:

1. Forward pass: Pass the batch of data through the network.

    predictions = model.forward(batch)

2. Calculate the loss: Compare the predictions with the true labels.

    loss = loss_function(predictions, batch.labels)

3. Backward pass: Calculate the gradients of the loss with respect to the model's parameters.

    gradients = model.backward(loss)

4. Update parameters: Use an optimizer (e.g., gradient descent) to update the model's weights and biases.

    optimizer.step(gradients)

5. Evaluate the model on a validation set (optional, but highly recommended).

    validation_loss = model.evaluate(validation_data)

```
print(f"Epoch {epoch}, Validation Loss:
{validation_loss}")
```

In this loop:

1. We iterate over the epochs.
2. For each epoch, we iterate over the batches provided by the data loader.
3. For each batch, we perform a forward pass to get the model's predictions.
4. We calculate the loss by comparing the predictions with the true labels.
5. We perform a backward pass (backpropagation) to calculate the gradients.
6. We use an optimizer to update the model's parameters based on the gradients.
7. Optionally, we evaluate the model on a validation set at the end of each epoch to monitor its performance and prevent overfitting.

By using data loaders, batching, and training for multiple epochs, you can efficiently train neural networks on large datasets and achieve good performance.

9.6 Evaluating Neural Network Performance

After you've trained a neural network, it's crucial to assess how well it performs. This process, called model evaluation, helps you understand how accurately your network can make predictions on unseen data. It's not enough to know that your network performs well on the data it was trained on; you need to know if it can generalize to new, previously unseen examples.

The way you evaluate a neural network depends on the type of machine learning problem you're solving: classification or regression.

Evaluation in Classification

In classification problems, the goal is to assign a data point to one of several categories. For example, you might want to classify emails as spam or not spam, or classify images as cats, dogs, or birds.

Here are some common metrics for evaluating the performance of neural networks in classification tasks:

1. Accuracy

Accuracy is the simplest and most intuitive metric. It measures the proportion of data points that the network correctly classifies.

Accuracy = (Number of correct predictions) / (Total number of predictions)

For example, if your network correctly classifies 90 out of 100 images, its accuracy is 90%.

Limitations of Accuracy

While accuracy is easy to understand, it can be misleading, especially when dealing with imbalanced datasets. An imbalanced dataset is one where the classes are not represented equally.

For instance, consider a spam email classification problem where 99% of the emails are not spam and only 1% are spam. A network that always predicts "not spam" would achieve an accuracy of 99%, which seems very good. However, it would be completely useless because it fails to identify any spam emails.

2. Precision and Recall

To address the limitations of accuracy, especially in imbalanced datasets, we use precision and recall. These metrics are defined in the context of a specific class (e.g., the "positive" class).

Let's define some terms:

- True Positive (TP): The network correctly predicts a data point belongs to the positive class.
- False Positive (FP): The network incorrectly predicts a data point belongs to the positive class when it actually belongs to the negative class.
- True Negative (TN): The network correctly predicts a data point belongs to the negative class.
- False Negative (FN): The network incorrectly predicts a data point belongs to the negative class when it actually belongs to the positive class.

Precision

Precision measures how many of the data points that the network predicted as positive were actually positive. It's a measure of how "precise" the network's positive predictions are.

Precision = TP / (TP + FP)

For example, if your network predicts 100 emails as spam, but only 80 of them are actually spam, the precision is 80%.

Recall (Sensitivity)

Recall measures how many of the actual positive data points the network correctly identified as positive. It's a measure of how "sensitive" the network is to the positive class.

Recall = TP / (TP + FN)

For example, if there are 100 actual spam emails, and your network correctly identifies only 70 of them as spam, the recall is 70%.

3. F1-Score

The F1-score is the harmonic mean of precision and recall. It provides a balanced measure of a network's performance, considering both false positives and false negatives.

F1-Score = 2 (Precision Recall) / (Precision + Recall)

A higher F1-score indicates better performance, especially in imbalanced datasets.

4. Area Under the ROC Curve (AUC)

The Receiver Operating Characteristic (ROC) curve plots the true positive rate (TPR, which is the same as recall) against the false positive rate (FPR) at various threshold settings. The Area Under the ROC Curve (AUC) measures the overall performance of the network across all possible classification thresholds.

An AUC of 0.5 indicates random guessing, while an AUC of 1 indicates perfect classification. A higher AUC generally indicates better performance.

Code Example: Evaluating Classification Performance in Rust

(A full implementation would require a trained model and a validation set, but I can show how to calculate the metrics given predictions and true labels.)

Rust

```rust
use ndarray::Array1;


// Function to calculate accuracy
fn calculate_accuracy(predictions: &Array1<i32>,
targets: &Array1<i32>) -> f64 {
```

```rust
    let correct_predictions = predictions
        .iter()
        .zip(targets.iter())
        .filter(|(&p, &t)| p == t)
        .count() as f64;

    correct_predictions / predictions.len() as
f64

}


// Function to calculate precision and recall
(for binary classification)
fn calculate_precision_recall(predictions:
&Array1<i32>, targets: &Array1<i32>) -> (f64,
f64) {
    let mut true_positives = 0;
    let mut false_positives = 0;
    let mut false_negatives = 0;


    for i in 0..predictions.len() {
        if predictions[i] == 1 && targets[i] == 1
{
            true_positives += 1;
        } else if predictions[i] == 1 &&
targets[i] == 0 {
            false_positives += 1;
        } else if predictions[i] == 0 &&
targets[i] == 1 {
            false_negatives += 1;
```

```
        }
    }

    let precision = if true_positives +
false_positives > 0 {

        true_positives as f64 / (true_positives +
false_positives) as f64

    } else {

        0.0

    };
    let recall = if true_positives +
false_negatives > 0 {

        true_positives as f64 / (true_positives +
false_negatives) as f64

    } else {

        0.0

    };


    (precision, recall)

}


// Function to calculate F1-score (for binary
classification)
fn calculate_f1_score(precision: f64, recall:
f64) -> f64 {
    if precision + recall > 0.0 {
        2.0 * (precision * recall) / (precision +
recall)
```

```rust
    } else {
        0.0
    }
}


fn main() {
    // Example: Binary classification predictions
and true labels
    let predictions = array![1, 0, 1, 1, 0, 1, 0,
0, 1, 0];
    let targets =    array![1, 0, 0, 1, 1, 1, 0,
1, 0, 0];


    // Calculate accuracy
    let accuracy =
calculate_accuracy(&predictions, &targets);
    println!("Accuracy: {:.2}", accuracy);


    // Calculate precision and recall
    let (precision, recall) =
calculate_precision_recall(&predictions,
&targets);
    println!("Precision: {:.2}", precision);
    println!("Recall: {:.2}", recall);


    // Calculate F1-score
    let f1_score = calculate_f1_score(precision,
recall);
```

```rust
    println!("F1-Score: {:.2}", f1_score);
}
```

Evaluation in Regression

In regression problems, the goal is to predict a continuous value. For example, you might want to predict house prices, temperature, or stock prices.

Here are some common metrics for evaluating the performance of neural networks in regression tasks:

- Mean Squared Error (MSE): Calculates the average of the squared differences between the predicted values and the actual values.[1] Lower MSE indicates better performance.
- Root Mean Squared Error (RMSE): The square root of the MSE. It has the same units as the target variable, making it easier to interpret than MSE.
- R-squared (Coefficient of Determination): Measures the proportion of the variance in the target variable that is explained by the model.[2] It ranges from 0 to 1, with higher values indicating a better[3] fit.

Code Example: Evaluating Regression Performance in Rust

Rust

```rust
use ndarray::Array1;


// Function to calculate Mean Squared Error (MSE)
fn calculate_mse(predictions: &Array1<f64>,
targets: &Array1<f64>) -> f64 {
    let diff = predictions - targets;
    (diff.dot(&diff)) / predictions.len() as f64
```

```rust
}


// Function to calculate R-squared
fn calculate_r_squared(predictions: &Array1<f64>,
targets: &Array1<f64>) -> f64 {
    let ss_res = (predictions - targets).map(|x|
x.powi(2)).sum();

    let ss_tot = (targets -
targets.mean().unwrap()).map(|x|
x.powi(2)).sum();

    1.0 - (ss_res / ss_tot)
}


fn main() {
    // Example: Regression predictions and true
values
    let predictions = array![260000.0, 310000.0,
400000.0, 490000.0, 540000.0];
    let targets     = array![250000.0, 320000.0,
410000.0, 480000.0, 550000.0];


    // Calculate MSE
    let mse = calculate_mse(&predictions,
&targets);
    println!("Mean Squared Error (MSE): {:.2}",
mse);


    // Calculate R-squared
```

```
    let r_squared =
calculate_r_squared(&predictions, &targets);

    println!("R-squared: {:.2}", r_squared);
}
```

By using these metrics, you can effectively evaluate the performance of your neural networks and make informed decisions about how to improve them.

9.7 Introduction to Popular Neural Network Architectures

While the basic feedforward neural network we discussed earlier provides a foundation, researchers have developed various specialized architectures tailored to specific types of data and tasks.

Let's take a look at a few prominent ones:

1. Convolutional Neural Networks (CNNs)

Convolutional Neural Networks (CNNs) have revolutionized computer vision and are the dominant architecture for tasks such as image recognition, object detection, and image segmentation.

Understanding Convolution

At the heart of CNNs is the operation of convolution. Instead of connecting every neuron in one layer to every neuron in the next layer (as in a fully connected layer), CNNs use small filters that slide over the input image.

Here's how convolution works:

- Filters (Kernels): A filter is a small matrix of weights. For example, a 3x3 filter.
- Feature Maps: The filter slides across the input image, performing element-wise multiplications with the

corresponding pixels and summing the results. This produces a new feature map, which represents the response of the filter at each location in the image.

- Shared Weights: A crucial aspect of CNNs is that the same filter is used across the entire image. This weight sharing significantly reduces the number of parameters the network needs to learn, making it more efficient and less prone to overfitting.

CNN Architecture

A typical CNN architecture consists of several layers:

- Convolutional Layers: These layers apply convolution operations with learnable filters to extract features from the input image. Multiple convolutional layers can be stacked to learn increasingly complex features.
- Pooling Layers: These layers reduce the spatial dimensions of the feature maps, making the network more robust to small shifts and distortions in the input. Common pooling operations include max pooling and average pooling.
- Fully Connected Layers: After several convolutional and pooling layers,[1] the high-level features are fed into one or more fully connected layers, which perform the final classification or regression.

Example: A Simple CNN Architecture for Image Classification

Input Image -> Convolutional Layer (32 filters, 3x3) -> Pooling Layer (Max Pooling, 2x2) -> Convolutional Layer (64 filters, 3x3) -> Pooling Layer (Max Pooling, 2x2) -> Fully Connected Layer (128 neurons) -> Output Layer (10 neurons, Softmax)

In this example:

- The input image is processed by two convolutional layers to extract features like edges, textures, and shapes.
- Pooling layers reduce the spatial dimensions after each convolutional layer.
- The fully connected layer combines the extracted features to make the final classification.
- The output layer has 10 neurons, one for each class (e.g., for classifying images into 10 different categories), and uses the softmax activation function to produce a probability distribution over the classes.

Why CNNs for Images?

CNNs excel at image processing because:

- Local receptive fields: Each neuron in a convolutional layer only sees a small local region of the input image, allowing the network to learn local patterns.
- Translation invariance: The shared weights of the filters make the network robust to small shifts in the input image.
- Hierarchical feature learning: Deeper layers learn increasingly complex and abstract features.

2. Recurrent Neural Networks (RNNs)

Recurrent Neural Networks (RNNs) are designed to process sequential data, such as:

- Text (sequences of words)
- Time series (sequences of measurements over time)
- Speech (sequences of audio signals)

The Recurrent Connection

The key feature of RNNs is the **recurrent connection**, which allows them to maintain a "memory" of past information.

In a traditional feedforward network, the output of a layer depends only on the current input. In an RNN, the output of a layer at a given time step also depends on the output of the same layer at the previous time step. This allows the RNN to process sequences of varying lengths and capture dependencies between elements in the sequence.

RNN Architecture

An RNN can be thought of as a loop that processes one element of the sequence at a time. The hidden state, which acts as the network's memory, is updated at each time step based on the current input and the previous hidden state.

Example: A Simple RNN for Text Processing

Imagine you want to build a neural network that predicts the next word in a sentence.

1. The input is a sequence of words, represented as numerical vectors (e.g., word embeddings).
2. The RNN processes the words one at a time.
3. At each time step, the RNN receives the input word and the hidden state from the previous time step.
4. The RNN updates its hidden state based on the current word and the previous hidden state.
5. The output of the RNN at each time step is a prediction of the next word.

Challenges with Simple RNNs

Simple RNNs can suffer from the vanishing gradient problem, making it difficult to train them to capture long-range dependencies in the data.

Long Short-Term Memory (LSTM) and Gated Recurrent Unit (GRU)

To address the vanishing gradient problem, more sophisticated RNN architectures have been developed, such as:

- Long Short-Term Memory (LSTM): Introduces a more complex memory cell with gates that control the flow of information.
- Gated Recurrent Unit (GRU): A simplified version of LSTM with fewer parameters.

LSTMs and GRUs can learn long-range dependencies more effectively than simple RNNs and have become the standard for many sequence modeling tasks.

3. Transformers

Transformers are a relatively new type of neural network architecture that has achieved state-of-the-art results in natural language processing (NLP) and is increasingly being used in other areas like computer vision.

Attention Mechanism

The key innovation of transformers is the attention mechanism. Unlike RNNs, which process sequences sequentially, transformers process all elements of the sequence in parallel. The attention mechanism allows the model to weigh the importance of different parts of the input sequence when processing a^2 particular element.

How Attention Works

Instead of relying on recurrent connections to maintain a hidden state, transformers use attention to directly access relevant information from the entire input sequence. For example, when processing the word "it" in the sentence "The dog chased the cat, and it ran away," the attention mechanism allows the model to attend to the word "cat" to determine what "it" refers to.

Transformer Architecture

A typical transformer architecture consists of:

- Self-Attention Layers: These layers allow the model to attend to different parts of the input sequence to capture relationships between them.
- Feedforward Neural Networks: These layers process the attended information.
- Encoder and Decoder: Transformers often have an encoder-decoder structure. The encoder processes the input sequence into a representation, and the decoder generates the output sequence based on that representation.

Advantages of Transformers

- Parallelism: Transformers can process sequences in parallel, making them much faster to train than RNNs, especially on long sequences.
- Long-range dependencies: Attention allows transformers to capture dependencies between distant elements in a sequence more effectively than RNNs.
- State-of-the-art performance: Transformers have achieved remarkable results in various NLP tasks, such as machine translation, text summarization, and question answering.

Neural networks come in many different architectures, each with its own strengths and weaknesses. CNNs excel at image processing, RNNs are well-suited for sequential data, and transformers have revolutionized natural language processing. The choice of architecture depends heavily on the specific task and the type of data you're working with.

Chapter 10: Working with Deep Learning Frameworks (Rust Bindings)

While Rust is a powerful language for implementing machine learning algorithms, the deep learning landscape is currently dominated by frameworks like TensorFlow and PyTorch, which are primarily written in Python. This chapter explores how you can leverage these existing frameworks from Rust, combining their capabilities with Rust's performance and safety.

10.1 Overview of Popular Deep Learning Frameworks (TensorFlow, PyTorch)

The field of deep learning has been significantly shaped by the development of powerful and flexible software frameworks. These frameworks provide the tools and abstractions necessary to build, train, and deploy complex neural networks efficiently. While Rust is emerging as a language for high-performance machine learning, the deep learning "heavy lifting" is still largely done with frameworks built in other languages, most notably Python.

Let's take a closer look at two of the most popular and influential deep learning frameworks: TensorFlow and PyTorch.

TensorFlow

TensorFlow is an open-source deep learning framework originally developed by Google. It's a comprehensive platform that provides a wide range of tools and libraries for various machine learning tasks.

Key Features of TensorFlow

- Computational Graph: TensorFlow represents the computations involved in a neural network as a directed graph.
  - Each node in the graph represents an operation, such as matrix multiplication, addition, or applying an activation function.
  - The edges in the graph represent the data (tensors) that flow between these operations.
  - This graph-based representation allows TensorFlow to optimize the computations for efficient execution on various hardware platforms.
- Eager Execution: While TensorFlow's original design focused on defining the computation graph statically before execution, it also offers eager execution.
  - Eager execution provides a more imperative, Python-like programming style where operations are executed immediately as they are encountered in the code.
  - This can make development and debugging more intuitive, especially for beginners.
- High-Level APIs: TensorFlow provides high-level APIs, such as Keras, which simplify the process of building and training neural networks.
  - Keras offers a user-friendly[1] interface for defining network architectures, compiling models, and training them with minimal code.
- Production Deployment: TensorFlow has strong capabilities for deploying models in production environments.
  - TensorFlow Serving is a system for deploying trained models to servers, making them accessible via APIs.
  - TensorFlow Lite is a lightweight version of TensorFlow for deploying models on mobile and embedded devices.

- Large Community and Ecosystem: TensorFlow has a large and active community, which means you can find extensive documentation, tutorials, and pre-trained models.
  - This vast ecosystem makes it easier to get started with TensorFlow and find solutions to common problems.

Example: Building a Simple Neural Network with TensorFlow Keras (Python)

Here's a Python example using TensorFlow's Keras API to build a simple neural network for a classification task:

Python

```python
import tensorflow as tf

from tensorflow import keras

from tensorflow.keras import layers


# 1. Define the model architecture.
model = keras.Sequential([
    layers.Dense(64, activation='relu',
input_shape=(784,)),  # Input layer and first
hidden layer
    layers.Dense(64, activation='relu'),
# Second hidden layer
    layers.Dense(10, activation='softmax')
# Output layer (10 classes, softmax for
probability distribution)
])
```

```python
# 2. Compile the model.
model.compile(optimizer='adam',
              loss='categorical_crossentropy', #
Common loss for multi-class classification
              metrics=['accuracy'])         #
Track accuracy during training


# 3. Load the data (e.g., MNIST handwritten
digits).
(x_train, y_train), (x_test, y_test) =
keras.datasets.mnist.load_data()
x_train = x_train.reshape(60000,
784).astype('float32') / 255.0 # Flatten and
normalize
x_test = x_test.reshape(10000,
784).astype('float32') / 255.0
y_train = keras.utils.to_categorical(y_train,
num_classes=10) # One-hot encode the labels
y_test = keras.utils.to_categorical(y_test,
num_classes=10)


# 4. Train the model.
model.fit(x_train, y_train, epochs=5,
batch_size=32)


# 5. Evaluate the model.
loss, accuracy = model.evaluate(x_test, y_test)
print('Test loss:', loss)
print('Test accuracy:', accuracy)
```

This example demonstrates how Keras simplifies the process of building, compiling, training, and evaluating a neural network in TensorFlow.

PyTorch

PyTorch is another popular open-source deep learning framework, primarily developed by Facebook. It has gained significant traction, particularly in the research community, due to its flexibility and intuitive design.

Key Features of PyTorch

- Dynamic Computation Graph: PyTorch uses a dynamic computation graph, also known as define-by-run.
    - This means that the computation graph is constructed as the code executes, allowing for greater flexibility and easier debugging.
    - You can change the graph structure on the fly, which is very useful for research and experimentation.
- Tensor Computation with GPU Acceleration: PyTorch provides efficient tensor operations, similar to NumPy, with seamless GPU acceleration.
    - Tensors are the fundamental data structure in PyTorch, representing multi-dimensional arrays.
- Pythonic Interface: PyTorch has a Pythonic design, making it easy to learn and use for those familiar with the Python data science ecosystem.
- Active Research Community: PyTorch is favored by many researchers, leading to a rich ecosystem of pre-trained models, libraries, and cutting-edge research implementations.

Example: Building a Simple Neural Network with PyTorch (Python)

Here's a Python example using PyTorch to build a similar neural network as the TensorFlow example:

Python

```python
import torch
import torch.nn as nn
import torch.nn.functional as F
import torch.optim as optim
from torchvision import datasets, transforms


# 1. Define the model architecture as a class.
class Net(nn.Module):
    def __init__(self):
        super(Net, self).__init__()
        self.fc1 = nn.Linear(784, 64)  # Input layer to first hidden layer
        self.fc2 = nn.Linear(64, 64)   # First hidden layer to second hidden layer
        self.fc3 = nn.Linear(64, 10)   # Second hidden layer to output layer


    def forward(self, x):
        x = F.relu(self.fc1(x))        # Apply ReLU activation
        x = F.relu(self.fc2(x))        # Apply ReLU activation
```

```python
        x = F.softmax(self.fc3(x), dim=1) # Apply
Softmax activation

        return x


# 2. Load the data (e.g., MNIST handwritten
digits).
train_loader = torch.utils.data.DataLoader(
    datasets.MNIST('../data', train=True,
download=True,
                    transform=transforms.Compose([
                        transforms.ToTensor(),

transforms.Normalize((0.1307,), (0.3081,))
                    ])),
    batch_size=32, shuffle=True)
test_loader = torch.utils.data.DataLoader(
    datasets.MNIST('../data', train=False,
transform=transforms.Compose([
                        transforms.ToTensor(),

transforms.Normalize((0.1307,), (0.3081,))
                    ])),
    batch_size=32, shuffle=True)


# 3. Instantiate the model and define an
optimizer.
model = Net()
optimizer = optim.Adam(model.parameters())
```

```
# 4. Train the model.
for epoch in range(5):
    for batch_idx, (data, target) in
enumerate(train_loader):
        optimizer.zero_grad()           # Clear
gradients
        output = model(data)            # Forward
pass
        loss = F.nll_loss(output, target) #
Calculate loss (negative log likelihood loss for
classification)
        loss.backward()                 # Backward
pass (calculate gradients)
        optimizer.step()                # Update
parameters
        if batch_idx % 100 == 0:
            print('Epoch: {} [{}/{} ({:.0f}%)]
    Loss: {:.6f}'.format(
                epoch, batch_idx * len(data),
len(train_loader.dataset),
                100. * batch_idx /
len(train_loader), loss.item()))


# 5. Evaluate the model.
correct = 0
total = 0
with torch.no_grad():
    for data, target in test_loader:
```

```
output = model(data)

_, predicted = torch.max(output.data, 1)

total += target.size(0)

correct += (predicted ==
target).sum().item()


print('Accuracy of the network on the 10000 test
images: %d %%' % (

    100 * correct / total))
```

In conclusion, both TensorFlow and PyTorch have significantly contributed to the advancement of deep learning, empowering researchers and developers to build and deploy sophisticated neural networks. TensorFlow excels in production deployment and large-scale applications, while PyTorch is often favored in research and experimentation due to its flexibility and intuitive nature.

10.2 Exploring Existing Rust Bindings for Deep Learning Frameworks

As you might know, the deep learning landscape is largely dominated by frameworks like TensorFlow and PyTorch. While Rust offers compelling advantages for machine learning, these frameworks are primarily built with other languages, particularly Python. To leverage the power of these frameworks within Rust, one approach is to use Rust bindings.

Rust bindings essentially act as a bridge, allowing Rust code to interact with libraries written in other languages, such as the C++ libraries that underpin TensorFlow and PyTorch.

Challenges and Considerations

Creating and maintaining robust bindings to complex frameworks like TensorFlow and PyTorch is a significant undertaking. These frameworks are constantly evolving, which means that bindings need to be updated frequently to keep pace. Additionally, deep learning frameworks often have intricate APIs with a large number of functions and data structures, making it challenging to create a complete and accurate Rust interface.

Therefore, the availability and maturity of Rust bindings can vary. It's important to be aware of the current state of these bindings and their limitations before relying on them for your projects.

TensorFlow Bindings

TensorFlow has an official set of Rust bindings. However, the level of support and the API they expose can change. It's crucial to refer to the official TensorFlow documentation and the TensorFlow Rust repository on GitHub for the most up-to-date information.

Historically, the TensorFlow Rust bindings have presented some challenges in terms of completeness and ease of use compared to the Python API. The TensorFlow team has been working to improve this, but the situation is dynamic.

Key things to check for TensorFlow Rust bindings:

- Official Documentation: Always refer to the official TensorFlow documentation for Rust.
- GitHub Repository: Check the TensorFlow GitHub repository for the latest status, examples, and any potential issues.
- Community Support: See how active the community is and whether there are many users successfully using the bindings in practice.

PyTorch Bindings (tch-rs)

PyTorch has a more actively maintained and user-friendly set of Rust bindings, primarily provided by the tch-rs crate. tch-rs aims to provide a reasonably comprehensive interface to the PyTorch C++ API, allowing you to perform various deep learning tasks from Rust.

Using tch-rs

To use tch-rs, you need to add it as a dependency in your Cargo.toml file:

Ini, TOML

[dependencies]

tch = "0.13" # **Check crates.io for the latest version**

Here's a basic example of how to use tch-rs to load a pre-trained model and perform inference:

Rust

```rust
use tch::{Device, Kind, Tensor, CModule}; // Import necessary modules from tch


fn main() -> Result<(), tch::TchError> {

    // 1. Set the device (CPU or GPU).

    let device = Device::cuda_if_available(); // Use GPU if available, otherwise use CPU


    // 2. Load a pre-trained model (e.g., a serialized PyTorch model).
```

```rust
    let model =
CModule::load("path/to/your/model.pt")?.to(device
); // Ensure the model is on the correct device


    // 3. Create an input tensor.

    let input_data = Tensor::from_slice(&[1.0,
2.0, 3.0, 4.0], &[1, 4], Kind::Float).to(device);
// Example input tensor


    // 4. Perform inference (forward pass) by
calling the model.

    let output_tensor =
model.forward(&[input_data])?; // Pass the input
tensor as a slice


    // 5. Print the output tensor.

    println!("Output tensor: {:?}",
output_tensor);


    Ok(())

}
```

Let's break down this example:

Import necessary modules:

- We import Device, Kind, and Tensor from tch to work with tensors and devices.
- We import CModule to load a pre-trained PyTorch model.

Set the device:

- We use Device::cuda_if_available() to automatically use a CUDA-enabled GPU if one is available; otherwise, it defaults to the CPU. This ensures that the code runs on the appropriate hardware.

Load a pre-trained model:

- We use CModule::load() to load a pre-trained PyTorch model from a file. The file path "path/to/your/model.pt" should be replaced with the actual path to your model file. The model is then moved to the selected device (CPU or GPU) using .to(device).

Create an input tensor:

- We create a sample input tensor using Tensor::from_slice(). This function creates a tensor from a slice of data, and we specify the shape of the tensor as [1, 4] (1 row, 4 columns) and the data type as Kind::Float (32-bit floating-point numbers). The tensor is also moved to the selected device.

Perform inference:

- We call the model.forward() method, passing the input tensor as a slice, to perform the forward pass and obtain the model's output.

Print the output:

- We print the output tensor using println!().

Key Considerations for Using Bindings

When working with Rust bindings to deep learning frameworks, keep these points in mind:

- API Coverage: The bindings might not cover the entire API of the underlying framework. You might need to use the framework's core functionalities, and you might not have access to all the high-level niceties.
- Version Compatibility: Ensure that the versions of the bindings and the deep learning framework are compatible. Mismatches can lead to errors or unexpected behavior.
- Error Handling: Pay close attention to error handling. Deep learning frameworks often use exceptions, which need to be translated into Rust's Result type for safe and idiomatic error handling.
- Memory Management: Be mindful of memory management, especially when passing data between Rust and the framework's C++ libraries. You might need to use smart pointers or other techniques to ensure memory safety.
- Performance: While Rust bindings can offer good performance, there might still be some overhead associated with the language boundary.

Using Rust bindings to deep learning frameworks allows you to leverage the power of these frameworks while benefiting from Rust's safety and performance. While the landscape of Rust bindings is still evolving, crates like tch-rs provide a promising way to integrate PyTorch into your Rust projects. As the Rust ML ecosystem matures, we can expect even better and more comprehensive solutions for working with deep learning frameworks.

10.3 Using Foreign Function Interface (FFI) for Interoperability

Rust's Foreign Function Interface (FFI) is a powerful mechanism that allows Rust code to interact with code written in other programming languages, most commonly C and C++. This capability is crucial when working with deep learning frameworks, as many of them have core libraries written in these languages.

Why Use FFI?

You might wonder why we need FFI in the first place.

Why not just write everything in Rust? Here are a few key reasons:

- Existing Libraries: Many powerful and well-established libraries are written in C or C++. Deep learning frameworks like TensorFlow and PyTorch have highly optimized C++ backends for performing the heavy computations. It would be a massive undertaking to rewrite these from scratch in Rust. FFI allows us to leverage these existing libraries without reinventing the wheel.
- Performance: C and C++ are often used for performance-critical code, and FFI allows Rust to tap into that performance. This is especially important in deep learning, where speed is paramount.

- Hardware Interaction: Some hardware-specific functionalities or drivers might only be available through C APIs. FFI enables Rust to interact with this hardware.

How FFI Works

FFI essentially creates a bridge between Rust code and code from another language.

It involves the following key aspects:

1. Declaring Foreign Functions: In your Rust code, you declare the signatures of the functions that you want to call from the external library (e.g., a C++ library). You do this using the extern keyword. This tells the Rust compiler that these functions are defined outside of Rust.
2. Data Type Conversion: Rust and other languages often represent data differently. You need to convert data between Rust types and the types expected by the foreign functions. This can involve things like:
   - Converting Rust's String to a C-style string (*const c_char).
   - Converting Rust's vectors and slices to raw pointers and lengths.
   - Defining Rust structs that mirror the layout of C++ classes.
3. Calling Foreign Functions: Once the foreign functions are declared and the data is converted, you can call those functions from your Rust code as if they were regular Rust functions.
4. Memory Management: This is a critical aspect of FFI. You need to be very careful about memory allocation and deallocation to prevent memory leaks or other memory-related errors. Rust's ownership system doesn't directly apply to memory managed by other languages, so you must manage it manually in these cases.

5. Safety: FFI is inherently unsafe because the Rust compiler cannot guarantee the memory safety of the code you're calling. You have to ensure that the foreign functions are called correctly and that the data being passed is valid.

Example: Calling a C Function from Rust

Let's start with a simple example to illustrate the basic principles of FFI.

Suppose you have a C function that adds two integers:

C

```c
// sum.c

#include <stdio.h>


int sum(int a, int b) {

  printf("C: a = %d, b = %d\n", a, b);

  return a + b;

}
```

Here's how you can call this function from Rust:

Rust

```rust
use std::os::raw::c_int; // Import the C integer
type.
```

```rust
// 1. Declare the foreign function signature
using `extern`.

extern "C" {

    fn sum(a: c_int, b: c_int) -> c_int;

}


fn main() {

    // 2. Call the foreign function.

    let a = 5;

    let b = 10;

    let result = unsafe { sum(a, b) }; // FFI
calls are inherently unsafe.


    println!("Rust: sum({}, {}) = {}", a, b,
result);

}
```

In this example:

1. We import the c_int type from Rust's std::os::raw module. This type represents a C integer, ensuring that we use the correct data type when calling the C function.
2. We declare the sum function using the extern "C" block.
   - extern "C" tells the Rust compiler that this function uses the C calling convention. This is important because different programming languages might use

different ways of passing arguments and returning values.

- ○ Inside the extern block, we provide the function signature, including the types of the arguments and the return type, exactly as they are defined in the C code.
3. We call the sum function from Rust within an unsafe block.
   - ○ FFI calls are considered unsafe because the Rust compiler cannot guarantee the safety of the code being called. The C function could potentially do anything, including accessing invalid memory or causing a crash. It's the programmer's responsibility to ensure that the call is safe.

Working with Pointers

When dealing with more complex data structures, such as strings or arrays, you'll often need to use pointers when working with FFI.

Example: Passing a String from Rust to C

Here's an example of passing a Rust string to a C function:

Rust

```rust
use std::ffi::CString;

use std::os::raw::c_char;

use std::ptr;



// C function that takes a C-style string

extern "C" {
```

```rust
    fn print_string(s: *const c_char);

}


fn main() {

    // 1. Create a Rust String.

    let rust_string = "Hello from
Rust!".to_string();


    // 2. Convert the Rust String to a C-style
string using CString.

    let c_string =
CString::new(rust_string).unwrap(); // Ensure no
null bytes in the string


    // 3. Get a raw pointer to the C-style
string.

    let c_string_ptr = c_string.as_ptr();


    // 4. Call the C function, passing the
pointer.

    unsafe {

        print_string(c_string_ptr);

    }
```

}

In this example:

1. We create a Rust String.
2. We convert the Rust String to a C-style string using CString::new().
   - o A C-style string is a null-terminated byte string, which is the format that C functions expect.
   - o CString ensures that the string is null-terminated and doesn't contain any internal null bytes, which would cause problems for C functions.
   - o The unwrap() call is used to handle potential errors during the conversion (e.g., if the Rust string contains a null byte).
3. We get a raw pointer to the C-style string using c_string.as_ptr().
4. We call the C function print_string, passing the raw pointer.
   - o It's the caller's responsibility to ensure that the pointer is valid for the duration of the C function call.

Memory Management Across the FFI Boundary

Memory management is crucial when working with FFI. You need to be very careful about who is responsible for allocating and deallocating memory.

- Rust Allocation, Rust Deallocation: If Rust allocates the memory (e.g., creating a String or a Vec), Rust is responsible for deallocating it. You don't need to do anything special.
- C/C++ Allocation, C/C++ Deallocation: If the C/C++ code allocates the memory, the C/C++ code is responsible for deallocating it. You must ensure that the C/C++ code provides a way to free the memory, and you must call that function from Rust when you're done with the data.

- C/C++ Allocation, Rust Deallocation: This is generally unsafe and should be avoided if possible. If you must do this, you need to be extremely careful to ensure that the memory is deallocated correctly and that you're using the correct deallocation function (e.g., free() for memory allocated with malloc()).

Example: Passing a Vector from Rust to C++

(This is a more complex example and assumes you have a C++ library with a function that takes a pointer and a length)

Rust

```rust
use std::os::raw::{c_float, c_int, c_void};


// 1. Declare the foreign function.

extern "C" {

    fn process_data(data: *const c_float, length: c_int, output: *mut c_void);

}


fn main() {

    // 2. Create a Rust Vec of f32 values.

    let rust_data: Vec<f32> = vec![1.0, 2.0, 3.0, 4.0, 5.0];

    let length = rust_data.len() as c_int;
```

```rust
    // 3. Convert the Rust Vec to a raw pointer.

    let data_ptr = rust_data.as_ptr() as *const
c_float;


    // 4. Create a buffer for the output from
C++

    let mut output_buffer: Vec<f32> = vec![0.0;
10];  // Example output buffer

    let output_ptr = output_buffer.as_mut_ptr()
as *mut c_void;


    // 5. Call the C++ function.

    unsafe {

        process_data(data_ptr, length,
output_ptr);

    }

    // 6. Convert the output data

    println!("Output data from C++: {:?}",
output_buffer);

}
```

Safety Considerations

FFI is inherently unsafe because you're interacting with code that
the Rust compiler cannot verify for memory safety.

You must take extra precautions to prevent undefined behavior:

- Valid Pointers: Ensure that any pointers you pass to foreign functions are valid and point to memory that is properly allocated.
- Data Ownership: Be very clear about who owns the memory. If C/C++ allocates memory, make sure C/C++ is responsible for deallocating it.
- Calling Conventions: Use the correct calling convention (usually "C") when declaring foreign functions.
- Exception Handling: Foreign functions might use exceptions (in C++) to signal errors. You need to handle these appropriately, typically by checking the return value of the function.

10.4 Leveraging Pre-trained Models in Rust

One of the great advantages of deep learning is the availability of pre-trained models. These models have been trained by experts on massive datasets and can perform well on a variety of tasks without requiring you to train them from scratch. This can save you a tremendous amount of time and computational resources.

What are Pre-trained Models?

A pre-trained model is a neural network that has already been trained on a large dataset for a specific task. The learned weights and biases of the network are saved and can be reused for other related tasks.

For example:

- A model trained on a massive dataset of images (like ImageNet) can be used as a starting point for tasks like image classification, object detection, and image segmentation.

- A model trained on a large corpus of text can be used for tasks like text classification, sentiment analysis, and machine translation.

Why Use Pre-trained Models?

There are several compelling reasons to leverage pre-trained models:

- Reduced Training Time: Training a deep neural network from scratch can take days or even weeks, requiring significant computational resources and energy. Pre-trained models allow you to skip this lengthy process.
- Improved Performance: Pre-trained models have often been trained on much larger datasets than you might have access to, enabling them to learn more generalizable features and achieve better performance.
- Feature Extraction: You can use a pre-trained model as a feature extractor. This involves feeding your data through the pre-trained network and taking the activations of an intermediate layer as the features for your task.
- Fine-tuning: You can fine-tune a pre-trained model on your specific dataset. This involves training the model further on your data, updating its weights to adapt it to your particular task. Fine-tuning is often much faster and more effective than training a model from scratch.

How to Use Pre-trained Models in Rust

The process of using pre-trained models in Rust typically involves these steps:

1. Choose a Framework: Select a deep learning framework that has pre-trained models available for your task. TensorFlow and PyTorch are the most common choices.

2. Obtain the Pre-trained Model: Download the pre-trained model from a model zoo or repository. These models are usually stored in a specific file format (e.g., a .pb file for TensorFlow, a .pt file for PyTorch).
3. Load the Model: Load the pre-trained model into your Rust program using the appropriate bindings or FFI.
4. Preprocess Input Data: Prepare your input data to match the format expected by the pre-trained model. This might involve resizing images, normalizing values, or tokenizing text.
5. Perform Inference: Feed the preprocessed input data to the model to obtain predictions.
6. Post-process Output: Process the model's output into a usable format for your application.

Example: Using a Pre-trained Model with PyTorch and Rust (tch-rs)

Let's walk through an example of using a pre-trained image classification model (ResNet) with PyTorch and Rust using the tch-rs crate.

Rust

```rust
use tch::{Device, Kind, Tensor, CModule};

use tch::vision::resnet;

use tch::nn::Module;


fn main() -> Result<(), tch::TchError> {

    // 1. Set the device (CPU or GPU).

    let device = Device::cuda_if_available();
```

```rust
// 2. Load a pre-trained ResNet-18 model from
Torchvision.

let mut model =
resnet::resnet18(true).to(device); // true: load
pre-trained weights



// 3. Prepare an input image (replace with
your actual image loading).

// For this example, we'll create a dummy
tensor.  In a real application, you'd

// load an image from a file, resize it,
normalize it, and convert it to a tensor.

let input_tensor =
Tensor::from_slice(&[0.0_f32; 3 * 224 * 224],
&[1, 3, 224, 224], Kind::Float).to(device); //
[1, 3, 224, 224] shape: 1 image, 3 channels,
224x224 size



// 4. Perform inference (forward pass).

let output_tensor =
model.forward(&[input_tensor])?; //  Pass the
input tensor as a slice



// 5. Post-process the output (e.g., get the
predicted class).
```

```rust
    let probabilities = output_tensor.softmax(1);
// Apply softmax to get probabilities along the
channel dimension (1).

    let (_max_probability, predicted_class) =
probabilities.max1(1, false); // Get the class
with the highest probability

    let predicted_class_id =
predicted_class.int64_value(&[0]); // Extract the
class ID as an integer.



    println!("Predicted class: {}",
predicted_class_id);



    Ok(())

}
```

In this example:

1. We set the device to either a CUDA-enabled GPU or the CPU.
2. We load a pre-trained ResNet-18 model using resnet::resnet18(true). The true argument tells the function to download and load the pre-trained weights from Torchvision. We move the model to the selected device.
3. We create a dummy input tensor. Important: In a real application, you would replace this with code that loads an image from a file, preprocesses it to match the input requirements of the ResNet model (e.g., resizing to 224x224 pixels, normalizing the pixel values), and converts it into a PyTorch tensor.

4. We perform inference by calling the model's forward method with the input tensor.
5. We post-process the output tensor:
    - We apply the softmax function to the output to get a probability distribution over the classes.
    - We use maxi to get the class with the highest probability.
    - We extract the predicted class ID as an integer.

This example shows how to load a pre-trained model and use it for inference in Rust using tch-rs. You can adapt this approach to use other pre-trained models and perform different tasks.

Fine-tuning Pre-trained Models

In many cases, you'll want to adapt a pre-trained model to your specific task and dataset. This is called **fine-tuning**. Instead of using the model as a fixed feature extractor, you train it further on your own data, updating its weights to improve its performance on your particular problem.

Fine-tuning typically involves these steps:
1. Load the pre-trained model: Load the model as described above.
2. Freeze some layers: Often, you'll freeze the weights of the earlier layers of the network, which learn general features (like edges and textures in images), and only train the later layers, which learn task-specific features.
3. Modify the output layer: You'll usually need to modify the output layer to match the number of classes or the output format required for your task.
4. Train on your data: Train the model on your dataset using an optimization algorithm like Adam, updating the weights of the trainable layers.

Fine-tuning can significantly improve performance with less training data and computational resources compared to training a model from scratch.

10.5 Building Custom Layers or Operations in Rust and Integrating with Frameworks

In some advanced scenarios, you might need to go beyond the pre-defined layers and operations provided by deep learning frameworks.

You might want to:

- Implement a novel neural network layer with a specific computation.
- Optimize a particular operation for your hardware or application.
- Integrate custom algorithms or logic into your deep learning model.

In such cases, you can leverage Rust's performance and control to build custom layers or operations and then integrate them into frameworks like TensorFlow or PyTorch. This allows you to combine the flexibility and ecosystem of these frameworks with the speed and efficiency of Rust.

The Challenge of Integration

The main challenge lies in bridging the gap between Rust and the deep learning framework, which are typically written in Python and have core components in C++. This requires careful handling of data transfer, memory management, and ensuring safety across the language boundary.

General Approach

The general approach involves these steps:

1. Implement the Custom Layer/Operation in Rust: You write the core logic of your custom layer or operation in Rust, often using crates like ndarray for efficient numerical computation.
2. Create a C Interface: You define a C-compatible interface for your Rust code. This involves declaring the functions that you want to call from the deep learning framework using the extern "C" keyword and using C-compatible data types.
3. Build a Shared Library: You compile your Rust code into a shared library (e.g., a .so file on Linux, a .dll file on Windows, or a .dylib file on macOS).
4. Load the Shared Library in the Framework: You load the shared library into your deep learning framework (usually in Python) using a library like ctypes (for Python) to access the functions you defined.
5. Wrap the Operation as a Layer: You create a custom layer or operation in the deep learning framework, using the framework's API, and within that layer, you call the foreign function to execute your Rust code.

Example: Implementing a Custom Activation Function in Rust and Integrating with PyTorch

Let's illustrate this process with a simplified example: implementing a custom activation function in Rust and integrating it into PyTorch.

1. Implement the Custom Activation Function in Rust

First, we define our custom activation function in Rust. For this example, let's create a simple activation function that squares the input:

Rust

```rust
use std::os::raw::c_float;



// 1. Define the custom activation function in
Rust with a C-compatible signature.

#[no_mangle] // Disable name mangling to make the
function name predictable in the shared library.

pub extern "C" fn square_activation(x: c_float)
-> c_float {

    x * x

}
```

In this code:

- #[no_mangle] attribute: This is crucial for FFI. It tells the Rust compiler not to mangle the name of the function. Name mangling is a process that the compiler uses to generate unique names for symbols, but it makes it difficult to link to the function from other languages. By disabling name mangling, we ensure that the function has the simple name "square_activation" in the compiled shared library.
- pub extern "C": This declares the function as a foreign function that can be called from C. "C" specifies the calling convention, which is the standard way that C functions are called.
- We use c_float from std::os::raw to ensure that the data type is compatible with C's float.
- The function takes a single c_float as input and returns a c_float, performing the squaring operation.

2. Build a Shared Library

Next, we need to compile this Rust code into a shared library. Add this to your Cargo.toml:

Ini, TOML

```toml
[lib]

crate-type = ["cdylib"] #  "cdylib" creates a
C-compatible shared library.
```

Then, build the project in release mode:

Bash

cargo build --release

This will create a shared library file (e.g., libmy_custom_layer.so on Linux, my_custom_layer.dll on Windows, or libmy_custom_layer.dylib on macOS) in the target/release directory.

3. Create a Python Wrapper

Now, we create a Python script to load the shared library and define a custom PyTorch function that calls our Rust function using ctypes:

Python

```python
import torch

import torch.nn as nn

import ctypes

from ctypes import c_float, CDLL
```

```python
# 1. Load the shared library.

#    The path to the library will depend on your
operating system and where you compiled it.

try:

    my_lib =
CDLL("target/release/libmy_custom_layer.so")  #
Linux

except:

    try:

        my_lib =
CDLL("target/release/my_custom_layer.dll") #
Windows

    except:

        my_lib =
CDLL("target/release/libmy_custom_layer.dylib") #
macOS



# 2. Define the function signature using ctypes.

my_lib.square_activation.restype = c_float  #
Specify the return type

my_lib.square_activation.argtypes = [c_float] #
Specify the argument types
```

```python
# 3. Create a custom PyTorch function that calls
the Rust function.

class SquareActivation(torch.autograd.Function):

    @staticmethod

    def forward(ctx, input_tensor):

        # Convert the input tensor to a float

        x = input_tensor.item()

        # Call the Rust function using ctypes.

        output =
my_lib.square_activation(c_float(x))

        # Convert the result back to a PyTorch
tensor.

        output_tensor = torch.tensor(output,
dtype=input_tensor.dtype,
device=input_tensor.device)

        ctx.save_for_backward(input_tensor) #
Save input for gradient calculation in backward

        return output_tensor


    @staticmethod

    def backward(ctx, grad_output):

        # Calculate the gradient of the square
function (2*x) in python.
```

```python
        input_tensor, = ctx.saved_tensors

        grad_input = 2.0 * input_tensor * grad_output

        return grad_input


square_activation_layer = SquareActivation.apply


# 4. Create a PyTorch module that uses the custom
activation function.


class MyModule(nn.Module):

    def __init__(self):

        super(MyModule, self).__init__()

        self.linear = nn.Linear(1, 1) # A linear layer


    def forward(self, x):

        x = self.linear(x)

        x = square_activation_layer(x) # Use our custom activation function

        return x
```

```python
# 5. Use the custom layer in a PyTorch model.

if __name__ == "__main__":

    import torch

    # Create a dummy input tensor

    input_tensor = torch.randn(1, 1)

    # Instantiate the module

    model = MyModule()

    # Perform a forward pass

    output_tensor = model(input_tensor)

    # Print the output

    print("Output tensor: ", output_tensor)

    #Print the gradient.

    output_tensor.backward()

    print("Gradient: ", input_tensor.grad)
```

In this example, we:
1. Load the shared library using ctypes.CDLL.
2. Define the function signature of the square_activation function using ctypes.
3. Create a custom PyTorch function, SquareActivation, by subclassing torch.autograd.Function.
   - In the forward method, we call the Rust function using ctypes, convert the input tensor to a float, pass it to the Rust function, and convert the result back to a PyTorch tensor.

- ○ We also save the input tensor using ctx.save_for_backward so that we can use it in the backward method to calculate the gradient.
- ○ The backward method calculates the gradient of the square function (2*x) and multiplies it by the gradient of the output. This is the crucial part that allows the custom function to be used in backpropagation.
4. Create a PyTorch module, MyModule, that uses our custom activation function.
5. In main:
   - ○ We create a dummy input tensor.
   - ○ Instantiate the module
   - ○ Perform a forward pass
   - ○ Print the output and the gradient.

This example demonstrates how to define a custom operation in Rust and integrate it into PyTorch using FFI. This allows you to leverage Rust's performance for specific parts of your neural network while using PyTorch for the overall architecture and training process.

Chapter 11: Deploying ML Models Built with Rust

You've built and trained a fantastic machine learning model in Rust. Now comes the crucial step: getting that model out into the real world so people or other systems can actually use it. This chapter will guide you through various deployment strategies for your Rust-powered ML models.

11.1 Model Serialization and Deserialization in Rust

When you train a machine learning model, you're essentially finding the optimal set of parameters (weights, biases, and other internal values) that define how the model makes predictions. To use this trained model later, you need a way to store these parameters and reload them when needed.

This process involves two key steps:

- Serialization: Converting the model's state (its parameters) into a format that can be easily stored in a file, database, or transmitted over a network. You can think of this as taking a snapshot of your model's brain and saving it in a file.
- Deserialization: The reverse process of taking the stored representation of the model's state and reconstructing the model in memory so you can use it to make predictions. This is like loading the snapshot of the brain back into a new instance of your model.

Why is Serialization/Deserialization Important?

Consider these scenarios:

- Saving a trained model: You've spent hours training a complex neural network. You want to save your progress so you can use the trained model later without having to retrain it every time you run your program.

- Loading a pre-trained model: You want to use a model that someone else has already trained (e.g., a pre-trained image recognition model). You need to load the model's parameters from a file.
- Deploying a model: You want to deploy your model as part of a web service or application. You need to transfer the model's parameters to the server or application where it will be used.

In all these cases, serialization and deserialization are essential for persisting and transferring your model's state.

Serde: Rust's Powerhouse for Serialization

Rust provides a fantastic crate called serde that makes serialization and deserialization incredibly easy and efficient. Serde is a generic serialization framework that supports many different data formats.

Key Features of Serde

- Derive Macros: Serde uses derive macros (#[derive(Serialize, Deserialize)]) to automatically generate the code for serializing and deserializing your data structures. This greatly simplifies the process and reduces boilerplate code.
- Data Format Agnostic: Serde itself doesn't dictate the format of the serialized data. You choose a separate Serde format crate (like serde_json or serde_bincode) to handle the actual serialization and deserialization. This design allows you to easily switch between different formats without changing your core data structures.
- Performance: Serde is designed to be efficient, providing fast serialization and deserialization.
- Flexibility: Serde is highly configurable and customizable, allowing you to handle complex serialization scenarios.

- Safety: Serde works within Rust's safety guarantees, minimizing the risk of memory corruption or other errors.

Serialization with Serde

To use Serde, you first need to add it as a dependency in your Cargo.toml file:

Ini, TOML

```
[package]

# ... other package information ...



[dependencies]

serde = { version = "1.0", features = ["derive"]
}

serde_json = "1.0" # Or serde_bincode,
serde_cbor, etc.
```

The features = ["derive"] part is crucial. It tells Serde that you want to use its derive macros. You'll also need to include a crate for the specific data format you want to use (e.g., serde_json for JSON, serde_bincode for the Bincode format).

Now, let's say you have a Rust struct that represents the parameters of a linear regression model:

Rust

```
use serde::{Serialize, Deserialize};
```

```
// 1. Define a struct to hold your model's
parameters.

#[derive(Serialize, Deserialize, Debug)] //
Derive the Serialize and Deserialize traits.

struct LinearRegressionModel {

    weights: Vec<f64>,

    bias: f64,

}
```

The #[derive(Serialize, Deserialize, Debug)] annotation is the key to making this struct serializable and deserializable with Serde.

- Serialize: This trait tells Serde how to convert an instance of LinearRegressionModel into a serialized representation (e.g., a JSON string or a sequence of bytes).
- Deserialize: This trait tells Serde how to convert a serialized representation back into an instance of LinearRegressionModel.
- Debug: This trait enables pretty-printing of struct instances, useful for debugging.

Here's how you can serialize an instance of this struct to a JSON string:

```
Rust

use serde::{Serialize, Deserialize};

use serde_json::Result; // Use serde_json's
Result type.



#[derive(Serialize, Deserialize, Debug)]
```

```rust
struct LinearRegressionModel {

    weights: Vec<f64>,

    bias: f64,

}



fn main() -> Result<()> {

    // 2. Create an instance of the struct with
your model's parameters.

    let model = LinearRegressionModel {

        weights: vec![0.5, 0.2],    // Example
weights

        bias: 0.1,                          // Example
bias

    };



    // 3. Serialize the struct to a JSON string.

    let serialized_model =
serde_json::to_string(&model)?;



    // 4. Print the JSON string.

    println!("Serialized Model (JSON):\n{}",
serialized_model);
```

```
    Ok(())
```

}

In this example:

1. We define the LinearRegressionModel struct and annotate it with #[derive(Serialize, Deserialize, Debug)].
2. We create an instance of LinearRegressionModel with some example data. In a real-world scenario, these values would be the learned parameters from your trained model.
3. We use serde_json::to_string(&model) to serialize the model instance into a JSON string.
   - serde_json::to_string(): This function takes a reference to a value that implements the Serialize trait (which our struct does because of the #[derive] annotation) and converts it into a JSON string.
   - ?: The question mark operator is used for concise error handling. If the serialization fails, the error is propagated up the call stack.
4. We print the resulting JSON string.

If you were to use Bincode, a compact binary format, the serialization would look like this:

Rust

```
use serde::{Serialize, Deserialize};

use bincode::Result;


#[derive(Serialize, Deserialize, Debug)]

struct LinearRegressionModel {

    weights: Vec<f64>,
```

```rust
    bias: f64,

}


fn main() -> Result<()> {

    // 1. Create an instance of the struct.

    let model = LinearRegressionModel {

        weights: vec![0.5, 0.2],

        bias: 0.1,

    };



    // 2. Serialize the struct to a byte vector
using bincode.

    let serialized_model =
bincode::serialize(&model)?;



    // 3. Print the serialized data (bytes).

    println!("Serialized Model (Bincode): {:?}",
serialized_model);



    Ok(())

}
```

The main difference is that we use bincode::serialize(&model) instead of serde_json::to_string(&model), and the result is a Result<Vec<u8>, bincode::Error> (a vector of bytes) instead of a JSON string.

Deserialization with Serde

Deserialization is the reverse process of serialization: you take the serialized data and turn it back into a Rust data structure.

Here's how you can deserialize the JSON string from the previous example back into a LinearRegressionModel instance:

Rust

```rust
use serde::{Serialize, Deserialize};

use serde_json::Result;


#[derive(Serialize, Deserialize, Debug)]

struct LinearRegressionModel {

    weights: Vec<f64>,

    bias: f64,

}


fn main() -> Result<()> {

    // 1. A JSON string representing the
serialized model data.
```

```rust
let serialized_model = r#"{

    "weights": [0.5, 0.2],

    "bias": 0.1

}"#;



// 2. Deserialize the JSON string back into a
LinearRegressionModel instance.

let deserialized_model: LinearRegressionModel
= serde_json::from_str(serialized_model)?;



// 3. Use the deserialized model.

println!("Deserialized Model: {:?}",
deserialized_model);



    Ok(())

}
```

In this example:

1. We have a JSON string (serialized_model) that represents the serialized data. Note the use of a raw string literal r#"{...}"#, which allows us to include double quotes without escaping.
2. We use serde_json::from_str(serialized_model) to deserialize the JSON string back into a LinearRegressionModel struct.

- serde_json::from_str(): This function takes a string slice (&str) containing the JSON data and attempts to convert it into a Rust value of the specified type (LinearRegressionModel in this case).
- ?: The question mark operator propagates any errors that occur during deserialization.

3. We can then use the deserialized_model as a regular Rust struct.

If you were using Bincode, the deserialization would look like this:

Rust

```
use serde::{Serialize, Deserialize};

use bincode::Result;



#[derive(Serialize, Deserialize, Debug)]

struct LinearRegressionModel {

    weights: Vec<f64>,

    bias: f64,

}



fn main() -> Result<()> {

    // 1. A byte vector representing the
serialized model data

    let serialized_model: Vec<u8> = vec![
```

```
        161, 105, 0, 0, 0, 0, 0, 0, 0, 0, 0, 63,
153, 153, 153, 153, 153, 153, 61, 153,

        153, 153, 153, 153, 153, 63, 205, 204,
204, 204, 204, 205, 63,

    ];



    // 2. Deserialize the byte vector into a
LinearRegressionModel instance.

    let deserialized_model: LinearRegressionModel
= bincode::deserialize(&serialized_model[..])?;


    // 3. Use the deserialized model.

    println!("Deserialized Model: {:?}",
deserialized_model);



    Ok(())

}
```

The key difference is that we use bincode::deserialize(&serialized_model[..]) and pass it a byte slice (&[u8]) representing the serialized data in the Bincode format.

Choosing a Serialization Format

Serde supports a wide variety of serialization formats, each with its own advantages and disadvantages.

When choosing a format for your machine learning models, consider the following:

- Human Readability: If you need to inspect or edit the serialized data manually, a human-readable format like JSON is a good choice.
- Performance: If you need the fastest possible serialization and deserialization, especially for large models, a binary format like Bincode is generally preferred.
- File Size: Binary formats like Bincode tend to produce smaller files than text-based formats like JSON, which can be important for storage and transmission.
- Cross-Language Compatibility: If you need to share your models with applications written in other languages, you might need to choose a format that is widely supported, such as JSON or Protocol Buffers.

For machine learning models, especially when performance and file size are critical, Bincode is often a good choice for serialization.

11.2 Building Standalone Executables for Model Inference

One of the simplest and most direct ways to deploy a machine learning model built with Rust is to create a standalone executable. This means creating a program that contains everything it needs to run on a target machine without requiring any external dependencies or a complex runtime environment.

This approach is particularly suitable for scenarios where:

- The model will be used on a single machine or a small number of machines.
- You want to avoid the overhead of setting up a server or a web service.
- You need very low latency inference.

- The application has specific deployment requirements.

The Process: From Trained Model to Executable

Here's a breakdown of the process:

1. Train and Serialize Your Model: The first step, of course, is to train your machine learning model using your chosen algorithm and Rust crates (like ndarray). Once the model is trained, you need to serialize its learned parameters (weights, biases, etc.) to a file. We typically use Serde for this, as discussed in the previous section.

2. Create a New Rust Project: You'll create a new Rust project that will be responsible for loading the serialized model and performing inference (making predictions). This will be the core of your standalone executable.

3. Add Dependencies: In your Cargo.toml file, you'll need to add the necessary dependencies:
   - serde and serde_json (or serde_bincode) for deserializing the model data.
   - ndarray or any other crates you use for numerical computation and data manipulation.

4. Load the Model: In your Rust code, you'll read the serialized model data from the file and deserialize it back into the appropriate Rust data structures (structs) that represent your model.

5. Implement Inference Logic: You'll write a function that takes the input data, feeds it to your loaded model, and performs the necessary calculations to generate predictions. This is where you'll use the forward pass of your neural network or the prediction equation of your linear regression model, for example.

6. Build the Executable: You'll use Cargo to build your Rust project in release mode. This creates an optimized executable that is ready for deployment.

7. Deploy: To deploy your model, you simply distribute the executable file along with the serialized model data file to the target machine. The user can then run the executable to perform inference.

Example: Standalone Executable for Linear Regression

Let's create a simplified example of deploying a linear regression model as a standalone executable.

1. Train and Serialize the Model (Conceptual)

For this example, we'll skip the actual training part and assume you have a trained linear regression model.

Imagine you've trained it, and the resulting weights and bias are:

- weights: [2.0, 3.0]
- bias: 5.0

You would then serialize these values using Serde as shown in the previous section. Let's assume you've serialized it to a file named "model.json".

2. Create a New Rust Project

Create a new Rust project using Cargo:

Bash

```
cargo new linear_regression_inference

cd linear_regression_inference
```

3. Add Dependencies to Cargo.toml

Open Cargo.toml and add the following dependencies:

Ini, TOML

```
[package]

name = "linear_regression_inference"

version = "0.1.0"

authors = ["Your Name <your.email@example.com>"]

edition = "2021"


[dependencies]

serde = { version = "1.0", features = ["derive"]
}

serde_json = "1.0"

ndarray = "0.15.1"
```

4. Load the Model and Implement Inference Logic in src/main.rs

Now, let's write the Rust code to load the serialized model and perform inference:

Rust

```
use ndarray::Array1;

use ndarray::Array2;

use serde::{Serialize, Deserialize};
```

```rust
use std::fs::File;

use std::io::Read;


// 1. Define the struct that matches the
serialized model data.

#[derive(Serialize, Deserialize, Debug)]

struct LinearRegressionModel {

    weights: Array1<f64>,

    bias: f64,

}


// 2. Function to perform inference with the
loaded model.

fn predict(model: &LinearRegressionModel,
features: &Array2<f64>) -> Array1<f64> {

    // Perform the linear regression calculation:
y = Xw + b

    features.dot(&model.weights) + model.bias

}


fn main() -> Result<(), Box<dyn
std::error::Error>> {

    // 3. Load the serialized model from a file.
```

```rust
    let mut file = File::open("model.json")?; //
Open the "model.json" file

    let mut serialized_model = String::new();

    file.read_to_string(&mut serialized_model)?;
// Read the entire file content into a string


    // 4. Deserialize the model data from the
string.

    let model: LinearRegressionModel =
serde_json::from_str(&serialized_model)?;


    // 5. Print some info.

    println!("Model loaded successfully. Weights:
{}, Bias: {}", model.weights, model.bias);


    // 6. Sample input data for inference.

    let input_data = array![[5.0, 10.0], [2.5,
7.5], [8.0, 12.0]]; // Shape: (3, 2) - 3 data
points, 2 features each


    // 7. Perform inference using the loaded
model.

    let predictions = predict(&model,
&input_data);
```

```
    println!("Predictions for input data:\n{}",
predictions);



    Ok(())

}
```

5. Build the Executable

Build the Rust project in release mode to create an optimized executable:

Bash

cargo build --release

The executable will be located in the target/release directory (e.g., target/release/linear_regression_inference on Linux/macOS, target\release\linear_regression_inference.exe on Windows).

6. Deploy the Executable

To deploy your model:

1. Copy the executable (e.g., linear_regression_inference) and the serialized model file (e.g., model.json) to the target machine.
2. Ensure that the target machine has the necessary system libraries that your Rust program depends on. For most Rust programs, this is usually not a concern, as Rust binaries are often statically linked.
3. The user can then run the executable from the command line. The executable will load the model from the model.json file, perform inference on any input data you provide to it, and print the predictions.

Real-World Application: Image Classification CLI

You could create a command-line tool that takes an image as input and uses a pre-trained image classification model (e.g., ResNet) to predict the image's class. The executable would:

1. Load the pre-trained model.
2. Read the image file from the command-line argument.
3. Preprocess the image (resize, normalize).
4. Convert the image data into a tensor.
5. Perform inference using the model.
6. Print the predicted class.

This tool could then be used on any machine without requiring a complex setup or a running server.

11.3 Deploying Rust ML Models to Servers (Web APIs with Rust Frameworks)

In many real-world applications, you won't be running your machine learning model directly on the user's machine. Instead, you'll deploy it to a server, where it can receive requests and provide predictions over a network. This is commonly done by creating a web API.

A web API (Application Programming Interface) allows other applications to communicate with your ML model using standard web protocols, such as HTTP. This enables you to:

- Provide ML capabilities to various clients, such as web applications, mobile apps, or other services.
- Centralize your ML model, making it easier to manage and update.
- Scale your ML service to handle a large number of requests.

Rust's web frameworks, such as Actix Web and Rocket, make it efficient and straightforward to build these web APIs.

General Workflow

Here's a typical workflow for deploying a Rust ML model as a web API:

1. Train and Serialize Your Model: You'll train your machine learning model using your preferred Rust libraries and then serialize its parameters (weights, biases, etc.) using Serde. This creates a file (or a byte array) containing the model's state.
2. Set Up a Rust Web Project: You'll create a new Rust project using a web framework like Actix Web or Rocket. This project will define the API endpoints and handle the communication with clients.
3. Add Dependencies: In your Cargo.toml file, you'll add the necessary dependencies:
   - The web framework (e.g., actix-web, rocket).
   - serde and serde_json (or serde_bincode) for handling data serialization and deserialization in the API.
   - ndarray or any other crates you need for numerical computation and data manipulation.
4. Load the Model: When the web server starts, you'll load the serialized model data from the file (or other storage) into memory. This makes the model's parameters available for making predictions.
5. Define API Endpoints: You'll define API endpoints that clients can use to send data to your model and receive predictions. For example, you might define a /predict endpoint that accepts input features and returns the model's output.
6. Implement Inference Logic: Within your API endpoints, you'll:
   - Extract the input data from the client's request (e.g., from the request body).

- Preprocess the input data as needed (e.g., convert it into an ndarray::Array2).
- Feed the data to your loaded model to obtain predictions.
- Format the predictions into a suitable response (e.g., a JSON object).
7. Run the Web Server: You'll start the Rust web server, which will listen for incoming requests on a specific address and port and handle them according to the defined API endpoints.
8. Deploy: Finally, you'll deploy your Rust web application to a server, making your ML model accessible to clients over the network.

Example: Deploying a Linear Regression Model with Actix Web

Let's walk through a simplified example of deploying a linear regression model as a web API using Actix Web.

1. Train and Serialize the Model (Conceptual)

As before, we'll assume you have a trained linear regression model with weights and bias. You've serialized it to a JSON file named "model.json".

2. Set Up a Rust Web Project with Actix Web

First, make sure you have Rust and Cargo installed. Then, create a new Rust project:

Bash

cargo new linear_regression_api

cd linear_regression_api

Add Actix Web, Serde, and Serde JSON to your Cargo.toml:

Ini, TOML

```ini
[package]

name = "linear_regression_api"

version = "0.1.0"

authors = ["Your Name <your.email@example.com>"]

edition = "2021"


[dependencies]

actix-web = "4"        # Use the latest version

serde = { version = "1.0", features = ["derive"] }

serde_json = "1.0"

ndarray = "0.15.1"
```

3. Implement the Web API in src/main.rs

Now, let's write the Rust code to create the web API:

Rust

```rust
use actix_web::{web, App, HttpResponse, HttpServer, Responder};

use serde::{Serialize, Deserialize};

use ndarray::Array1;
```

```rust
use ndarray::Array2;

use std::fs::File;

use std::io::Read;

use actix_web::rt::System;


// 1. Define the struct to hold the model
parameters.  Import Serialize and Deserialize

#[derive(Serialize, Deserialize, Debug)]

struct LinearRegressionModel {

    weights: Array1<f64>,

    bias: f64,

}


// 2. Function to perform inference with the
loaded model.

fn predict(model: &LinearRegressionModel,
features: &Array2<f64>) -> Array1<f64> {

    features.dot(&model.weights) + model.bias

}


// 3. Define the API endpoint for making
predictions.
```

```rust
async fn predict_handler(req_body: web::Bytes) ->
impl Responder {

    // 4. Deserialize the input data from the
request body (assuming JSON format).

    let input_data: Vec<Vec<f64>> = match
serde_json::from_slice(&req_body) {

        Ok(data) => data,

        Err(e) => return
HttpResponse::BadRequest().body(format!("Invalid
input data: {}", e)),

    };


    // 5. Convert the input data into an
ndarray::Array2.

    let input_array = Array2::from_shape_vec(

        (input_data.len(), input_data[0].len()),
// (number of data points, number of features)

input_data.into_iter().flatten().collect::<Vec<f6
4>>(), // Flatten the 2D vector into a 1D vector

    )

    .unwrap();


    // 6. Load the model from the file (in a real
application, load this once at startup).
```

```rust
    let mut file =
File::open("model.json").unwrap(); //  Open the
model file

    let mut serialized_model = String::new();

    file.read_to_string(&mut
serialized_model).unwrap();   // Read the file
into a string

    let model: LinearRegressionModel =
serde_json::from_str(&serialized_model).unwrap();
// Deserialize



    // 7. Perform inference using the loaded
model.

    let predictions = predict(&model,
&input_array);



    // 8. Serialize the predictions to JSON and
return them as the response.

    HttpResponse::Ok().json(&predictions)

}



fn main() -> std::io::Result<()> {

    // 9. Set up and run the Actix Web server.

    let system = System::new(); //create system
```

```
let res = system.block_on(async { //block

    HttpServer::new(|| {

        App::new()

            .route("/predict",
web::post().to(predict_handler)) // Define the
/predict endpoint to handle POST requests

    })

        .bind("127.0.0.1:8080")? // Bind the
server to localhost and port 8080

        .run()

        .await

});

system.run()?; //run

Ok(())

}
```

Key points in this example:

- We define a LinearRegressionModel struct (which should match the structure of your serialized model).
- We have a predict function that takes the loaded model and input features and returns the predictions.
- The predict_handler function is the Actix Web handler for the /predict endpoint:
    - It deserializes the input data from the request body (assumed to be JSON) into a Rust data structure.
    - It converts the input data into an ndarray::Array2.

- It loads the serialized model from the "model.json" file. In a production environment, you'd load this once when the server starts, not on every request.
- It calls the predict function to get the model's predictions.
- It serializes the predictions to JSON and returns them as the HTTP response.
- The main function sets up and starts the Actix Web server, defining the /predict endpoint and associating it with the predict_handler function.

4. Build and Run

Build and run the server:

Bash

cargo build --release

cargo run --release

Now, your model is accessible as a web API at http://127.0.0.1:8080/predict. You can send POST requests to this endpoint with your input data in JSON format, and the server will respond with the model's predictions in JSON format.

Deployment

To deploy this to a production server, you'll need to:

1. Copy the compiled executable (from target/release) and the model.json file to your server.
2. Configure a process manager (like systemd on Linux) to run your executable as a service.
3. Set up a reverse proxy (like Nginx or Apache) to forward requests to your application.

4. Ensure that your server has the necessary system libraries. For statically linked Rust executables, this is usually minimal.

11.4 Integrating ML Models into Existing Rust Applications

Instead of deploying your ML model as a separate service, you might want to incorporate it directly into an existing Rust application. This approach offers several advantages, particularly in scenarios where low latency and offline functionality are crucial.

Why Integrate Directly?
- Low Latency: Calling a model within the same application eliminates the network overhead associated with making requests to a separate server. This can significantly reduce the time it takes to get predictions, which is critical for real-time applications.
- Offline Functionality: By embedding the model directly into your application, you enable it to function even when there's no network connectivity. This is essential for applications that need to work in disconnected environments, such as mobile apps or embedded systems.
- Simplified Deployment: Deploying a single application is often simpler than deploying a separate server and managing communication between them.
- Resource Efficiency: For certain use cases, it can be more efficient to have a single process that handles both the application logic and the ML inference, rather than having two separate processes communicating over a network.

The Process: Integrating a Model into a Rust Application

Here's a general process for integrating a trained ML model into an existing Rust application:

1. Train and Serialize Your Model: This step is the same as in the previous deployment scenario. You train your model using your chosen Rust libraries and then serialize its parameters (weights, biases, etc.) to a file using Serde.
2. Add Dependencies: In your existing Rust application's Cargo.toml file, add the necessary dependencies:
   - serde and serde_json (or serde_bincode) for deserializing the model data.
   - ndarray or any other crates you need for numerical computation and data manipulation.
3. Load the Model: In your Rust application's code, you'll read the serialized model data from the file and deserialize it back into the appropriate Rust data structures (structs) that represent your model. This usually happens during the application's initialization process.
4. Implement Inference Logic: You'll write a function or method within your application that takes the input data, feeds it to the loaded model, and performs the necessary calculations to generate predictions. This is where you'll use the forward pass of your neural network or the prediction equation of your linear regression model.
5. Use the Model for Inference: Wherever you need to make predictions in your application's code, you'll call the inference function, passing it the input data and using the loaded model.

Example: Integrating a Linear Regression Model into a Rust CLI Application

Let's say you have an existing Rust command-line application that predicts house prices based on user-provided input. You've trained a linear regression model in Rust and serialized it to a file named "model.json".

Here's how you can integrate the model into your CLI application:

Rust

```rust
use ndarray::Array1;
use ndarray::Array2;
use serde::{Serialize, Deserialize};
use std::fs::File;
use std::io::Read;
use std::io;

// 1. Define the struct to hold the model
parameters.
#[derive(Serialize, Deserialize, Debug)]
struct LinearRegressionModel {
    weights: Array1<f64>,
    bias: f64,
}

// 2. Function to perform inference with the
loaded model.
fn predict_price(model: &LinearRegressionModel,
size: f64, bedrooms: f64) -> f64 {
    // Prepare the input features as a 2D array
(1 sample, 2 features).
    let features = array![[size, bedrooms]];
    // Perform the linear regression calculation:
y = Xw + b
    let predicted_price =
features.dot(&model.weights) + model.bias;
    predicted_price[0] // Extract the scalar
prediction from the 1D array
}
```

```rust
fn main() -> Result<(), Box<dyn
std::error::Error>> {
    // 3. Load the serialized model from a file
during application initialization.
    let mut file = File::open("model.json")?;
    let mut serialized_model = String::new();
    file.read_to_string(&mut serialized_model)?;
    let model: LinearRegressionModel =
serde_json::from_str(&serialized_model)?;

    println!("House Price Predictor CLI
Application");

    loop {
        // 4. Get user input.
        println!("Enter house size (in square
feet):");
        let mut size_input = String::new();
        io::stdin().read_line(&mut size_input)?;
        let size: f64 =
size_input.trim().parse()?;

        println!("Enter number of bedrooms:");
        let mut bedrooms_input = String::new();
        io::stdin().read_line(&mut
bedrooms_input)?;
        let bedrooms: f64 =
bedrooms_input.trim().parse()?;

        // 5. Perform inference using the loaded
model and user input.
        let predicted_price =
predict_price(&model, size, bedrooms);
        println!("Predicted house price: ${:.2}",
predicted_price);
```

```
        println!("Do you want to predict another
house price? (yes/no)");
        let mut continue_input = String::new();
        io::stdin().read_line(&mut
continue_input)?;
        if continue_input.trim().to_lowercase()
!= "yes" {
            break;
        }
    }

    println!("Exiting application.");
    Ok(())
}
```

In this example:

1. We define the LinearRegressionModel struct to hold the model's parameters, matching the structure of the serialized data.
2. We create a predict_price function that takes the loaded model and user-provided house size and bedroom count as input and returns the predicted price. Note how the input is shaped into a (1,2) ndarray array.
3. In the main function:
   - We load the serialized model from the "model.json" file at the start of the application.
   - We enter a loop to interact with the user, prompting them to enter house size and bedroom count.
   - We parse the user input and call the predict_price function to get the prediction.
   - We print the predicted price and ask the user if they want to make another prediction.

This approach allows you to embed the ML model directly into your CLI application, making it self-contained and easy to distribute. The application can then perform predictions without relying on external services or network connections.

11.5 Considerations for Edge Deployment with Rust

Edge deployment involves running machine learning models on devices with limited resources, such as:

- Mobile phones
- Embedded systems (e.g., microcontrollers)
- IoT (Internet of Things) devices
- Sensors
- Robotics

Instead of relying on powerful servers in a data center, edge deployment brings the ML processing closer to the data source, enabling real-time decision-making, reducing latency, and improving privacy.

Rust's unique characteristics make it a compelling choice for edge deployment of ML models. Its performance, memory efficiency, and small binary sizes are crucial advantages in resource-constrained environments. However, deploying ML models to the edge also presents specific challenges that you need to consider.

Key Challenges and Considerations

Here are some key challenges and considerations for deploying ML models on edge devices with Rust:

1. Model Size

Edge devices typically have limited storage capacity. Therefore, the size of your ML model is a critical factor. Larger models require more storage space, which might not be available on a small device.

- Model Compression: Techniques to reduce the size of your model:
  - Quantization: Reducing the precision of the model's weights (e.g., from 32-bit floating point to 8-bit integers).
  - Pruning: Removing less important connections or neurons from the network.
  - Distillation: Training a smaller "student" model to mimic the behavior of a larger "teacher" model.

Example: Model Quantization

Rust

```
//pseudo code
// // 1. Convert weights from f32 to i8 (simplified illustration)
// fn quantize_weights(weights: ArrayD<f32>) -> ArrayD<i8> {
//     // Scale and round float weights to i8 range
//     let scaled_weights = (weights * 127.0).map(|&x| x.round() as i8);
//     scaled_weights
// }
```

Quantization reduces model size, but you'll need to perform inference using integer arithmetic, which may require a specialized runtime or hardware.

2. Inference Speed

Edge devices often have limited processing power, so inference speed is crucial, especially for real-time applications. You need to optimize your model and inference code to minimize latency.

- Operator Fusion: Combining multiple operations into a single kernel to reduce overhead.
- Efficient Data Structures: Using appropriate data structures (like ndarray with efficient memory layout) to optimize memory access.
- Hardware Acceleration: Leveraging any available hardware acceleration on the device, such as specialized processors or GPUs.

Example: Optimized Inference Function

Rust

```
use ndarray::Array1;
use ndarray::Array2;

// fn predict_efficient(model: &MyModel,
features: &Array2<f32>) -> Array1<f32> {
//      // Optimized inference, e.g., using a more
efficient matrix multiplication
//      //  (This is a placeholder, actual
optimization would be more complex)
//      features.dot(&model.weights) + model.bias
// }
```

3. Resource Constraints

Edge devices have limited memory (both RAM and flash storage), processing power, and energy budgets. Your ML application must be designed to operate within these constraints.

- Memory Usage: Carefully manage memory allocation and deallocation to avoid memory leaks and excessive memory consumption. Rust's ownership system helps with this.
- Power Consumption: Minimize computations and optimize code for energy efficiency, especially for battery-powered devices.

4. Heterogeneous Hardware

Edge devices come with a wide variety of hardware architectures, including:

- ARM processors (common in mobile phones and embedded systems)
- Microcontrollers with very limited resources
- Specialized AI accelerators

You might need to adapt your code or use different libraries to target specific hardware.

5. Real-time Requirements

Many edge applications have strict real-time requirements. For example, a self-driving car's object detection system must process data with minimal delay.

- Deterministic Execution: Ensure that your code's execution time is predictable and consistent. Avoid operations with variable or unbounded execution times.
- Interrupt Handling: For real-time systems, you might need to handle interrupts from sensors or other devices.

6. Security

Security is paramount when deploying ML models to edge devices, as these devices can be vulnerable to attacks.

- Model Protection: Protect your model from being extracted or tampered with.
- Secure Communication: If your edge device communicates with a central server, use secure communication protocols (e.g., HTTPS).
- Firmware Updates: Implement secure mechanisms for updating your model and application firmware.

7. Rust's Advantages for Edge Deployment

Rust's features make it well-suited for addressing these challenges:

- Performance: Rust's speed allows you to perform complex computations efficiently on resource-constrained devices.
- Memory Efficiency: Rust's lack of garbage collection and fine-grained control over memory usage help you minimize memory footprint.
- Small Binary Size: Rust produces small, self-contained executables, which is crucial for devices with limited storage.
- Safety: Rust's memory safety guarantees prevent common errors like buffer overflows and data races, which are especially critical in security-sensitive edge applications.
- Cross-Platform Compatibility: Rust can be compiled for a wide range of architectures, making it suitable for diverse edge devices.

Deploying machine learning models to the edge with Rust requires careful consideration of the device's limitations and the application's requirements. By focusing on model optimization, efficient resource management, and leveraging Rust's strengths, you can create robust, high-performance ML applications that run directly on edge devices.

Chapter 12: Exploring Advanced ML Techniques in Rust

This chapter provides a glimpse into some advanced machine learning techniques and discusses how Rust can be used to implement them or integrate with existing frameworks.

12.1 Introduction to Reinforcement Learning Concepts and Potential Rust Implementations

Reinforcement learning (RL) is a fascinating area of machine learning that differs significantly from the supervised and unsupervised learning we've discussed so far. Instead of learning from labeled data or finding hidden patterns in unlabeled data, RL is about training an **agent** to make decisions in an **environment** to maximize a certain type of reward.

A Different Kind of Learning

Think of it like teaching a dog a new trick. You don't give the dog a list of correct actions; instead, you reward the dog when it does something right and perhaps punish it (or simply withhold the reward) when it does something wrong. The dog learns to associate its actions with the consequences and gradually develops a strategy to get the most rewards.

Reinforcement learning works on similar principles.

Key Concepts in Reinforcement Learning

To understand RL, let's define its core components:

- Agent: This is the "brain" of the system, the decision-maker. It could be a robot, a game-playing program, or even a trading algorithm.

- Environment: This is the external system that the agent interacts with. It could be a physical space, a simulated game, or a financial market.
- State: This is a representation of the environment at a particular moment. It's the information the agent uses to make a decision. For example, in a game, the state might be the current position of all the pieces on the board.
- Action: This is what the agent does in response to the current state. In the maze example, the actions could be "move forward," "turn left," or "turn right."
- Reward: This is a scalar value that the agent receives from the environment after taking an action. The reward signals how desirable the action was. A positive reward indicates a good action, while a negative reward (or punishment) indicates a bad action.
- Policy: This is the agent's strategy for choosing actions. It's a mapping from states to actions, telling the agent what to do in each state. The goal of RL is to learn an optimal policy that maximizes the agent's cumulative reward.
- Value Function: This is an estimate of the expected future rewards that the agent will receive starting from a given state (or state-action pair). It helps the agent to evaluate the long-term consequences of its actions.

The RL Process

The interaction between the agent and the environment unfolds in a sequence of steps:

1. Initialization: The environment starts in an initial state.
2. State Observation: The agent observes the current state of the environment.
3. Action Selection: The agent selects an action based on its current policy.
4. Action Execution: The agent executes the chosen action in the environment.

5. Reward Reception: The environment provides the agent with a reward, indicating the immediate consequence of the action.
6. State Transition: The environment transitions to a new state, which depends on the previous state and the agent's action.
7. Iteration: The process repeats from step 2, with the agent observing the new state and choosing the next action.

The agent's goal is to learn a policy that maximizes its cumulative reward over time. This means it needs to learn not only which actions lead to immediate rewards but also which actions lead to states that will yield future rewards.

Example: Reinforcement Learning in Robotics

Let's consider a classic example of reinforcement learning in robotics: training a robot to navigate a maze.

- Agent: The robot.
- Environment: The maze, with walls, open paths, and a goal location.
- State: The robot's current position within the maze (e.g., its coordinates).
- Action: The robot's possible movements, such as "move forward," "turn left," "turn right."
- Reward:
  - Positive reward: The robot receives a large positive reward when it reaches the goal.
  - Negative reward: The robot receives a small negative reward for each step it takes (to encourage efficiency) or a larger negative reward for hitting a wall.
  - Zero reward: The robot receives no reward for moving in an empty space.
- Policy: The robot's decision-making strategy, which maps its current position in the maze to a specific movement.

- Value Function: An estimate of how many steps it will take the robot to reach the goal from its current position. A higher value function indicates a more promising state (closer to the goal).

In this scenario, the robot starts at the beginning of the maze and explores its surroundings by taking actions. Initially, the robot's movements are random, and it receives rewards and penalties based on its actions. Through a reinforcement learning algorithm, the robot learns to associate certain actions with positive rewards (e.g., moving towards the goal) and other actions with negative rewards (e.g., hitting a wall). Over time, the robot refines its policy to navigate the maze more efficiently and reach the goal as quickly as possible.

Potential Rust Implementations

Rust's performance, memory safety, and concurrency features make it a compelling language for implementing reinforcement learning algorithms, especially in applications where:

- Performance is critical: Applications like robotics, real-time control systems, and high-frequency trading require very fast decision-making.
- Resource constraints are present: Embedded systems and mobile devices have limited processing power and memory, making Rust's efficiency a significant advantage.
- Safety and reliability are paramount: In applications like autonomous driving or healthcare, errors can have severe consequences, and Rust's safety guarantees can help prevent them.

While the reinforcement learning ecosystem in Rust is still developing, you could potentially build RL agents and environments using Rust, leveraging crates like:

- ndarray for efficient numerical computation and representation of states, actions, and rewards.
- rand for generating random actions and simulating environmental stochasticity.
- rayon for parallelizing simulations or experience replay.

Furthermore, you could explore ways to represent the agent, environment, and their interactions using Rust's powerful data structures and abstractions.

For example, you could define:

- Structs to represent the state of the environment and the agent's attributes.
- Enums to represent the possible actions the agent can take.
- Traits to define the agent's behavior and the environment's dynamics.

By combining Rust's performance with sound software engineering principles, you can create efficient, robust, and maintainable reinforcement learning systems.

12.2 Natural Language Processing with Rust

Natural Language Processing (NLP) is a branch of artificial intelligence that focuses on enabling computers to understand,[1] interpret, and generate human language.[2] It's a field that bridges the gap between human communication and machine understanding, and it's essential for a wide range of applications, from search engines and chatbots to machine translation and sentiment analysis.

While Python has been the dominant language in NLP due to its rich ecosystem of libraries and frameworks, Rust's performance, reliability, and memory safety make it an attractive option for building efficient and robust NLP systems, especially in production environments or when dealing with large volumes of text data.

Key NLP Tasks and Concepts

Before we discuss Rust's role in NLP, let's briefly touch upon some fundamental NLP tasks and concepts:

- Tokenization: The process of breaking down a text into smaller units called tokens. Tokens can be words, subwords, or characters. For example, the sentence "The quick brown fox" can be tokenized into the words ["The", "quick", "brown", "fox"].
- Part-of-Speech (POS) Tagging: The process of labeling each word in a text with its corresponding part of speech, such as noun, verb,[3] adjective, etc. This helps to understand the grammatical structure of the sentence.
- Named Entity Recognition (NER): The task of identifying and classifying named entities in a text, such as people, organizations, locations, and dates.
- Sentiment Analysis: The process of determining the emotional tone or attitude expressed in a text, such as positive, negative, or neutral.
- Machine Translation: The task of automatically translating text from one language to another.
- Text Summarization: The process of generating a concise summary of a longer text while preserving its key information.
- Question Answering: The task of automatically answering questions posed in natural language.

Rust Libraries for NLP

The Rust NLP ecosystem is still evolving, but there are several libraries that provide functionalities for various NLP tasks.

1. Tokenization

Tokenization is a fundamental step in most NLP pipelines, and Rust offers libraries to perform this task efficiently.

- tokenizers Crate: This crate, originally written in Rust and also available with bindings for other languages, provides high-performance tokenization for various languages and models, including BERT, GPT, and more. It offers several tokenization algorithms and supports various normalization and preprocessing steps.

Example: Tokenization with the tokenizers Crate

(This example assumes you have the tokenizers crate in your Cargo.toml)

Rust

```rust
use tokenizers::tokenizer::{Tokenizer,
TokenizerImpl, Model, Normalizer, PreTokenizer,
PostProcessor};

use tokenizers::models::bpe::BpeTrainer;

use tokenizers::normalizers::strip::Strip;

use
tokenizers::pre_tokenizers::whitespace::Whitespac
e;

use tokenizers::Encoding;


fn main() -> Result<(), Box<dyn
std::error::Error>> {

    // 1. Define the training data.
```

```
let sentences = [

        "The quick brown fox jumps over the lazy
dog.",

        "A journey of a thousand miles begins
with a single step.",

        "The best way to predict the future is to
invent it.",

    ];
```

```
// 2. Create a tokenizer model (e.g., BPE -
BytePairEncoding).

    let vocab_size = 500;

    let mut trainer =
BpeTrainer::new(vocab_size);

    let mut tokenizer: TokenizerImpl<_, _, _, _>
=
TokenizerImpl::new(Model::Bpe(Default::default())
);
```

```
    //3. Create a normalizer

    let normalizer = Strip::new(true, true);
```

```
// 4. Pretokenize

    let pre_tokenizer = Whitespace::default();
```

```rust
    // 5. Train the tokenizer.

    tokenizer.with_normalizer(normalizer);

    tokenizer.with_pre_tokenizer(pre_tokenizer);


    tokenizer.train_from_iterator(sentences.iter(),
    trainer, None)?;


    // 6. Encode a sentence.

    let encoding: Encoding =
    tokenizer.encode("The quick brown fox", false)?;

    println!("Tokens: {:?}",
    encoding.get_tokens());

    println!("Token IDs: {:?}",
    encoding.get_ids());


    Ok(())

}
```

In this example, we:

1. Define a set of sentences as our training data.
2. Create a BpeTrainer with a vocabulary size of 500. BPE is a subword tokenization algorithm that can handle words not seen during training.
3. Create a TokenizerImpl and associate it with the BPE model.

4. Train the tokenizer on the training sentences.
5. Encode a sample sentence using the trained tokenizer. The encoding contains the tokens and their corresponding IDs.

2. Rust BERT

rust-bert is a Rust crate that provides pre-trained transformer models and utilities for various NLP tasks. Transformer models, such as BERT, have achieved state-of-the-art results in many NLP tasks.

Example: Sentiment Analysis with Rust BERT

(This example assumes you have the rust-bert crate and a pre-trained model)

Rust

```
use
rust_bert::pipelines::sequence_classification::{S
equenceClassificationModel,
SequenceClassifierConfig, ClassificationOption};



fn main() -> Result<(), Box<dyn
std::error::Error>> {

    // 1. Load a pre-trained sentiment analysis
model.

    let config_path = "path/to/config.json"; //
Path to the model configuration file

    let weights_path = "path/to/model.ot"; //
Path to the model weights file (e.g., a .ot file
for ONNX)
```

```rust
    let sequence_classifier_config =
SequenceClassifierConfig::new("distilbert-base-un
cased", config_path);

    let model =
SequenceClassificationModel::new(sequence_classif
ier_config, weights_path)?;


    // 2. Define the input texts.

    let input_texts = [

        "This is a great movie!",

        "The food was terrible.",

        "I had a neutral experience.",

    ];


    // 3. Perform sentiment analysis.

    let predictions = model.predict(input_texts,
ClassificationOption::default())?;


    // 4. Print the predictions.

    for (text, prediction) in
input_texts.iter().zip(predictions.iter()) {

        println!("Text: \"{}\", Sentiment: {:?}",
text, prediction);
```

```
    }


    Ok(())

}
```

In this example, we:

1. Load a pre-trained sentiment analysis model (you would need to provide the paths to the model's configuration and weights).
2. Define a set of input texts.
3. Use the model's predict method to get the sentiment predictions for each text.
4. Print the original texts along with their predicted sentiments.

Framework Integration

Rust can also be used in conjunction with existing deep learning frameworks like PyTorch and TensorFlow for NLP tasks. This typically involves using FFI (Foreign Function Interface) to call functions from these frameworks' C++ APIs. This is useful for incorporating custom Rust-based NLP components into a larger deep learning pipeline.

12.3 Computer Vision in Rust: Image Processing Crates and Deep Learning Integration

Computer vision is a field of artificial intelligence that empowers computers to "see" and interpret visual information from the world, such as images and videos.

It involves a wide range of tasks, including:

- Image classification: Identifying the main object or scene in an image (e.g., "cat," "dog," "landscape").
- Object detection: Locating and identifying multiple objects within an image (e.g., detecting cars and pedestrians in a street scene).
- Image segmentation: Partitioning an image into multiple regions or objects (e.g., separating the foreground from the background).
- Image processing: Manipulating images to enhance them, extract features, or prepare them for further analysis (e.g., resizing, filtering, color correction).

Rust can play a significant role in building efficient and reliable computer vision systems, especially when performance and resource constraints are critical.

Rust Crates for Image Processing

Rust provides several crates that offer functionalities for various image processing tasks:

- image Crate: This crate is a versatile library for reading, writing, and manipulating images in various formats. It supports a wide range of image formats, such as JPEG, PNG, GIF, TIFF, and more. You can use it to load images from files, decode them, perform pixel-level operations, and encode and save images.
- imageproc Crate: Building on top of the image crate, imageproc provides a collection of image processing algorithms and operations. This includes:
    - Filtering: Applying kernels to blur, sharpen, or detect edges in images.
    - Resizing: Scaling images up or down.
    - Color manipulation: Adjusting brightness, contrast, and color balance.

- Drawing: Drawing shapes, text, and other graphics on images.
- Geometric transformations: Rotating, translating, and warping images.

Example: Basic Image Processing with Rust

Let's illustrate how to use the image and imageproc crates to perform some basic image processing operations:

Rust

```rust
use image::{open, ImageOutputFormat};

use imageproc::filter::gaussian_blur;

use std::fs::File;

use std::path::Path;


fn main() -> Result<(), Box<dyn std::error::Error>> {

    // 1. Open an image file.

    let img = open("input.jpg")?; // Replace "input.jpg" with your image path


    // 2. Resize the image.

    let resized_img =
image::imageops::resize(&img, 800, 600,
image::imageops::FilterType::Triangle);
```

```rust
// 3. Apply a Gaussian blur filter.

let blurred_img = gaussian_blur(&resized_img,
5.0); // 5.0 is the standard deviation (sigma)



// 4. Save the processed image.

let output_path = Path::new("output.jpg");

let mut output_file =
File::create(output_path)?;

blurred_img.write_to(&mut output_file,
ImageOutputFormat::Jpeg(80))?; // 80 is the JPEG
quality



println!("Image processed and saved to
output.jpg");



Ok(())

}
```

In this example, we:

1. Open an image file named "input.jpg" using the open
   function from the image crate.
2. Resize the image to 800x600 pixels using
   image::imageops::resize, specifying the Triangle filter for
   interpolation.

3. Apply a Gaussian blur to the resized image using imageproc::filter::gaussian_blur, with a standard deviation of 5.0.
4. Save the processed image as a JPEG file named "output.jpg" using the write_to method, specifying a JPEG quality of 80.

Deep Learning Integration for Computer Vision

While Rust crates like image and imageproc provide essential image processing functionalities, many advanced computer vision tasks, such as object detection and image segmentation, rely on deep learning models.

To leverage the power of deep learning in your Rust-based computer vision applications, you can integrate with existing deep learning frameworks like TensorFlow or PyTorch.

This typically involves the following steps:

1. Preprocess the image: Use Rust crates like image and imageproc to load, decode, and preprocess the image data as needed. This might involve resizing, normalizing, and converting the image into a suitable format for the deep learning model.
2. Transfer the image data to the deep learning framework: Convert the processed image data into a tensor representation that can be fed into the deep learning model. You might need to use FFI (Foreign Function Interface) or Rust bindings to the framework to do this.
3. Perform inference with the deep learning model: Use the deep learning framework's API to run the model on the image data and obtain the predictions.
4. Post-process the output: Convert the model's output (which is typically a tensor) into a usable format for your application, such as bounding boxes for object detection or a segmentation mask.

Example: Image Classification with Rust and PyTorch (Conceptual)

(A full example would require setting up a PyTorch model and handling memory transfer with torch-rs, which is more involved. This example outlines the core idea.)

Rust

```
//pseudo

// use image::{open, DynamicImage,
GenericImageView};

// use tch::{Device, Kind, Tensor};

//

// fn main() -> Result<(), Box<dyn
std::error::Error>> {

//      // 1. Load an image.

//      let img = open("image.jpg")?;

//      let img_rgb = img.to_rgb8();

//

//      // 2. Preprocess the image (resize and
normalize).

//      let resized_img =
image::imageops::resize(&img_rgb, 224, 224,
image::imageops::FilterType::Triangle);

//      let normalized_img =
normalize_image(resized_img);   // Custom function
for normalization
```

```
//

//      // 3. Convert the image data to a tensor
(for PyTorch).

//      let img_array: Vec<f32> =
normalized_img.into_raw();

//      let img_tensor = Tensor::from_slice(

//          &img_array,

//          &[1, 3, 224, 224], // Shape:
[batch_size, channels, height, width]

//          Kind::Float,

//      ).to(Device::Cpu);

//

//      // 4. Load a pre-trained PyTorch model
(e.g., ResNet).

//      // let model = ...; // Load your
pre-trained model

//

//      // 5. Perform inference.

//      // let output_tensor =
model.forward(&[img_tensor])?;

//

//      // 6. Post-process the output tensor to
get the predicted class.
```

```
//          // let probabilities =
output_tensor.softmax(1);

//          // let predicted_class =
probabilities.argmax(1);

//

//          // 7. Print the predicted class.

//          // println!("Predicted class: {}",
predicted_class);

//

//          Ok(())

// }
```

This example outlines the process of using Rust to load and preprocess an image, convert it into a tensor, and then pass it to a pre-trained PyTorch model for inference.

12.4 Generative Models

You're likely familiar with machine learning models that make predictions or classifications based on input data. These are called discriminative models. But there's another exciting category of models called generative models.

Instead of predicting an output from a given input, generative models learn the underlying probability distribution of the data itself. In simpler terms, they learn how the data is generated. Once trained, they can then generate new data that is similar to the data they were trained on.

Think of it this way:

- Discriminative Model: Learns to distinguish between different categories or predict a specific value. For example, a model that classifies emails as spam or not spam, or a model that predicts house prices.
- Generative Model: Learns to create new examples of the data. For example, a model that can generate new images of faces, new musical pieces, or new sentences that resemble human writing.

What Can Generative Models Do?

Generative models have a wide range of applications, including:

- Image Generation: Creating new images that look like they belong to a specific category, such as generating realistic-looking faces, animals, or landscapes.
- Text Generation: Generating new text, such as poems, articles, or code, that resembles the style and content of the training data.
- Music Composition: Creating new musical pieces that sound like they were composed by a human.
- Drug Discovery: Generating new molecular structures that have desired properties for drug development.
- Data Augmentation: Creating synthetic data to augment training sets, which can improve the performance of other machine learning models.
- Anomaly Detection: Identifying unusual or rare data points by learning the distribution of normal data and then detecting data points that deviate significantly from it.

How Do Generative Models Work?

The basic idea is that we want the model to learn a function that can produce new data points that look like they came from the same distribution as our training data. But how do we achieve this?

There are several different approaches, but they often involve these key elements:

1. Learning a Latent Space: Many generative models learn a lower-dimensional space called a "latent space" to represent the essential features of the data. Think of this latent space as a compressed representation of the data. For example, if you're generating images of faces, the latent space might capture features like hair color, eye shape, and face structure.
2. Sampling from the Latent Space: To generate a new data point, the model samples a point from this latent space.
3. Decoding to Data Space: The sampled point is then passed through a decoding function (often a neural network) that transforms it back into the original data space, creating a new data point that resembles the training data.

Popular Types of Generative Models

Let's briefly discuss two popular types of generative models:

- Variational Autoencoders (VAEs): VAEs are a type of generative model that learns a probabilistic latent space.
  - An encoder network maps the input data to a distribution in the latent space (typically a Gaussian distribution).
  - A decoder network then samples from this latent distribution and maps it back to the data space to generate new data.
  - VAEs are trained to minimize the difference between the input data and the generated data, while also encouraging the latent distribution to be well-behaved.

- Generative Adversarial Networks (GANs): GANs involve two neural networks: a generator and a discriminator.
  - The generator network generates new data samples from random noise.
  - The discriminator network tries to distinguish between real data samples from the training set and fake samples generated by the generator.
  - The generator and discriminator are trained in an adversarial process: the generator tries to fool the discriminator, while the discriminator tries to correctly classify real and fake samples. This[1] creates a feedback loop that drives both networks to improve, resulting in the generator being able to produce increasingly realistic data.

Example: Generating Images with a GAN (Conceptual)

Let's say you want to train a GAN to generate images of cats.

1. Generator: The generator network takes random noise as input and outputs an image that it hopes will look like a cat.
2. Discriminator: The discriminator network takes an image as input (either a real image of a cat from your dataset or a fake image generated by the generator) and tries to classify it as either "real" or "fake."
3. Training: The generator and discriminator are trained in a game-like fashion:
   - The generator tries to get better at generating images that can fool the discriminator.
   - The discriminator tries to get better at distinguishing between real and fake images.

As this process continues, both networks improve, and the generator learns to produce increasingly realistic images of cats.

Potential in Rust

Rust's performance and memory safety make it a compelling language for implementing and deploying generative models, especially in applications where:

- High performance is required: Generating high-resolution images or complex sequences can be computationally intensive.
- Real-time generation is needed: Applications like interactive art or real-time simulations might benefit from the speed of Rust.
- Resource constraints exist: Deploying generative models on edge devices or in embedded systems might require the efficiency that Rust provides.

While the Rust ecosystem for generative models is still evolving, you could potentially use Rust to:

- Implement custom generative model architectures.
- Optimize the training and inference process for specific hardware.
- Build high-performance applications that leverage generative models.

12.5 Ethical Considerations in High-Performance ML

As machine learning systems become more powerful and are integrated into more aspects of our lives, it's crucial to consider the ethical implications of their development and use. High-performance ML, while offering many potential benefits, also amplifies these ethical concerns due to its increased capabilities and potential for wider deployment.

The Double-Edged Sword of High Performance

High-performance ML allows us to tackle increasingly complex problems and build systems that can process vast amounts of data with incredible speed and accuracy.

This can lead to breakthroughs in various fields, such as:

- Healthcare: Faster and more accurate disease diagnosis, personalized medicine.
- Scientific discovery: Accelerated research in fields like drug discovery, materials science, and climate modeling.
- Autonomous systems: More capable self-driving cars, robots, and other autonomous devices.

However, this increased power also brings greater responsibility. High-performance ML systems can have a more significant impact on individuals and society, and if not developed and deployed ethically, they can exacerbate existing problems or create new ones.

Key Ethical Considerations

Here are some of the most pressing ethical considerations in the context of high-performance ML:

1. Bias

Machine learning models learn from the data they are trained on. If this data reflects existing societal biases, the model can perpetuate and even amplify those biases. High-performance ML systems, with their increased accuracy and efficiency, can amplify these biases on a larger scale and at a faster rate, leading to unfair or discriminatory outcomes.

For example:

- Facial recognition systems: If trained primarily on images of one ethnicity, a high-performance facial recognition system might be less accurate at recognizing individuals from other ethnicities, leading to biased results in applications like law enforcement or security.

- Loan approval systems: If trained on historical data that reflects discriminatory lending practices, a high-performance loan approval system might perpetuate those biases, denying loans to qualified individuals from certain groups.

2. Fairness

Fairness in ML goes beyond simply avoiding bias in the data. It involves considering the broader societal impact of ML systems and ensuring that they treat all groups of people equitably.

High-performance ML systems, due to their increased capability, can be deployed in situations where fairness is paramount, such as:

- Criminal justice: Risk assessment tools used in sentencing or parole decisions.
- Education: Systems that allocate resources or evaluate student performance.
- Employment: Algorithms used for hiring or promotion decisions.

In these contexts, it's crucial to ensure that high-performance ML systems are not only accurate but also fair and do not discriminate against individuals based on protected attributes like race, gender, or religion.

3. Transparency and Explainability

High-performance ML often involves complex models, such as deep neural networks, which can be difficult to understand and interpret. These models are often referred to as "black boxes" because it's hard to know exactly why they make a particular prediction.

This lack of transparency and explainability can be problematic, especially in high-stakes applications:

- Medical diagnosis: A high-performance AI system that recommends a treatment plan should ideally be able to explain its reasoning to a doctor.
- Autonomous driving: A self-driving car needs to be able to justify its actions in case of an accident.
- Financial decisions: An algorithm that denies someone a loan should provide a clear explanation of why.

If we don't understand how a high-performance ML system arrives at its decisions, it can be difficult to:

- Identify and correct errors or biases.
- Ensure that the system is behaving as intended.
- Build trust with users.
- Comply with regulations that require explainability.

4. Privacy

Machine learning models learn from data, and that data often contains sensitive personal information. High-performance ML models, with their ability to extract subtle patterns, can pose significant privacy risks.

For example:

- Facial recognition: A high-performance facial recognition system can identify individuals from images, raising concerns about surveillance and tracking.
- Personalized recommendations: A system that recommends products or services based on user data can learn sensitive information about their preferences and behaviors.

It's crucial to develop and deploy high-performance ML systems in ways that protect user privacy.

This involves techniques like:

- Differential privacy: Adding noise to data to prevent the identification of individual data points.
- Federated learning: Training models on decentralized devices without sharing the raw data.
- Privacy-preserving machine learning: Developing ML algorithms that can operate on encrypted data.

5. Misuse

The capabilities of high-performance ML can be misused for malicious purposes. As these systems become more powerful, the potential for harm increases.

Some examples include:

- Deepfakes: High-performance generative models can create highly realistic fake videos or audio recordings, which can be used to spread misinformation or manipulate public opinion.
- Autonomous weapons: High-performance computer vision and decision-making systems can be used to create autonomous weapons that can make life-or-death decisions without human intervention.
- Targeted disinformation: High-performance NLP models can be used to generate highly persuasive and targeted disinformation campaigns.

The Importance of Ethical Considerations

It is absolutely crucial to approach the development and deployment of high-performance ML systems with a strong sense of responsibility and a commitment to ethical principles.

We must strive to:

- Develop and use these technologies in ways that benefit humanity and promote fairness.
- Mitigate potential risks and harms.
- Engage in open and transparent discussions about the ethical implications of our work.
- Establish guidelines and regulations to ensure the responsible development and use of AI.

The choices we make today will shape the future of AI and its impact on society.

Chapter 13: The Rust ML Ecosystem: Libraries and Tools

While the Rust machine learning ecosystem is still maturing, it offers a growing collection of powerful libraries and tools that you can use to build high-performance ML applications. This chapter provides an overview of the key components.

13.1 Numerical Computation Libraries (e.g., ndarray, nalgebra)

Numerical computation is the foundation upon which much of machine learning is built.[1] Whether you're manipulating data, performing complex calculations, or implementing algorithms, you'll need efficient and reliable tools to handle the underlying mathematics. Rust provides several libraries for numerical computation, and two of the most prominent are ndarray and nalgebra.

ndarray: Your Go-To for N-Dimensional Arrays

The ndarray crate provides a powerful and flexible data structure for working with n-dimensional arrays in Rust. If you're familiar with NumPy in Python, you can think of ndarray as its Rust equivalent, though with some key differences due to Rust's memory management.

What is an N-Dimensional Array?

At its core, ndarray lets you work with arrays that can have any number of dimensions.

This is incredibly useful for representing various types of data:

- Vectors: A 1-dimensional array, like $[1, 2, 3]$.
- Matrices: A 2-dimensional array, like:

[[1, 2, 3],

[4, 5, 6]]

- Tensors: Arrays with three or more dimensions. For example, a 3D array could represent a volume of data, and a 4D array could represent a batch of images (batch size, height, width, channels).

Key Features of ndarray

- Efficient Storage: ndarray stores array data in contiguous memory blocks, which is crucial for performance. This layout allows the CPU to access data quickly and efficiently.
- Array Views: ndarray allows you to create "views" of existing arrays, which are like lightweight references that let you access a portion of the array without copying the underlying data. This is very useful for working with subsets of your data without incurring unnecessary overhead.
- Broadcasting: ndarray supports broadcasting, a powerful feature that allows you to perform operations on arrays with different shapes under certain conditions. This can significantly simplify your code and make it more expressive.
- Integration with Rust: ndarray works seamlessly with Rust's ownership and borrowing system, ensuring memory safety and preventing common errors.
- Parallelism: ndarray can be used in conjunction with libraries like Rayon to parallelize computations across multiple CPU cores.

Code Example: Working with ndarray

Let's look at some examples of how to create and manipulate arrays with ndarray:

Rust

```rust
use ndarray::Array1; // Import the Array1 type
(for vectors).

use ndarray::Array2; // Import the Array2 type
(for matrices).

use ndarray::array;    // Import the array! macro
(for convenient array creation).

use ndarray::Axis;


fn main() {
    // 1. Creating arrays:
    // Create a 1D array (vector) with specific
elements.
    let vector_a: Array1<f64> = array![1.0, 2.0,
3.0];
    println!("Vector a:\n{}", vector_a);


    // Create a 2x3 matrix with specific
elements.
    let matrix_b: Array2<f64> = array![[1.0, 2.0,
3.0], [4.0, 5.0, 6.0]];
    println!("Matrix b:\n{}", matrix_b);


     // Create a 2x2 matrix filled with zeros.
    let zeros_matrix: Array2<f64> =
Array2::zeros((2, 2));
    println!("Zeros Matrix:\n{}", zeros_matrix);


    // 2. Performing operations:
```

```rust
    // Element-wise addition.
    let matrix_c = array![[1.0, 1.0], [1.0,
1.0]];
    let matrix_sum = matrix_b + matrix_c;
    println!("Matrix Sum:\n{}", matrix_sum);


    // Scalar multiplication.
    let scaled_vector = vector_a * 2.0;
    println!("Scaled Vector:\n{}",
scaled_vector);


    // Matrix multiplication (dot product).
    let matrix_d = array![[2.0, 0.0], [0.0, 2.0],
[1.0, 1.0]];   // 3x2
    let result_matrix = matrix_b.dot(&matrix_d);
// 2x3 dot 3x2 => 2x2
    println!("Matrix Multiplication:\n{}",
result_matrix);


    // 3. Accessing elements and slicing:
    let first_element = matrix_b[[0, 0]]; //
Access element at row 0, column 0
    println!("First element of b: {}",
first_element);


    let first_row = matrix_b.row(0);          // Get
the first row as a view
    println!("First row of b: {}", first_row);
```

```rust
    let last_column = matrix_b.column(2);    //
Get the last column as a view

    println!("Last column of b:\n{}",
last_column);


    // 4. Iterating

    for element in matrix_b.iter() {

        println!("element from matrix b: {}",
element);

    }

}
```

In this example, we demonstrate how to create arrays, perform basic operations, access elements, and create views using ndarray.

nalgebra: Your Linear Algebra Toolkit

While ndarray excels at general-purpose array manipulation, nalgebra is a dedicated linear algebra library that provides a comprehensive set of tools for working with vectors, matrices, and other linear algebra objects.

Key Features of nalgebra

- Static and Dynamic Sizes: nalgebra supports both statically-sized matrices (where the dimensions are known at compile time) and dynamically-sized matrices (where the dimensions can vary at runtime). Statically-sized matrices can be more efficient when the dimensions are known in advance.
- Vectors, Matrices, and Transformations: nalgebra provides types for various linear algebra entities, including:
  - Vectors of different sizes (e.g., Vector2, Vector3, Vector4).

- Matrices of different sizes (e.g., Matrix2, Matrix3, Matrix4, Matrix3x4).
  - Dynamically sized matrices (DMatrix).
  - Transformations (e.g., rotations, translations, scaling).
- Mathematical Operations: nalgebra implements a wide range of linear algebra operations, such as:
  - Dot products
  - Matrix multiplication
  - Matrix transpose
  - Matrix inverse
  - Determinant
  - Eigenvalue decomposition
  - And more.
- Integration with Rust: nalgebra works seamlessly with Rust's ownership and borrowing system, ensuring memory safety and preventing common errors.

Code Example: Working with nalgebra

Here's an example of how to perform some linear algebra operations using nalgebra:

Rust

```rust
use nalgebra::{Vector3, Matrix3, Matrix4,
Point3, Isometry3, Translation3};


fn main() {
    // 1. Creating vectors and matrices:
    // Create a 3D vector.
    let vector_a = Vector3::new(1.0, 2.0, 3.0);
    println!("Vector a:\n{}", vector_a);
```

```rust
    // Create a 3x3 matrix.
    let matrix_b = Matrix3::new(
        1.0, 2.0, 3.0,
        4.0, 5.0, 6.0,
        7.0, 8.0, 9.0,
    );
    println!("Matrix b:\n{}", matrix_b);


    // Create a 4x4 transformation matrix
(rotation and translation).
    let rotation = Matrix3::new(
        0.0, -1.0, 0.0,
        1.0, 0.0, 0.0,
        0.0, 0.0, 1.0,
    );
    let translation = Vector3::new(10.0, 20.0,
30.0);
    let isometry =
Isometry3::from_parts(Translation3::from(translat
ion), rotation);
    let transformation_matrix: Matrix4<f64> =
isometry.to_homogeneous();
    println!("Transformation Matrix:\n{}",
transformation_matrix);


    // 2. Performing operations:
    // Vector addition.
```

```rust
    let vector_c = vector_a + Vector3::new(4.0,
5.0, 6.0);
    println!("Vector Addition:\n{}", vector_c);


    // Matrix multiplication.
    let matrix_c = matrix_b * Matrix3::new(
        9.0, 8.0, 7.0,
        6.0, 5.0, 4.0,
        3.0, 2.0, 1.0,
    );
    println!("Matrix Multiplication:\n{}",
matrix_c);


    // Matrix-vector multiplication.
    let vector_d = matrix_b * vector_a;
    println!("Matrix-Vector Multiplication:\n{}",
vector_d);


    // Inverse of a matrix
    let matrix_b_inverse =
matrix_b.try_inverse().unwrap();
    println!("Inverse of Matrix b:\n{}",
matrix_b_inverse);


    //Transform a point
    let point_e = Point3::new(1.0, 2.0, 3.0);
    let transformed_point = transformation_matrix
* point_e;
```

```
    println!("Transformed Point:\n{}",
transformed_point);

}
```

In this example, we demonstrate how to create vectors, matrices, and transformations, and how to perform operations like addition, multiplication, and inversion using nalgebra.

Choosing Between ndarray **and** nalgebra

Both ndarray and nalgebra are valuable tools, but they serve slightly different purposes:

- ndarray: Focuses on providing an efficient and flexible n-dimensional array type for general-purpose numerical computation. It's a good choice for tasks where you primarily need to store and manipulate data in array-like structures, such as data preprocessing, feature engineering, and working with data that naturally fits into grids.
- nalgebra: Focuses on providing a comprehensive set of linear algebra tools, including vectors, matrices, transformations, and various linear algebra operations.[2] It's a better choice when you need to perform more advanced linear algebra calculations, such as those involved in geometry, computer graphics, robotics, and some machine learning algorithms.

In many machine learning applications, you'll likely use both crates: ndarray to store and manipulate your data and nalgebra to perform specific linear algebra operations when needed.

13.2 Data Manipulation and Analysis Crates

Before you can feed your data into a machine learning model, you often need to perform a series of operations to clean, transform, and prepare it. This process, known as data preprocessing, is a vital step in the machine learning pipeline. While the Rust ecosystem is still developing libraries with the breadth of functionality of Python's Pandas, you can leverage Rust's strengths and other crates to handle these tasks efficiently.

Here are some of the key Rust crates that you can use for data manipulation and analysis:

1. Rust's Standard Library (std::collections)

Rust's standard library provides several essential data structures that are fundamental for data manipulation.

- HashMap<K, V>: This is a hash table that stores key-value pairs. It allows you to efficiently look up values based on their associated keys. HashMap is useful for tasks like:
    - Feature encoding: Creating mappings between categorical values and numerical representations.
    - Data aggregation: Grouping data by certain criteria and calculating statistics.
    - Building lookup tables: Storing and retrieving data based on unique identifiers.
- HashSet<T>: This is a collection that stores unique values of type T. It allows you to quickly check if a value is present in the set. HashSet is useful for:
    - Data cleaning: Removing duplicate entries from your dataset.
    - Feature selection: Identifying unique categories in a categorical feature.
    - Set operations: Performing operations like union, intersection, and difference on sets of data points.

Example: Using HashMap for Feature Encoding

Let's say you have a dataset of customer information, and one of the features is "city," which is a categorical variable. To use this feature in a machine learning model, you need to convert it into a numerical representation. One way to do this is using label encoding, where you assign a unique integer to each city.

Here's how you can use a HashMap to create a label encoder in Rust:

Rust

```rust
use std::collections::HashMap;


fn create_label_encoder(cities: &[String]) ->
HashMap<String, i32> {
    let mut encoder = HashMap::new();
    let mut label = 0;

    for city in cities {
        if !encoder.contains_key(city) {
            encoder.insert(city.clone(), label);
            label += 1;
        }
    }
    encoder
}


fn encode_cities(cities: &[String], encoder:
&HashMap<String, i32>) -> Vec<i32> {
    let mut encoded_cities = Vec::new();
    for city in cities {
```

```rust
        encoded_cities.push(encoder[city]);
    }
    encoded_cities
}


fn main() {
    // 1. Sample data: A list of cities.
    let cities = vec![
        "New York".to_string(),
        "London".to_string(),
        "Tokyo".to_string(),
        "New York".to_string(),
        "Paris".to_string(),
        "London".to_string(),
    ];


    // 2. Create a label encoder using a HashMap.
    let city_encoder =
create_label_encoder(&cities);
    println!("City Encoder: {:?}", city_encoder);


    // 3. Encode the cities using the encoder.
    let encoded_cities = encode_cities(&cities,
&city_encoder);
    println!("Encoded Cities: {:?}",
 encoded_cities);
}
```

In this example:

1. We define a function create_label_encoder that takes a slice of String representing city names and returns a HashMap that maps each unique city name to an integer label.
2. We iterate over the cities, and for each unique city, we insert it into the HashMap with a corresponding integer label.
3. We define a function encode_cities that takes a slice of city names and the encoder HashMap and returns a vector of integers, where each integer represents the label-encoded city.
4. In the main function, we create a sample list of cities, create a label encoder, and then use the encoder to encode the cities into a vector of integers.

2. itertools

The itertools crate provides a wealth of iterator adapters and combinators that can significantly simplify data processing and transformation tasks. Iterators are a powerful concept in Rust, allowing you to process sequences of data in a concise and efficient way. itertools enhances the standard Rust iterators with many useful methods.

Example: Grouping and Aggregating Data with itertools

Let's say you have a dataset of sales records, and you want to group the sales by product category and calculate the total sales for each category. You can use itertools to achieve this efficiently.

Rust

```rust
use itertools::Itertools;


// Represents a single sales record.
struct SalesRecord {
```

```rust
    product_category: String,

    sales_amount: f64,

}


fn main() {
    // 1. Sample data: A vector of sales records.
    let sales_data = vec![
        SalesRecord { product_category:
"Electronics".to_string(), sales_amount: 1000.0
},
        SalesRecord { product_category:
"Clothing".to_string(), sales_amount: 500.0 },
        SalesRecord { product_category:
"Electronics".to_string(), sales_amount: 1500.0
},
        SalesRecord { product_category:
"Books".to_string(), sales_amount: 200.0 },
        SalesRecord { product_category:
"Clothing".to_string(), sales_amount: 700.0 },
        SalesRecord { product_category:
"Electronics".to_string(), sales_amount: 2000.0
},
    ];


    // 2. Group sales records by product category
and calculate total sales.
    let category_sales = sales_data.into_iter()
```

```rust
            .group_by(|record|
record.product_category.clone()) // Group by
product category.

            .into_iter()

            .map(|(category, group)| {

                // For each group (category),
calculate the sum of sales amounts.

                let total_sales = group.fold(0.0,
|acc, record| acc + record.sales_amount);

                (category, total_sales) // Return a
tuple of (category, total_sales).

            })

            .collect::<Vec<_>>(); // Collect the
results into a vector.


    // 3. Print the results.

    println!("Sales by Category:");

    for (category, total_sales) in category_sales
{

        println!("{}: ${:.2}", category,
total_sales);

    }

}
```

In this example:

1. We define a struct SalesRecord to represent a single sales record.
2. We create a sample vector of SalesRecord structs.
3. We use itertools to group the sales records by product_category and then use fold to calculate the total sales for each category.

- group_by(): This method groups the sales records based on the product_category field. It returns an iterator that yields pairs of (category, group), where the group is an iterator over the sales records in that category.
- into_iter(): We convert the grouped iterator into a regular iterator.
- map(): For each group, we use map() to transform it into a tuple of (category, total_sales).
  - fold(): Inside the map(), we use fold() to iterate over the sales records in the group and calculate the sum of the sales_amount field.
- collect(): We collect the resulting tuples into a Vec.

4. We print the results, showing the total sales for each product category.

3. Polars

Polars is a DataFrame library for Rust, designed for high-performance data manipulation and analysis. It's similar to Pandas in Python but leverages Rust's speed and efficiency. Polars uses the Apache Arrow columnar memory format, which allows for very fast data processing.

Example: Data Manipulation with Polars

(A full example would involve reading from a file, which adds complexity. This shows the core idea.)

Rust

```rust
use polars::prelude::*;


fn main() -> Result<(), PolarsError> {
    // 1. Create a DataFrame.
```

```rust
    let df = df!(

        "Name" => &["Alice", "Bob", "Charlie",
"Alice", "Bob"],

        "Age" => &[25, 30, 35, 25, 30],

        "City" => &["New York", "London",
"Tokyo", "New York", "London"],

        "Sales" => &[100.0, 200.0, 150.0, 120.0,
250.0],

    )?;

    println!("Original DataFrame:\n{}", df);


    // 2. Group by "City" and calculate the mean
"Sales".
    let grouped_df = df.groupby(["City"])?

        .select(["Sales"])

        .agg_mean()?;
    println!("Sales by City:\n{}", grouped_df);


    // 3. Filter the DataFrame for rows where
"Age" is greater than 30.
    let filtered_df =
df.filter(col("Age").gt(30))?;

    println!("Filtered DataFrame (Age >
30):\n{}", filtered_df);


    // 4. Add a new column "Sales_x_2" which is
"Sales" times 2.
```

```
    let df_with_new_column =
df.with_column(col("Sales") * 2.0)?;

    println!("DataFrame with Sales x 2:\n{}",
df_with_new_column);


    Ok(())

}
```

In this example, we:

1. Create a DataFrame using the df! macro.
2. Group the DataFrame by the "City" column and calculate the mean "Sales" for each city.
3. Filter the DataFrame to keep only the rows where the "Age" column is greater than 30.
4. Add a new column named "Sales_x_2" to the DataFrame, which is calculated by multiplying the "Sales" column by 2.

These examples demonstrate how Rust crates can be used to perform common data manipulation and analysis tasks. While the ecosystem is still developing, the available tools provide a solid foundation for building efficient and robust data processing pipelines.

13.3 Machine Learning Model Building Libraries

While the Rust machine learning ecosystem is still evolving compared to Python's mature offerings, there are several libraries that provide implementations of various machine learning algorithms. These libraries allow you to build and train models directly in Rust, leveraging the language's performance and safety benefits.

It's important to note that the Rust ML library landscape is dynamic. New crates are being developed, and existing ones are being actively improved. Therefore, it's always a good idea to check the latest versions and documentation on crates.io and GitHub.

Here are a couple of notable crates that you can use to build machine learning models in Rust:

1. Linfa

Linfa is a relatively young but promising machine learning framework for Rust. It aims to provide a comprehensive toolkit for building machine learning applications, drawing inspiration from Python's scikit-learn.

Key Features of Linfa

- Classical ML Algorithms: Linfa implements a range of common machine learning algorithms, including:
    - Linear regression
    - Logistic regression
    - K-means clustering
    - Gaussian mixture models
    - Support vector machines
    - Decision trees
- Modular Design: Linfa is designed to be modular, allowing you to pick and choose the algorithms you need.
- Focus on Performance: Linfa leverages Rust's performance capabilities to provide efficient implementations of ML algorithms.
- Integration with ndarray: Linfa uses ndarray for numerical computations, ensuring seamless integration with Rust's array manipulation library.

Example: Linear Regression with Linfa

Here's a basic example of how to perform linear regression using Linfa:

Rust

```rust
use linfa::prelude::*;
use linfa::linear_regression::LinearRegression;
use ndarray::array;


fn main() {
    // 1. Sample data: Feature matrix (X) and
target variable (y).
    let features = array![
        [1.0, 2.0],
        [2.0, 3.0],
        [3.0, 4.0],
        [4.0, 5.0],
        [5.0, 6.0],
    ]; // Shape: (5, 2) - 5 data points, 2
features
    let targets = array![3.0, 5.0, 7.0, 9.0,
11.0]; // Shape: (5,) - corresponding target
values


    // 2. Create a Linear Regression model.
    let model = LinearRegression::default();
```

```
// 3. Train the model using the fit method.
let trained_model = model.fit(&features,
&targets);


// 4. Make predictions on new data.
let test_features = array![[6.0, 7.0], [7.0,
8.0]]; // Shape: (2, 2) - 2 new data points
let predictions =
trained_model.predict(&test_features);
println!("Predictions: {}", predictions);
}
```

In this example:

1. We create a sample dataset with features X and target values y.
2. We create a LinearRegression model with default parameters.
3. We train the model using the fit method, passing the features and targets. This returns a trained LinearRegression model.
4. We use the trained model's predict method to make predictions on new data (test_features).

2. SmartCore

SmartCore is another Rust crate that provides a set of machine learning algorithms. It aims to offer a comprehensive and efficient toolkit for various ML tasks.

Key Features of SmartCore

- Supervised Learning: SmartCore includes algorithms for:
  - Linear regression
  - Logistic regression

- ○ Support vector machines
- ○ Decision trees
- ○ Random forests
- Unsupervised Learning: Algorithms[1] for:
  - ○ K-means clustering
  - ○ PCA
- Model Selection: Tools for cross-validation and grid search.
- Metrics: Functions for evaluating model performance.

Example: K-Means Clustering with SmartCore

Rust

```rust
use smartcore::cluster::kmeans::{KMeans,
KMeansParams};

use smartcore::linalg::basic::DenseMatrix;


fn main() -> Result<(), Box<dyn
std::error::Error>> {
    // 1. Sample data:  Data points in 2D space.
    let data = DenseMatrix::from_2d_vec(&vec![
        vec![1.0, 2.0],
        vec![1.3, 2.2],
        vec![4.0, 7.0],
        vec![4.2, 6.1],
        vec![9.0, 8.0],
        vec![8.8, 9.1],
    ])?;


    // 2. Set the parameters for K-Means.
```

```rust
    let k = 2; // Number of clusters.

    let params =
KMeansParams::default().with_k(k).with_max_iter(1
00);


    // 3. Run K-Means clustering.

    let model = KMeans::fit(&data, params)?;

    let clusters = model.predict(&data)?;


    // 4. Print the cluster assignments.

    println!("Cluster assignments: {:?}",
clusters);


    // 5. Get the centroids

    let centroids = model.centroids();

    println!("Centroids:\n {:?}", centroids);


    Ok(())

}
```

In this example, we perform k-means clustering on a set of 2D data points using SmartCore.

Choosing a Library

Both Linfa and SmartCore are valuable resources. The best choice depends on the specific algorithms you need and the API that you find most comfortable. For a broader set of algorithms, SmartCore might be more suitable, while Linfa is tailored to be similar to scikit-learn.

The Future of Rust ML Libraries

The Rust ML library ecosystem is still evolving. As the language gains more traction in the machine learning community, we can expect to see more libraries and tools emerge, offering a wider range of algorithms and functionalities. Keep an eye on the Rust ML community and crates.io for the latest developments.

13.4 Visualization Tools and Integration with Rust

Visualization is a crucial part of the machine learning workflow. It allows you to:

- Explore your data: Gain insights into the patterns, distributions, and relationships within your dataset.
- Debug your models: Understand how your model is performing and identify potential issues.
- Communicate your results: Effectively present your findings to others.

While Rust's visualization ecosystem is still developing, you have several options for creating visualizations in your Rust ML projects.

1. plotters Crate

The plotters crate is a pure-Rust plotting library that enables you to create a variety of static plots, such as:

- Line charts
- Scatter plots
- Bar charts
- Histograms
- Box plots

plotters is well-suited for generating visualizations directly within your Rust applications, without relying on external tools or languages.

Example: Creating a Simple Scatter Plot with plotters

Here's a basic example of how to create a scatter plot using plotters:

Rust

```rust
use plotters::prelude::*;
use std::fs::File;


fn main() -> Result<(), Box<dyn
std::error::Error>> {
    // 1. Define the output file.
    let file = File::create("scatter_plot.svg")?;
    let root = SVGBackend::new(&file, (800,
600)).into_drawing_area();


    // 2. Set up the chart.
    let mut chart = ChartBuilder::on(&root)
        .caption("Scatter Plot", ("sans-serif",
30))
        .set_x_label_area_size(40)
        .set_y_label_area_size(40)
        .build_cartesian_2d(0f64..10f64,
0f64..100f64)?;


    // 3. Draw the gridlines.
```

```
chart.configure_mesh().draw()?;


// 4. Define the data points.
let data_points = [
        (1.0, 10.0),
        (2.0, 20.0),
        (3.0, 30.0),
        (4.0, 40.0),
        (5.0, 50.0),
        (6.0, 60.0),
        (7.0, 70.0),
        (8.0, 80.0),
        (9.0, 90.0),
        (10.0, 100.0),
    ];


// 5. Draw the data points as circles.
chart.draw_series(
        data_points.iter().map(|&(x, y)|
Circle::new((x, y), 3,
ShapeStyle::filled().with_color(&RED))),
    )?;


// 6. Write the chart to the file.
root.present()?;
```

```
    println!("Scatter plot saved to
scatter_plot.svg");

    Ok(())

}
```

In this example, we:

1. Create an SVG file to store the plot.
2. Set up the chart with a caption and axis labels.
3. Draw gridlines on the chart.
4. Define the data points as an array of (x, y) coordinates.
5. Draw the data points as circles with a red fill color.
6. Save the chart to the SVG file.

This generates a scatter plot saved as an SVG file. You can then open this file in a web browser or image viewer.

2. Integration with Python Visualization Libraries

A common approach is to leverage the rich visualization capabilities of Python libraries like Matplotlib, Seaborn, and Plotly.

This typically involves:

1. Performing the computationally intensive parts of your ML pipeline in Rust.
2. Transferring the data from Rust to Python.
3. Using a Python visualization library to create the plots.

Using PyO3 for Python Integration

The PyO3 crate facilitates embedding Python within Rust applications and vice-versa. It allows you to call Python code from Rust and pass data between the two languages.

Example: Visualizing Data with Matplotlib from Rust

(A full example requires a Python environment with matplotlib installed and more elaborate data transfer)

Rust

```
//pseudo
// use pyo3::prelude::*;
// use ndarray::Array2;
//
// fn visualize_data(data: &Array2<f64>) ->
PyResult<()> {
//      Python::with_gil(|py| {
//          // 1. Import the necessary Python
modules.
//          let plt =
py.import("matplotlib.pyplot")?;
//
//          // 2. Convert the Rust ndarray::Array2
to a Python NumPy array.
//          let data_np =
PyArray::from_ndarray(py, data)?;
//
//          // 3. Create a scatter plot using
Matplotlib.
//          plt.plot(data_np.getattr("[:, 0]")?,
data_np.getattr("[:, 1]")?, "o")?; // data_np[:,
0], data_np[:, 1], 'o')
//          plt.title("Data Visualization")?;
//          plt.xlabel("Feature 1")?;
```

```
//            plt.ylabel("Feature 2")?;

//            plt.show()?;

//

//            Ok(())

//        })

// }

//

// fn main() {

//        // 1. Sample data.

//        let data = array![[1.0, 2.0], [2.0, 3.0],
[3.0, 4.0], [4.0, 5.0]]; // Shape: (4, 2)

//

//        // 2. Call the visualization function.

//        if let Err(e) = visualize_data(&data) {

//            eprintln!("Error visualizing data:
{}", e);

//        }

// }
```

In this conceptual example, we:

1. Use PyO3 to embed Python within our Rust application.
2. Import the matplotlib.pyplot module in Python.
3. Convert the Rust ndarray::Array2 to a NumPy array using PyArray::from_ndarray.
4. Use Matplotlib to create a scatter plot of the data.
5. Display the plot.

This approach allows you to leverage the extensive visualization capabilities of Python libraries like Matplotlib while performing the computationally intensive parts of your ML pipeline in Rust.

13.5 Community Resources and Projects in Rust ML

The Rust community is known for its welcoming and helpful nature, and this extends to the growing area of machine learning. Here are some resources and projects that can help you learn, contribute, and connect with other Rust ML enthusiasts:

1. Are We Learning Yet?

"Are we learning yet?" is a website dedicated to tracking the progress of machine learning in Rust. It provides a curated list of Rust crates, projects, and resources relevant to machine learning.

This website is a great starting point for anyone wanting to get an overview of the current state of Rust ML.

You can find information on:

- Fundamental libraries: Crates for numerical computation, data manipulation, and linear algebra.
- Machine learning algorithms: Crates that implement specific ML algorithms.
- Deep learning: Projects and bindings for deep learning frameworks.
- Tools: Crates for visualization, data processing, and other related tasks.
- Community resources: Links to forums, chat groups, and other places to connect with the Rust ML community.

You can find it here: https://www.arewelearningyet.com/

2. Rust ML Working Group

The Rust ML Working Group is a community effort focused on improving the Rust ML ecosystem. It brings together people interested in using Rust for machine learning to collaborate on projects, share knowledge, and discuss the future of the field.

While not a formal organization, the working group provides a central place for coordination and discussion. You can find information about their activities and how to get involved on the "Are We Learning Yet?" website and in various online Rust communities.

3. GitHub

GitHub is a treasure trove of open-source projects, and you can find many Rust projects related to machine learning there. Searching GitHub for keywords like "Rust machine learning," "Rust deep learning," or specific algorithm names (e.g., "Rust k-means") can lead you to interesting projects.

Here are some tips for finding relevant projects:

- Look for well-maintained repositories: Check the project's activity level (recent commits), the number of contributors, and the presence of clear documentation.
- Explore related crates: Crates listed on crates.io often have associated GitHub repositories where you can find more information and contribute.
- Search for specific algorithms: If you're interested in a particular algorithm, such as "decision trees" or "neural networks," search for Rust implementations on GitHub.

4. Rust Community Forums and Chat

The Rust community is known for being welcoming and helpful, and you can find support and connect with other Rust ML enthusiasts through various online channels:

- The Rust Forum: This is the official online forum for the Rust programming language. You can find discussions about various topics, including machine learning, and ask questions to get help from the community.
- Discord: Several Discord servers host Rust communities, and some have dedicated channels for machine learning.

Discord provides a more real-time and interactive way to chat with other developers.

5. Crates.io

Crates.io is the official package registry for Rust crates. You can find and discover Rust libraries for various machine learning-related tasks by searching for keywords like "machine learning," "neural network," "linear algebra," or specific algorithms.

When using crates from crates.io, it's essential to:

- Check the documentation: Ensure that the crate has clear and comprehensive documentation.
- Look at the activity and maintenance: See how actively the crate is being maintained and how frequently it's updated.
- Consider the dependencies: Check the crate's dependencies to ensure they are also well-maintained and reliable.

Getting Involved

The Rust ML ecosystem is still developing, which means there are plenty of opportunities to contribute and make a real impact.

Whether you're interested in:

- Developing new ML libraries or algorithms in Rust
- Improving existing crates
- Writing tutorials and documentation
- Creating tools for data processing or visualization
- Applying Rust ML to specific problem domains

Your contributions can help shape the future of machine learning in Rust.

The Rust community provides a supportive and collaborative environment for exploring machine learning. By utilizing the resources and engaging with other developers, you can learn, contribute, and build exciting ML projects with Rust.

Chapter 14: The Future of High-Performance ML with Rust

We've explored Rust's potential in machine learning and examined the tools and techniques available today. Now, let's look ahead and discuss the exciting future of high-performance ML with Rust.

14.1 Current Research and Development in Rust for ML

The Rust community is actively engaged in research and development to expand the capabilities of the language in the field of machine learning. While the ecosystem is still evolving, the focus is on leveraging Rust's strengths—performance, safety, and concurrency—to address the growing demands of modern ML.

Here are some key areas of current research and development:

1. Enhancing Core Libraries

A significant portion of the work involves improving and expanding the core libraries that underpin ML development in Rust.

- ndarray Improvements: The ndarray crate is crucial for numerical computation. Ongoing efforts aim to further optimize its performance, add more linear algebra operations, and improve its integration with other Rust libraries.
- Specialized Data Structures: Researchers are exploring and developing specialized data structures tailored for ML workloads. This could include structures optimized for storing and processing large datasets, handling sparse data efficiently, or representing specific types of tensors.

- Ecosystem Integration: There's a focus on making these core libraries work seamlessly together. This involves ensuring that data can be easily transferred between different crates and that they provide a consistent and intuitive API.

2. Developing Machine Learning Frameworks

While Rust may not yet have a single, dominant framework like Python's TensorFlow or PyTorch, there are ongoing projects aimed at providing higher-level abstractions for building ML models.

- New Frameworks: Developers are working on creating new frameworks that provide tools for defining neural network architectures, training models, and performing inference. These frameworks often leverage Rust's strengths for performance and efficiency.
- Integration with Existing Frameworks: Another approach is to create Rust bindings or interfaces for existing deep learning frameworks like TensorFlow and PyTorch. This allows Rust developers to utilize the capabilities of these established frameworks while still benefiting from Rust's performance in certain parts of the ML pipeline.

3. Exploring Novel Applications

Rust's unique features make it a compelling choice for specific ML applications, and researchers are actively exploring these areas:

- Edge AI: Rust's small binary sizes, low memory footprint, and ability to run on resource-constrained devices make it ideal for deploying ML models to the edge. This includes applications in IoT, embedded systems, and mobile devices.
- High-Performance Computing: Rust's speed and parallelism capabilities are being investigated for building high-performance ML systems that can handle massive

datasets and complex models, potentially leveraging distributed computing and cluster environments.

- Real-time Systems: Rust's deterministic performance and memory safety are valuable for applications that require real-time ML inference, such as robotics, autonomous systems, and financial trading.

4. Improving Tooling and Infrastructure

To make ML development in Rust more accessible and user-friendly, there's ongoing work on improving the tooling and infrastructure:

- Visualization: Developing libraries or integrations for visualizing data and model results within Rust.
- Model Serving: Creating tools for deploying trained models as services that can be easily consumed by other applications.
- Workflow Automation: Building tools to streamline the ML workflow, such as data processing pipelines, experiment management, and model deployment.

Example: A Potential Future Rust ML Workflow

To illustrate how these efforts might come together, here's a hypothetical example of a future Rust ML workflow:

1. Data Loading and Preprocessing: You use Rust crates to efficiently load and preprocess your data from various sources, leveraging Rust's memory management for optimal performance.
2. Model Definition: You define your neural network architecture using a Rust-based framework, taking advantage of Rust's type system to ensure correctness.
3. Training: You train your model using a high-performance optimization algorithm implemented in Rust, potentially

utilizing GPU acceleration through a dedicated Rust crate or a framework integration.

4. Inference: You deploy your trained model to an edge device, such as a Raspberry Pi, using a small, self-contained Rust executable that performs real-time inference.

5. Visualization: You use a Rust visualization library to create interactive plots of your model's performance and results.

This workflow demonstrates how Rust could be used to build a complete, high-performance ML application, from data processing to model deployment.

Current research and development in Rust for ML is focused on building a robust and efficient ecosystem of libraries and tools, with a strong emphasis on leveraging Rust's unique strengths. The ongoing work in areas like core library enhancement, framework development, hardware acceleration, and tooling will pave the way for a future where Rust is a viable and compelling choice for a wide range of machine learning applications.

14.2 Open Challenges and Opportunities

While Rust shows great promise for machine learning, the ecosystem is still evolving. This means there are both challenges to overcome and exciting opportunities for those who want to contribute.

Challenges

Here are some of the key challenges that the Rust ML community is currently facing:

- Ecosystem Maturity: Compared to languages like Python, Rust's ML ecosystem is still relatively young. While there are some excellent crates for specific tasks, there isn't yet a single, comprehensive framework that covers all aspects of machine learning, from data preprocessing to model building and deployment. This means that you might need to use a combination of different crates and potentially write more code yourself to achieve the same functionality that you'd get with a more mature framework.

- Ease of Use: While Rust is known for its safety and performance, it can have a steeper learning curve than languages like Python, especially for those new to systems programming. Making Rust ML libraries more user-friendly and providing clear, concise documentation and examples is crucial for attracting a wider audience.
- Integration with Existing Frameworks: Deep learning is currently dominated by frameworks like TensorFlow and PyTorch, which have vast ecosystems and large communities. Seamlessly integrating Rust code with these frameworks can be challenging. While there are some efforts to create Rust bindings or use FFI (Foreign Function Interface), this area requires further development to make it easier to leverage pre-trained models and existing infrastructure.
- Hardware Acceleration: Efficiently utilizing hardware accelerators like GPUs is essential for deep learning. While Rust can achieve good performance on CPUs, making the most of GPUs requires careful handling of memory transfers and kernel launches. Developing robust and easy-to-use abstractions for GPU programming in Rust ML is an ongoing challenge.

Opportunities

Despite these challenges, the Rust ML landscape is full of exciting opportunities:

- Building Core Infrastructure: There's a significant opportunity to contribute to the development of fundamental libraries and tools that will form the

foundation of the Rust ML ecosystem. This includes libraries for:
- Efficient tensor operations and linear algebra
- Data manipulation and preprocessing
- Automatic differentiation
- Neural network building blocks

- Developing Specialized Frameworks: Rust's strengths make it well-suited for building high-performance, specialized ML frameworks for specific domains. For example:
  - A framework for real-time computer vision applications.
  - A library for time series analysis with a focus on low latency.
  - A framework for reinforcement learning in resource-constrained environments.
- Improving Tooling: There's a need for better tooling to support the development, deployment, and monitoring of ML systems in Rust. This includes:
  - Visualization tools that can be used directly from Rust.
  - Tools for model serving and deployment.
  - Debugging and profiling tools tailored for ML workloads.
- Contributing to Open-Source Projects: Existing Rust ML projects are always looking for contributors. You can help by:
  - Implementing new features
  - Improving performance
  - Writing documentation
  - Fixing bugs
  - Creating examples
- Education and Outreach: Creating high-quality educational resources, such as tutorials, blog posts, and workshops, is crucial for growing the Rust ML community and making the technology more accessible to a wider audience.

The challenges in Rust ML development present exciting opportunities to shape the future of machine learning. Your contributions can help build a powerful, performant, and safe ecosystem for developing and deploying ML solutions.

14.3 The Role of Rust in Edge AI and Embedded Systems

You've probably heard a lot about artificial intelligence (AI) and machine learning (ML) in recent years. While much of the focus has been on large-scale models running in the cloud, there's a growing trend towards deploying these models on smaller, less powerful devices.[1] This is where Edge AI and embedded systems come into play, and Rust is poised to be a key player in this space.

What is Edge AI?

Edge AI refers to running machine learning models directly on devices at the "edge" of the network, rather than relying on a central server in the cloud.[2]

These "edge devices" can be anything from:

- Mobile phones[3]
- Smart speakers[4]
- Wearable devices[5]
- Autonomous vehicles
- Industrial sensors
- Robots[6]

Instead of sending data to a cloud server for processing and receiving a response, edge AI devices process the data locally and make decisions in real-time.[7]

What are Embedded Systems?

Embedded systems are specialized computer systems designed to perform a dedicated function within a larger[8] device or system.[9] They are often characterized by limited resources, such as:

- Limited processing power[10]
- Small amounts of memory[11]
- Low power consumption requirements
- Real-time constraints

Examples of embedded systems include:

- Microcontrollers in household appliances (e.g., washing machines, refrigerators)[12]
- Engine control units in cars[13]
- Flight control systems in drones[14]
- Medical devices[15]
- Industrial control systems[16]

Why Edge AI and Embedded Systems?

There are several compelling reasons to move ML processing to the edge:

- Reduced Latency: Processing data locally eliminates the need to send data to a remote server and wait for a response.[17] This significantly reduces latency, enabling real-time decision-making.[18] For example, a self-driving car needs to process sensor data and make decisions in milliseconds.[19]
- Bandwidth Efficiency: Sending large amounts of data to the cloud consumes a lot of bandwidth. Edge AI reduces the amount of data that needs to be transmitted, saving bandwidth costs and reducing network congestion.[20]
- Increased Privacy: Processing data locally keeps sensitive information on the device, enhancing user privacy.[21] For

instance, a smart camera that recognizes faces locally doesn't need to send those images to the cloud.

- Improved Reliability: Edge devices can continue to function even when disconnected from the network.[22] This is crucial for applications that require high availability, such as industrial control systems or autonomous vehicles.

Challenges of Running ML on the Edge

However, running ML models on edge devices presents several challenges:

- Resource Constraints: Edge devices have limited processing power, memory, and energy budgets.[23] ML models need to be small and efficient to run on these devices.
- Model Optimization: Models need to be optimized for low latency and minimal resource consumption. This often involves techniques like model compression, quantization, and specialized hardware acceleration.
- Hardware Diversity: Edge devices come with a wide range of hardware architectures, making it challenging to develop software that runs on all of them.
- Power Consumption: Running ML models can be power-intensive, which is a major concern for battery-powered devices.[24]

Rust's Role in Edge AI and Embedded Systems

Rust's unique combination of features makes it exceptionally well-suited for addressing the challenges of deploying ML on edge devices and embedded systems:

- Performance: Rust provides performance comparable to C and C++, allowing you to execute ML computations efficiently on resource-constrained devices.[25]
- Memory Efficiency: Rust's lack of garbage collection and fine-grained control over memory allocation help you

minimize memory usage, which is crucial for devices with limited RAM.

- Small Binary Size: Rust produces small, self-contained executables that can be easily deployed to devices with limited storage.
- Safety: Rust's memory safety guarantees prevent common errors like buffer overflows and data races, which are critical in safety-critical applications such as autonomous systems or medical devices.[26]
- Cross-Platform Compatibility: Rust can be compiled for a wide range of architectures, including ARM (used in many mobile phones and embedded systems) and various microcontroller architectures.[27]

Examples of Rust in Edge AI and Embedded Systems

While the use of Rust in edge AI is still an emerging field, here are some potential and existing examples:

- Microcontroller ML: Rust can be used to implement very small ML models that run directly on microcontrollers, enabling applications like sensor data analysis, voice recognition, and simple control tasks in embedded devices.
- Robotics: Rust can be used to build high-performance, real-time control systems for robots, with integrated ML for perception and decision-making.[28]
- Autonomous Vehicles: Rust's safety and performance make it a strong candidate for implementing critical components of autonomous driving systems, such as perception, sensor fusion, and control.[29]
- Mobile Applications: Rust can be used to build performant and efficient mobile apps with embedded ML capabilities, allowing for offline functionality and real-time processing of data on the device.[30]

Rust's capabilities make it a powerful tool for bringing the benefits of machine learning to the edge and embedded systems. As the demand for efficient, reliable, and secure edge AI solutions grows, Rust is well-positioned to play a significant role in shaping the future of this exciting field.

14.4 Predictions for the Rust ML Ecosystem

Predicting the future is always tricky, but we can make some reasonable forecasts about how the Rust ML ecosystem is likely to evolve, based on current trends and the inherent strengths of the language.

Continued Growth and Maturation

The Rust community is vibrant and growing, and there's increasing interest in using Rust for machine learning.

We can expect this trend to continue, leading to:

- More Developers and Contributors: As more people discover Rust's potential for ML, we'll see a larger pool of developers contributing to the ecosystem. This will translate to more libraries, tools, and resources becoming available.
- Increased Investment: As the Rust ML ecosystem matures, it may attract more funding and support from companies and research institutions. This could lead to more rapid development and innovation.

Development of Specialized Libraries and Frameworks

Instead of trying to replicate the entire Python ML ecosystem in Rust, we're likely to see the emergence of specialized libraries and frameworks that leverage Rust's unique capabilities:

- High-Performance Computing Frameworks: Rust is well-suited for building frameworks that target high-performance computing environments, such as distributed systems and supercomputers, for demanding ML tasks.

- Edge AI Frameworks: We can expect to see frameworks optimized for deploying ML models on resource-constrained edge devices, taking advantage of Rust's small binary sizes and low memory footprint.
- Real-time ML Libraries: Rust's deterministic performance and memory safety make it a strong candidate for building libraries that provide real-time ML inference for applications like robotics, control systems, and autonomous vehicles.

Enhanced Interoperability

Given the dominance of Python in the current ML landscape, improved interoperability between Rust and Python is crucial.

We can anticipate further development in this area:

- Seamless Data Transfer: Tools and libraries will likely emerge to make it easier to move data between Rust and Python, allowing developers to use the strengths of both languages in a single ML pipeline.
- Integration with Popular Frameworks: We'll likely see better ways to integrate Rust code into TensorFlow and PyTorch, enabling developers to use Rust for performance-critical parts of their models while leveraging the vast capabilities of these frameworks.

Focus on Reliability and Safety

Rust's emphasis on safety will likely drive the development of more robust and reliable ML systems.

This will be particularly important in applications where safety is paramount, such as:

- Autonomous driving: Ensuring the safety of self-driving cars.
- Healthcare: Building reliable and trustworthy medical diagnosis and treatment systems.
- Robotics: Developing safe and predictable robot behavior.

Growing Community and Resources

The Rust ML community will continue to expand, leading to a richer ecosystem of resources:

- More Learning Materials: We can expect more tutorials, books, and online courses that teach how to use Rust for machine learning.
- Community-Driven Projects: More open-source projects will emerge, providing ready-to-use tools and examples for various ML tasks.
- Increased Collaboration: Collaboration between Rust developers and ML researchers will foster innovation and cross-pollination of ideas.

The future of machine learning with Rust looks promising. While still maturing, the Rust ML ecosystem is poised for significant growth, driven by the language's inherent advantages and the increasing demand for high-performance, reliable, and safe ML solutions.

14.5 Getting Involved in the Rust ML Community

The Rust community is renowned for its welcoming and helpful nature, and this extends to the machine learning space. There are many ways you can get involved, learn from others, and contribute to the development of this exciting field.

Why Contribute?

Contributing to the Rust ML community can be a rewarding experience for several reasons:

- Learn and Grow: You'll gain valuable knowledge and practical skills by working on real-world projects and collaborating with experienced developers.
- Make a Difference: Your contributions can help shape the future of machine learning in Rust and make the technology more accessible to a wider audience.
- Connect with Others: You'll become part of a vibrant and supportive community of like-minded individuals who share your passion for Rust and machine learning.
- Build Your Portfolio: Contributing to open-source projects can enhance your professional profile and showcase your abilities to potential employers.

Ways to Get Involved

Here are some concrete ways you can contribute to the Rust ML community:

1. Contribute to Existing Projects

Many Rust ML libraries and tools are open-source, hosted on platforms like GitHub. Contributing to these projects is a great way to get started.

Here's how you can find and contribute to projects:

- Explore GitHub: Search GitHub for repositories related to machine learning in Rust. Look for projects that are actively maintained and have a clear contribution process.
- Identify areas for improvement: Browse the project's issue tracker to find bug reports, feature requests, or documentation gaps. These are excellent starting points for contributions.

- Submit pull requests: If you find a bug or implement a new feature, submit a pull request (PR) to propose your changes to the project. Be sure to follow the project's contribution guidelines.

Example: Contributing to a Rust ML Library

Let's say you find a Rust ML library on GitHub that implements a particular algorithm, but you notice that the documentation for a specific function is lacking.

You can contribute by:

1. Forking the repository: Create your own copy of the repository on GitHub.
2. Creating a new branch: Create a branch in your forked repository for your documentation changes.
3. Improving the documentation: Update the code comments and documentation within the Rust code.
4. Submitting a pull request: Submit a PR to the original repository with your documentation improvements.

The project maintainers will review your changes, provide feedback, and potentially merge your contribution into the main branch.

2. Start New Projects

If you have an idea for a new ML library, tool, or application that you think would be valuable to the Rust community, consider starting your own project.

This gives you the opportunity to:

- Explore your interests: Work on a project that you're passionate about.
- Design the API: Create a library or tool with an API that you find intuitive and user-friendly.

- Shape the ecosystem: Contribute a new component to the Rust ML ecosystem.

Example: Creating a Rust Library for a Specific ML Task

Suppose you're interested in time series analysis and you notice that there isn't a dedicated, high-performance Rust library for this purpose.

You could create a new Rust crate that implements various time series analysis techniques, such as:

- Smoothing and filtering
- Autoregressive models
- Fourier analysis
- Wavelet analysis

You could then share your library on crates.io, making it available for others to use in their Rust projects.

3. Share Your Knowledge

Sharing your knowledge and experience is a valuable way to contribute to the Rust ML community and help others learn.

You can do this through various channels:

- Write blog posts: Share your insights, tutorials, and examples on your own blog or on platforms like Medium.
- Create tutorials: Develop step-by-step guides or video tutorials on how to use Rust for specific ML tasks.
- Give talks and presentations: Present your work and share your expertise at Rust meetups, conferences, or online webinars.
- Answer questions: Help others by answering questions on the Rust forum, Stack Overflow, or other online communities.

4. Participate in Online Communities

Engaging with the Rust community online is a great way to connect with other developers, ask questions, and stay up-to-date on the latest developments.

- The Rust Forum: This is the official online forum for the Rust programming language, and it often has discussions related to machine learning.
- Discord: Several Discord servers host Rust communities, and some have dedicated channels for machine learning and data science.
- Reddit: The r/rust subreddit is a good place to find news, articles, and discussions about Rust, including its applications in ML.

5. Attend Meetups and Conferences

Attending Rust meetups and conferences, whether online or in person, provides opportunities to:

- Network with other Rust developers: Meet people who share your interests and learn from their experiences.
- Learn from experts: Attend talks and workshops by experienced Rust developers and ML practitioners.
- Stay up-to-date: Hear about the latest developments in the Rust ML ecosystem.
- Share your work: Present your own projects and get feedback from the community.

The Rust ML community is a collaborative and growing space with numerous opportunities to contribute. By contributing to existing projects, starting new ones, sharing your knowledge, and participating in online and offline communities, you can play an active role in shaping the future of machine learning with Rust.

Conclusion

This book has equipped you with the foundational knowledge and practical skills to harness Rust's power in the field of machine learning. We've explored Rust's core strengths—its memory safety, performance, and concurrency—and how these attributes make it a compelling language for building efficient and reliable ML systems.

From understanding Rust's ownership model to implementing fundamental machine learning algorithms and delving into performance optimization techniques, you've gained the tools to tackle a range of ML challenges. We've also examined the broader Rust ML ecosystem, highlighting existing libraries and tools, and discussed the exciting potential of Rust in areas like edge computing and high-performance applications.

The journey doesn't end here. The field of machine learning is constantly evolving, and the Rust ML ecosystem is still maturing, presenting numerous opportunities for innovation and contribution. I encourage you to continue exploring, experimenting, and building upon the knowledge you've gained. The Rust community is a welcoming and supportive space, and your contributions can help shape the future of high-performance machine learning.